PHILOSOPHY GOES TO THE MOVIES

'Philosophy Goes to the Movies is very clearly and engagingly written. It has a particular claim on the attention of those preparing students for a systematic study of philosophy as well as providing a stimulating introduction in its own right.'
Stephen Mulhall, University of Oxford

'I think this is an excellent way to get to the material. Falzon writes clearly and at a level that undergraduates can understand. He seems as comfortable describing films as he is explaining the nature of a philosophical problem or view. It will make an outstanding text to use in introductory philosophy classes.'
Thomas Wartenberg, Mount Holyoke College, USA

Philosophy Goes to the Movies is a new kind of introduction to philosophy that makes use of film to help the reader's understanding of philosophical ideas. Drawing on art-house movies like *Antz* and *The Truman Show* and blockbusters such as *The Matrix*, Christopher Falzon introduces us to central areas of philosophical concern, including

- the theory of knowledge
- the self and personal identity
- ethics
- social and political philosophy
- science and technology
- critical thinking.

Falzon draws on the ideas of a diverse selection of thinkers, from Plato and Descartes to Marcuse and Foucault.

Ideal for the beginner, this book guides the student through philosophy using lively and illuminating cinematic examples including *Total Recall*, *Crimes and Misdemeanors*, *Monty Python and the Holy Grail*, *Antz* and *Wings of Desire*. It will also appeal to anyone interested in the philosophical dimensions of cinema.

Christopher Falzon is Lecturer in Philosophy at Newcastle University, Australia. He is the author of *Foucault and Social Dialogue* (Routledge, 1998).

PHILOSOPHY GOES TO THE MOVIES

An introduction to philosophy

Christopher Falzon

London and New York

First published 2002
by Routledge
11 New Fetter Lane, London EC4P 4EE

Simultaneously published in the USA and Canada
by Routledge
29 West 35th Street, New York, NY 10001

Routledge is an imprint of the Taylor & Francis Group

© 2002 Christopher Falzon

Typeset in Joanna by
Keystroke, Jacaranda Lodge, Wolverhampton
Printed and bound in Great Britain by
TJ International Ltd, Padstow, Cornwall

British Library Cataloguing in Publication Data
A catalogue record for this book is available from the British Library

Library of Congress Cataloging in Publication Data
A catalog record for this book has been requested

ISBN 0–415–23740–8 (hbk)
ISBN 0–415–23741–6 (pbk)

FOR PENNY, SARAH AND JOSHUA

CONTENTS

ACKNOWLEDGEMENTS

I am grateful to my editors at Routledge, Tony Bruce, Siobhan Pattinson and Sarah Howlett, for their support and patience; and to the anonymous readers to whom Routledge sent the manuscript, for their helpful editorial comments. I am also indebted to a number of people who read through all or part of the manuscript and provided invaluable comments: Sarah Bachelard, Jane Bennett, Penny Craswell, Winifred Lamb, Robert Nichols, Timothy O'Leary, John Quinn and Udo Thiel. I would also like to thank the many people who have offered advice and suggestions over the years regarding philosophical themes in movies. In particular, I am grateful to Elizabeth Coleman, William Connolly, Joanne Faulkner, Fran Gray, Kathleen Higgins, Roger Hillman, Genevieve Lloyd, Denis Loughry, Clare O'Farrell, Robert Pippin, Sarah Rice, Alison Ross, Undine Sellbach and Kimberley Tyrrell for their kind suggestions. I am also grateful to Robert Halliday and Timothy Shanahan, who generously made lists of philosophy-relevant films available on the internet, as well as to all those who contributed to those lists.

INTRODUCTION

Solveig Dommartin in *Wings of Desire*.
Credit: Road Movies/Argos Films/WDR (Courtesy Kobal)

This book is an introduction to philosophy that turns to films in order to illustrate and discuss philosophical ideas and themes. Its primary aim is, by spending some time at the movies, to introduce some of the ideas and arguments that have occupied philosophers over the years, to present philosophical ideas and arguments concerning knowledge, the self, morality and our social and political existence. The book is founded on the belief that films represent a kind of collective visual memory, a vast repository of images, through which many of these ideas and arguments can be illustrated and discussed.

Philosophy and film

At the outset it might be asked how films, which tend to make their points in the realm of 'action and appearance', rather than that of 'reflection and debate' (Perkins 1972, 69), can serve to illuminate philosophical ideas and arguments. Philosophy is often thought of as being austere and technical, concerned with abstract problems and universal principles, and far removed from anything so concrete and immediate as what is portrayed in the cinema. And philosophy itself has contributed to this perception. Within philosophy there is a degree of prejudice against the visual image. Philosophers have often portrayed the use of visual images as indicative of a more primitive or childlike form of thought, remote from the austere world of conceptual understanding, only appropriate for those who do not have access to more sophisticated means of expression. In essence, it is thought that images are concrete and particular, whereas philosophy is concerned with the abstract and the universal. This is a prejudice which arguably goes back a long way in philosophy,

3

to the Greek philosopher Plato (c.429–347 BC). In his book *The Republic*, Plato formulates a powerful and haunting myth, the myth of the cave. In this imaginative vision he portrays the philosophically unenlightened as captives who are bound so as to see only shadows before them on the wall of a cave, and who take these shadows for reality. Philosophical enlightenment, Plato argues, only comes when we escape from the cave and go out into the sunlight where we can see the real objects. Plato's claim is that sense experience only gives us access to shadows. To grasp the true nature of reality, which is the proper task of philosophy, we have to break free from dependence on sense experience and use reason alone.

On the face of it then, this would seem to represent a deep philosophical prejudice against the visual image as an avenue to philosophical enlightenment. And things look even less promising when we consider cinematic images, because the very structure of the modern cinema is reminiscent of Plato's cave. In the cinema also we sit in a darkened space, transfixed by images removed from the real world. So as cinema-goers we seem to be once again like Plato's captives, and it might seem that films would be no help whatsoever for an understanding of philosophy. Philosophy could only begin once we escape from the cinema. However, there is another way of looking at what Plato's cave has to tell us. With this myth, Plato himself makes use of a vivid image to illuminate his own philosophical position, to convey a sense of what he wants to say. The image Plato is using is not an illusion or mere appearance that we have to tear our eyes away from in order to start to do philosophy. Rather, it is playing a positive role in his philosophical discourse, as an illustration or illumination of his position; and hence it serves as pathway to the understanding of his philosophical thinking.

The use of images to illustrate philosophical positions and points in this way is not specific to Plato. Despite a lingering Platonic tendency to disparage the image in their 'official' pronouncements, philosophers have always resorted to a multitude of arresting and vivid visions to illustrate or clarify their position, to formulate a problem or to provide some basis for discussion. Philosophy is full of strange and wonderful images and inventions of this sort. A cursory survey of the philosophical literature reveals: a ring that confers invisibility, a ship that is transformed piece by piece into two distinct vessels, a donkey starving to death between two equal bales of hay, numerous visions of a perfect, utopian society, harrowing visions of life without authority of any kind, an evil demon that causes people to go wrong even in what they think is most obvious, a melting piece of wax, a missing shade of blue, a statue that smells roses, an island of idle South Sea islanders, a brain in a vat whose experiences are generated by a mad scientist, an 'experience machine' in which all desires will seem to be satisfied, a society in which people are chosen by lottery to be killed for their organs; the list goes on and on. As the contemporary French philosopher Michèle Le Doeuff puts it, in this literature there is 'a whole pictorial world sufficient to decorate even the driest "History of Philosophy"' (Le Doeuff 1989, 1).

So, Plato and his successors have often had recourse to vivid pictorial images to illustrate, illuminate and provoke philosophical thinking. It has even been argued, by Le Doeuff in particular, that images are not only illustrative but enter deeply into philosophical thinking, structuring the thought itself. On this view, the idea that the images philosophy employs are merely illustrative obscures the role they are playing in philosophical discourse. It thus helps philosophy to maintain a conception of itself as really concerned only with abstraction and universalization, and helps to shield these images, and the role they play in philosophical thinking, from critical examination. It allows philosophy to be uncritical about itself. My interest in images is not so much in the role of the image in philosophy as in the philosophy we can discern in the image. So my concern here is indeed with the image insofar as it is illustrative, insofar as it captures at a concrete level something about philosophical thought. Yet even here, the image is not merely illustrative. To recognize philosophical ideas, themes and perspectives illustrated in a concrete form is once again to call into question the perception that philosophy is remote from everyday existence, concerned only with abstraction and universalization. It is to bring philosophy down to earth in an important way, to show how philosophical issues and concerns enter deeply into our everyday experience. It is in this spirit that this introduction to philosophy turns to film, where the narrative is propelled primarily by images. In the cinema we have a galaxy of representations of characters, events and situations, in which philosophical ideas, themes and concerns find concrete embodiment, and to which we can turn in order to illuminate and provoke philosophical thinking.

There is a second possible concern about this recourse to films, this time not from the point of view of philosophy but of the films. In making use of cinematic images to tell us about philosophy, it might be argued, don't we run the risk of distorting the films in which they figure, of failing to treat films as films but instead reducing them to mere examples for philosophy? Isn't that to violate the integrity of the films we are discussing, to tear the relevant images out of their proper cinematic context, and to bend them to alien purposes? Shouldn't the theoretical discussion of films perhaps be left to film theorists, to those who are concerned with film as film? I would argue that films are rich texts that are able to sustain a range of readings. The approach adopted in this book provides one more perspective for thinking about film, in addition to those that arise in film theory. What is important is that, whatever approach one takes, due regard is paid to the particularity, the untidy, disorderly actuality, of the films themselves. And with regard to the specific approach being adopted here, there is no suggestion that reading cinematic images in this way exhausts what is going on in a film. Films do much more than serve as illustrations of philosophical themes. That they might do so can only amount to one aspect of what is going on.

This book does not only turn to films in order to help illustrate or illuminate philosophical themes. To identify philosophical positions, themes or questions that are being presented or worked through in particular films is also to understand something important about what is going on within these films, to say something about their intellectual and philosophical content. Once again it needs to be stressed that philosophical thinking and films are not diametrically opposed. Even if films tend to make their points in the realm of action and appearance, we should not be misled by this. For all their seeming 'naturalness' films are thoroughly constructed. As such they not only presuppose but also embody a multiplicity of ideas, conceptions of life and action, views of the world and so on; and philosophy, in reflecting on ideas, can tell us something about the intellectual content that films embody and explore. Moreover films have their own philosophical points to make, their own truth to reveal, their own insights into the human situation. They can address philosophical issues in a concrete way. As such they can also act as a corrective to philosophy, especially a philosophy that has lost itself in abstraction and universalization and has forgotten its connection to concrete existence. This is another reason why cinematic images are not simply illustrations for philosophy. It is also another reason why it is important that philosophy should turn to films with a due respect for what the film is saying; if it does, there is a chance that philosophers might learn something new.

Do these considerations apply to all films? It might be thought that philosophically significant issues are only embodied or illustrated in 'art house' movies or those belonging to 'respectable' genres, but this is a misconception. It is certainly true that some films have greater philosophical content than others, but philosophical issues are raised or invoked in a wide variety of films, both mainstream and art house, in a wide range of genres. It might be surprising to realize that a mainstream science fiction film like *Total Recall* (Paul Verhoeven, 1990) raises a wealth of interesting questions not only about personal identity but also about what we can be said to know. Of course one might argue that with sufficient ingenuity any film whatsoever could be made philosophically relevant, and this is quite true. However, the important point to note here is that some films require more ingenuity to make them philosophically relevant than others, and as a result there is a sense in which these films are being forced into philosophical service. Other films suggest themselves readily in connection with various philosophical themes. This circumstance also provides support for the claim that in identifying philosophical positions, themes or questions that are being presented or worked through in particular films, we are not simply imposing a significance upon them but bringing out something of what is going on within the films.

The philosophical approach

We have gone some way now without asking a fairly obvious question. What is philosophy? That is, what is the nature of philosophical thinking? What is distinctive about a philosophical approach? There are two things to note about this question. First of all, it is itself a philosophical question. And second, like most philosophical questions, it is difficult to come up with a straightforward or uncontroversial answer. The twentieth-century philosopher Bertrand Russell's facetious response was that philosophy is whatever gets taught in university departments of philosophy, but even this would be disputed by some philosophers. Nonetheless, it will be useful at this point to try to provide a general characterization of the philosophical enterprise; and in the spirit of the book, to do so with the help of some cinematic references.

Philosophy is often seen as dealing with the 'big questions'. That is, it is often seen as asking those large questions about the ultimate significance of life, about 'what it's all about', the sorts of questions that we are usually too busy to stop and think about. This is the view of philosophy that appears for example in the Monty Python comedy *The Meaning of Life* (Terry Jones, 1983), a series of sketches loosely based on the theme indicated in the title. Very loosely, as it happens. The question of life's meaning is not directly addressed until the middle of the film. At this point we find ourselves in a restaurant with two diners who are being offered a choice not of food but of conversations. One of the options on the menu is philosophy, and when diner Michael Palin asks what philosophy is, his waiter (John Cleese) replies that it is 'an attempt to construct a viable hypothesis to explain the meaning of life'. Palin wants Cleese to 'start them off', and so Cleese asks them whether they have ever wondered why they're here, on this planet, what it's all about? 'Nope!' replies Palin. Undeterred, Cleese informs them that 'throughout history there have been certain men and women who have tried to find the solution to the mysteries of existence – and we call these guys philosophers'.

This idea that philosophy is an inquiry into the meaning of life is of course something of a popular cliché, but it is nonetheless true that there are certain kinds of questions about the world and ourselves, large, vaguely unsettling questions, which have an unmistakably philosophical character. In Wim Wenders' film *Wings of Desire* (1987), which tells the story of two angels who watch over the citizens of Berlin, it is the children who ask these questions. As Damiel (Bruno Ganz), one of the observing angels, writes in his journal:

> When the child was a child, it was the time of these questions: Why am I me, and why not you? Why am I here and why not there? When did time begin, and where does space end? Isn't life under the sun just a dream? Isn't what I see, hear and smell only the illusion of a world before the world? Does evil actually exist, and are there people who are really evil? How can it be that I, who I am, didn't exist before I came to be and that someday the one who I am will no longer be the one I am?

Moreover, it makes sense to see these as the questions of children. They are questions that arise out of a sense of wonderment at the world, the amazement that comes with viewing the world through fresh eyes, without the baggage of accumulated preconceptions and habitual patterns of thought. As Damiel notes later in the film, when the child was a child 'it had no opinions about anything. It had no habits.' Nor do such questions necessarily disappear with adulthood. Though we often become weighed down by habit, routine and the practical demands of life, these searching, suggestive questions still arise from time to time, and are still able to intrigue and disturb us. And one way of thinking about philosophy is that it is what happens when we deliberately stand back from our ordinary habits and familiar routines, look at the world afresh, and systematically try to answer questions like these.

But this is still a fairly vague picture of what philosophy is. It might seem that in order to give it some substance we need to establish what it asks these questions about, to determine the subject area of philosophy. Other disciplines have a clear subject area. Physics asks questions about matter and energy; sociology asks questions about society; history asks questions about the past. So what is philosophy's subject matter? The problem is that philosophy asks its questions about a wide range of topics – about knowledge, about the self, our moral lives, our social and political existence and so on. In addition, it also seems to be able to take as its subject matter other disciplines and areas of thought in which human beings seek to understand the world and themselves. There is philosophy of science, philosophy of the social sciences, philosophy of religion, philosophy of history, philosophy of art; and at the moment we are asking a philosophical question about philosophy itself. So it is starting to look as if *anything* can be the subject matter for philosophy. But this in fact means that talking about philosophy's subject matter does not really help us to understand what philosophy is. We need to think once more about the kinds of questions that we are asking about these various areas, about what makes our reflections on them philosophical.

Indeed, philosophical reflection might be better seen as a certain kind of approach, a certain way of thinking that can be applied to all kinds of subject matter, both disciplines like science, psychology and history, and our everyday activities in the practical world. Here we come back to the idea that philo-sophical questions arise when we are not confined by familiar routines and habitual patterns of thought, when we look at things afresh. In our everyday activities and in disciplines we ordinarily proceed in the light of certain presuppositions, certain fundamental beliefs, concepts, principles and stan-dards. They represent the ground on which we stand, the background in terms of which we think, know and act. We do not ordinarily think about or question these presuppositions, but simply take them for granted. However we may also step back from what we are doing, from our existing forms of thinking and acting, in order to think about and critically weigh up the beliefs, principles or assumptions we are relying on. For example, we might ask whether any of the beliefs we have accumulated about the world can be trusted, whether anything our eyes and ears tell us about the world is true. Here we are no longer working within familiar frameworks of thought and action, but asking questions about the frameworks themselves; and this is a useful way of understanding philosophical reflection. As Jay Rosenberg puts it, philosophy is a 'second-order' discipline (Rosenberg 1996, 4). It is a form of reflection in which we try to think about, clarify and critically evaluate the most basic terms within which we think and act.

That philosophy is engaged in this kind of reflection helps explain why philosophical accounts are typically general in character, and address fundamental questions about what we think and do. It also helps explain why philosophy is sometimes seen as being remote, abstract and impractical, a matter of 'sitting and thinking' rather than 'going and seeing' (Emmet 1968, 12). Ordinarily we need to presuppose a good deal in order to get on with what we are doing. Scientists could not get on with doing science if they were constantly asking fundamental questions about what constitutes scientific knowledge; nor could we get on with our lives if we were constantly questioning our most basic beliefs. To stop and think about the underlying presuppositions of our activity would interfere with it. In philosophical reflection we necessarily have to stand back from our activities in order to think about the framework in terms of which we proceed. This does not mean however that philosophy is entirely detached from everyday life. The angels in *Wings of Desire* have this superhuman detachment, floating effortlessly above the world, but at the cost of being reduced to pure observers, merely recording what goes on down below. Indeed Damiel yearns to overcome his abstraction from life, to 'take the plunge' and become human, while recognizing that this means coming down to live in the midst of time, suffering and death. But it is only then, he thinks, that he will be able to experience for himself the child's amazement at the world in which it finds itself. And in the end, however abstract and impractical philosophy might seem to be, it begins with this wonderment at the world in which we find ourselves; and it always remains indirectly related to our worldly involvements, since it concerns itself with the presuppositions that underpin and structure them.

In thinking critically about the presuppositions behind our disciplines and everyday activities, philosophical reflection explores already existing frameworks of thinking and action. But philosophy also produces speculative visions and grand theories of its own, new frameworks for thinking about the world, for understanding knowledge, the self, our social and political existence. A philosophy, a systematic vision of the world, is a comprehensive way of thinking about and making sense of the world and ourselves. When we understand the work of an important thinker, we come to look at the world and ourselves through new eyes. Understood in this way, philosophy can be thought of as the first discipline, the origin of all the others. Philosophy concerned itself with ambitious speculation about the nature of reality, the self and proper forms of human society long before the emergence of independent disciplines like physics, psychology and sociology. These disciplines can be thought of as having split off from philosophy to become organized forms of thinking in their own right. This means that they have taken over areas formerly the province of philosophy alone; for example we are more likely now to turn to physics than philosophy to understand the ultimate nature of material reality. Nonetheless there remain areas that are primarily the concern of philosophers, such as logic, epistemology, ethics and aesthetics. And as we have seen, philosophy has also made the independent disciplines part of its subject matter, to the extent that it critically examines the basic assumptions they take for granted.

It should be added that in this activity of critical reflection, philosophy does not spare itself. Philosophical reflection includes thinking critically about philosophy's own accounts of the world. Stretching back to ancient Greece is a long series of philosophical accounts of the scope and limits of knowledge, the nature of the self, the proper forms of social and political life, and so on. These are not simply historical curiosities but continue to influence our thinking in the present. They raise basic questions, identify important problems, offer influential answers and develop positions that still have to be reckoned with, even if we end up rethinking or rejecting them. Thus, to think philosophically about knowledge, the self or social and political life is not to proceed in a vacuum, to start entirely from scratch, but to encounter and engage with the long history of philosophical thinking about these areas. New philosophical accounts always emerge, at least in part, out of the critique, rejection or reformulation of earlier philosophical positions; and these new accounts will in turn become the focus of critique, rejection or reformulation. The history of philosophy can itself be seen as an ongoing series of critiques, disputes, arguments and reformulations, an ongoing conversation as it were. And if this is so, it is a conversation that has been going on for well over two thousand years.

Overall then, philosophy can be thought of as reflection on the basic frameworks in terms of which we think about the world and ourselves. It both critically examines existing frameworks of thinking, and plays a role in creating new ones. Out of such philosophical questioning and reflection come very general ways of making sense of our situation, various philosophical accounts of the world and ourselves. At the same time, philosophy rarely produces final answers to its questions. Every philosophical account that emerges is in turn subjected to critical examination; and perhaps in the end this critical questioning is more important than coming up with final answers. Philosophy is always more than just a set of doctrines to be learnt, or thoughts to repeat. To do philosophy is above all to philosophize, to think about things rather than simply take them for granted. And this points us to one further aspect of philosophical reflection. To refuse to take things for granted, to think things through for ourselves, is crucially important for our intellectual independence. Out of philosophical reflection comes something more than general ways of making sense of the world; as we will see in more detail in the final chapter, philosophical reflection is linked in an important way with our freedom.

Overview of the book

The structure of this book has been dictated by broad areas of philosophical interest: knowledge, the self, morality and our social and political existence. Each chapter deals with a particular area. It will look at the kinds of questions and problems that have arisen in connection with it, and, in roughly historical order, at some of the main philosophical theories or accounts that have emerged in Western thought. In general, the starting point in each chapter will be ancient Greek philosophy, and in particular the views of Plato, who first posed many of the questions that remain to this day on the philosophical agenda. Reference will then be made where possible to what the medieval world has to say, to how things look from a world-view dominated by Christianity. We will finally turn to the kinds of positions characteristic of modern philosophy, the philosophy of our own era. This is philosophical thinking as it has developed since around the seventeenth century, beginning with the French philosopher René Descartes and including figures such as Thomas Hobbes, John Locke, David Hume, Immanuel Kant, John Stuart Mill and Karl Marx. Throughout, the views of contemporary thinkers and commentators will also be drawn on.

As to the philosophical themes and issues to be discussed, in the first chapter we will look at issues to do with knowledge; questions about the nature of knowledge, how we acquire it and what its scope and limits are. We will look at a number of the positions that have been put forward seeking to give answers to these kinds of questions, positions that have been developed in the area of philosophy known as epistemology or the theory of knowledge. In Chapter 2 we will turn to what we can know of ourselves, and discuss questions concerning the self and personal identity, such as: what is the nature of the self? Are reason and the passions in conflict within us? Is the self something distinguishable from the body? And what makes me the same person over time? Many of these issues are explored in the area of philosophy known as philosophy of mind. In Chapter 3, we will start to move outwards from the self, in order to consider questions about how we ought to conduct ourselves in the world, how we ought to deal with one another and how we ought to live, and indeed the question of why we should be moral at all. These are questions that are typically discussed in the area known as ethics or moral philosophy.

In Chapter 4 we will move even further afield, from issues centring on individual morality to issues concerning our life in a larger social order, issues that are typically dealt with in social and political philosophy. Here we will look at questions to do with the individual's relation to society, and at notions of political power. In Chapter 5 we will turn to issues arising from a particularly important aspect of contemporary social and political existence: the ever-increasing influence of science and technology on our lives, something that is also going to play a major part in structuring our future. Issues that emerge in this connection include the ethical implications of scientific activity, the question of whether technology is alienating or dehumanizing and the implications of new technologies such as genetic engineering. Finally, having looked at a number of philosophical accounts concerning knowledge, the self, morality and our social and political existence, we will turn in Chapter 6 to a consideration of philosophical reflection specifically as a critical enterprise, a critical evaluation of ways of thinking. This will involve looking at the nature of arguments, the fallacies and other problems that can get in the way of good arguments and sound thinking, and to conclude, the importance of being critical.

There is no suggestion that this represents a comprehensive survey of philosophical thought. Far from it. I have restricted myself as far as possible to philosophical accounts of areas we are all familiar with in everyday life, and have avoided philosophical thinking that concerns itself with specialized disciplines, such as the philosophy of science. Nor is every philosophically significant thinker discussed. Within the scope of a small volume like this it is of course necessary to be selective. The same can be said of the films that will be referred to in the course of the discussion. Not every philosophically interesting film has been, or possibly could be, mentioned. With regard to the films, there are at least four ways in which films link up with philosophical themes, and thus become useful for my purposes. First, films may have, as their subject matter, specific philosophers and their work, for example Roberto Rossellini's trilogy *Socrates* (1970), *Blaise Pascal* (1971) and *Augustine of*

Hippo (1975), and Derek Jarman's *Wittgenstein* (1993). Second, films may be made of literary works that were philosophically inspired, for example *The Stranger* (Sergio Gobbi and Luchino Visconti, 1967), based on Albert Camus's book, and *The Name of the Rose* (Jean-Jacques Annaud, 1986), based on Umberto Eco's novel. Third, films may explicitly and self-consciously make use of or invoke philosophical ideas and positions, such as *Dark Star* (John Carpenter, 1972), *Love and Death* (Woody Allen, 1975) and many of the Monty Python films including of course *The Meaning of Life*. Finally, films may present scenarios that, though not necessarily explicitly making use of philosophical ideas and themes, can be used to explore and discuss philosophical issues. A typical example would be *Twelve Angry Men* (Sidney Lumet, 1957).

In this book the bulk of the examples will come from the last two categories, which is to say they will either be philosophically self-conscious films, or films that in telling their story happen to make use of philosophically interesting ideas and themes without self-consciously seeking to do so. Although I am mainly drawing on fiction films in this discussion, I will occasionally also use television material when it seems apt. It is difficult, for example, to ignore a television show like *Star Trek: The Next Generation* for the discussion of a number of philosophically interesting issues. Nor could we neglect the immortal 'Argument Clinic Sketch' from *Monty Python's Flying Circus*. The films to be considered in connection with the various philosophical issues will in all cases be identified by their title, director and date of release, as for example in *The Crying Game* (Neil Jordan, 1992). Usually the actor playing a significant character will be referred to as well, as in Terry Molloy (Marlon Brando). In the final chapter, which deals with critical thinking and looks at various examples of arguments and fallacies drawn from films, I have as far as possible also provided references to the published scripts.

This book will hopefully be useful to its readers in a number of ways. As a basic introduction to philosophy that makes use of cinematic material, it is intended to be of use to those who are unfamiliar with philosophy, and who would like to gain acquaintance with some of its key ideas and themes, as well as to learn something of its history. In this regard it will also hopefully be useful for beginning students in philosophy, for whom it can provide a fresh avenue for thinking about philosophical topics, issues and problems that have come up in the classroom. Third, it is intended to provide a resource for teachers of philosophy, who can make use of the films indicated here to provide concrete illustrations of the material they are presenting. Considered not as an introduction to philosophy using film but as a way of using philosophy to illuminate aspects of films, the book also provides an interesting way of looking at and thinking about the movies. To that extent it also seeks to contribute to the cinematic experience.

1

PLATO'S PICTURE SHOW – THE THEORY OF KNOWLEDGE

A Clockwork Orange.
Credit: Warner Bros. (Courtesy The Ronald Grant Archive)

In Bernardo Bertolucci's 1970 film *The Conformist*, the protagonist, Marcello Clerici (Jean Louis Trintignant), joins the Italian Fascist movement and is sent to Paris to assassinate his former mentor, a philosophy professor. In one key scene, Clerici goes to visit the professor in his study. The professor reminds him that Plato's cave was the subject of his unfinished thesis. As they talk, Clerici remarks that when the professor entered the lecture room, he would always close the windows to keep out the light and noise. Clerici now goes to the window and closes the shutters himself, leaving only a shaft of light. He then recounts how the professor used to lecture on Plato's cave, and begins to recite the myth. So why does Clerici close the shutters? What is Plato's cave doing in Bertolucci's film? What is its significance for this tale of Fascist delusion? And what does this appearance tell us about the cave story itself? We will come back to these questions shortly, but in order to answer them it is necessary to pay a visit to Plato's cave itself.

Plato's cave

Plato's cave is one of philosophy's most memorable and haunting images. I have already said a little about it in the Introduction, but we can now start to explore it in more detail. In the *Republic*, Plato asks us to imagine prisoners in an underground cave with a fire behind them. The prisoners are bound so they can only see the shadows on the wall before them. These shadows are cast by puppets that are being carried by unseen figures behind them, moving up and down in front of the fire. The prisoners think that the shadows are the only things there are to see. If they are released from their bonds and forced to turn around to the fire and the puppets, they become bewildered and disoriented, and would much rather be left in their original state. Only a few can bear to realize that what they see are only shadows cast by the puppets, and these courageous few begin their journey of liberation that leads past the fire and eventually out of the cave. Here, outside the cave, they find not merely puppets but the real things, the objects of the real world (see Plato 1974, 514–18; these numbers refer to the standardized pagination which appears in the margins of most editions of the *Republic*).

What makes this image so compelling is its suggestion that we might be like these prisoners, that everything we ordinarily take to be reality might in fact be no more than a shadow, a mere appearance, and that the real world might be something quite different. In our ordinary experience, of course, we are perfectly familiar with the apparent as well as the real, and can usually tell the difference between them. The stick in water appears to be bent, but we can readily establish that it is really straight. But if absolutely everything that we encountered, everything in our ordinary experience, was merely an appearance, an illusion, and quite different from what was really the case, we would have no idea that we were being systematically deluded in this way. We would imagine that we had genuine access to reality, that what we saw was all that there was to see. And if anyone were able to pierce through this veil of appearances, and to grasp the true nature of reality, they would view those left behind as no more than prisoners confined to a world of illusion. To them everything that those left behind took to be solid reality would seem to be no more than shadows.

There are a number of ways in which the cave story can be interpreted. First of all, it can be read as 'an invitation to think, rather than to rely on the way things appear to us' (Blackburn 1994, 253). In other words, it is an invitation to engage in philosophical reflection. To start thinking philosophically about our beliefs, we have to abandon our unthinking confidence that what we ordinarily take to be knowledge really is knowledge. We have to become critical of received opinion and commonsense beliefs, beliefs that are presented to us as self-evident or unquestionable. Second, the cave story illustrates Plato's positive philosophical views about the nature of knowledge. Philosophers have always been interested in giving an account of knowledge, of the nature, scope and limits of what we can know – an area of philosophical reflection that has come to be known as epistemology. And the cave serves as a concrete representation of Plato's own epistemological position. It is a representation of his view that all that our senses reveal to us are mere shadows, mere appearances removed from reality. For Plato we are just like the prisoners in the cave to the extent that we think the world we ordinarily encounter through our five senses is the real one. In order to comprehend the world as it really is, we have to escape from this prison; we have to go beyond what is given to us in experience.

The cave image is also significant because it brings us to our first encounter between philosophy and the cinema. As I mentioned in the Introduction, it has often been noted that there are uncanny similarities between the cave Plato imagines and the modern cinema. As in Plato's 'picture show', so too in the cinema we sit in darkness, transfixed by mere images that are removed from reality. The very structure of the cinema parallels that of the cave. The cinema audience watches images projected onto a screen in front of them. These images are projected from a piece of film being moved past a light, behind them. And the images on this piece of film are themselves merely copies of the real things outside the cinema. There are some striking parallels here. Indeed, if anything, the cinema improves on the cave as a place of illusion. What are being projected on the cinema screen are not mere shadows, but sophisticated, highly realistic images. The history of the cinema is itself one of increasingly sophisticated representations of reality, with the progressive addition of sound and colour making the illusion more and more complete. Moreover, through seamless editing, films usually do not call attention to the fact that they are merely representations of reality up on the screen, not reality itself – the so-called 'reality effect'.

There is a sense then in which, as Ian Jarvie puts it in *Philosophy of the Film*, we recreate Plato's thought experiment every time we step into a cinema (see Jarvie 1987, 48). And it is always possible to think of the cinema itself in cave-like terms, as a refuge from reality, a place where we can go in order to escape from the outside world, to lose ourselves in deception, illusion and fantasy. However it is important to note that despite the clear similarities between the cinema and Plato's cave, there are also some significant differences. In particular, the kind of deception involved in Plato's account is much more profound than anything we might find in the cinema. If the cinematic image is a mere representation, an illusion, it is an illusion that we voluntarily subject ourselves to, which we allow ourselves to be taken in by and in full awareness of its status as an illusion. That we are not seriously taken in by the cinematic image reflects the fact mentioned earlier, that ordinarily we can distinguish perfectly well between illusion and reality, between the apparent and the real. We can do this even if the illusions are relatively sophisticated, like those we find in the cinema. Moreover, leaving the cinema and returning to the 'real world' all takes place within our ordinary experience, just as the distinctions we make between appearance and reality are ordinarily made within the realm of our ordinary experience. For Plato in contrast, it is ordinary experience as a whole that is illusory. In order to escape from illusion and to comprehend reality, we have to escape entirely from the realm of ordinary experience.

Now, Plato's account does not only have to do with knowledge, but also with a certain kind of liberation bound up with knowledge. Ignorance for Plato is not bliss, but rather a form of enslavement. We are prisoners insofar as we are prevented from grasping the true order of things by the limits of everyday experience, the limits of our commonsense understanding of the world. To gain knowledge is to escape from the imprisonment of our ordinary conception of the world. There is also a suggestion in Plato's account that ignorance can enslave us in a more concrete sense as well. Plato portrays the prisoners as mistaking for reality the shadows of puppets that are being carried by others. The implication is that we can be effectively enslaved or controlled by other people when we take for reality the images they feed to us, when we believe what they want us to believe. Only if we become critical, if we come to see these false images for what they are, will we be in a position to free ourselves from this kind of enslavement.

Seen in these terms, Plato's story of the cave, of imprisonment and its over-coming, starts to acquire wider resonances. It calls to mind first of all what is involved in the process of an individual's growing up, of leaving childhood behind and becoming an adult. This is more than simply a process of physical development. An important part of growing up is intellectual growth, in which we come to question the ideas and beliefs, along with the moral principles and standards, that have been fed to us by our parents, teachers and others over the years. When we are young, of course, we uncritically accept whatever we are told about the world. As a result we are very much influenced and determined in our thinking by the views, opinions and attitudes of those around us. As we grow up, however, we often find that many things we have hitherto accepted without question are in fact questionable, and may even be false. In so doing, we start to become critical, to examine our existing beliefs and standards, to sift through them and weigh them up. Such critical thinking is an important part of breaking away from dependence on others and of establishing our own identity, our own views on the world, and our intellec-tual and personal independence.

Second, the cave calls to mind forms of imprisonment and their over-coming in a wider social context. An important way in which people can be controlled or manipulated is by filling their heads with misleading or false images of the world. And this is a far more effective form of social manipulation than straightforward coercion, because here we are willingly doing what other people want us to do. Consider for example the advertising images manufacturers bombard us with, designed to make us think that their products are indispensable to our well-being or happiness. Or consider the role of political propaganda in fostering certain views of the world, or in orchestrating public opinion in various ways, in order to help bring about the political goals of others. And movies too have sometimes been seen as part of this, as instruments of cultural or political indoctrination, encouraging people to mistake a false cinematic reality for the reality of life in the world. So in this wider social and political context as well it would seem that we can become like Plato's prisoners, controlled by others because we take the images they present us with for reality. This is by no means to suggest that we are nothing more than passive, unthinking dupes, completely at the mercy of these images, as some commentators have supposed. We can still differentiate between appearance and reality. What the possibility of such deception means, once again, is that it is important to be critical. Becoming critical of these images imposed on us, seeing them for what they are and grasping the truth of our circumstances, is an important part of breaking away from this kind of subjection, of attaining some degree of independence in our lives.

These are some of the wider implications of the cave image, and they are often alluded to in cinematic portrayals that make use of the cave image. Let me cite some examples of this. First of all, as Erich Freiberger (1996) argues, *Cinema Paradiso* (Giuseppe Tornatore, 1989) makes use of the cave image, and indeed the parallel between the cave and the cinema, to portray the development of its main character Toto towards adulthood and intellectual independence. In the film, Toto (played as an adult by Jacques Perrin) tells the story of his childhood, and in particular, his childhood friendship with the projectionist at the local cinema. On Freiberger's reading, the local cinema can be seen as a cave-like place, in which the villagers are spellbound and seduced – in effect 'bound' – by the conventional opinions and standards of behaviour they see on the screen. But Toto has already begun to escape from this cultural confinement because he has turned away from the screen and has come to know the projectionist (Philippe Noiret) 'behind the scenes'. The liberating escape from the cave that Plato envisages is paralleled in the film's overall story, which traces how Toto gradually comes to escape from the narrow confines of small village life, and heads off into the wider world to gain an education.

In *Cinema Paradiso* the cave image figures in a tale that is primarily about an individual's journey out of childhood and intellectual confinement. The cave has also been used in order to comment on forms of confinement in a wider social and political context. Bertolucci's *The Conformist* is a good example of this. As Julie Annas notes in her *Introduction to Plato's* Republic (1981, 257–8), Bertolucci uses Plato's cave image quite deliberately and explicitly in the film to comment on the imprisoning delusions of Fascism (it does not appear in the Alberto Moravia book on which the film was based). Clerici, having closed the shutters and turned his old philosophy professor's office into a gloomy, cave-like place, recalls how the professor used to lecture on Plato's cave. In response, the professor compares the deluded prisoners in the cave with the inhabitants of Fascist Italy, blinded by propaganda. Since Clerici is himself one of those who has been trapped and blinded, one of the cave-dwellers, he is unaware of the irony of his own recollections. But Bertolucci underscores the professor's point, because there is enough light entering the room to cast shadows on the wall behind them. At one point in Clerici's exposition, as he is emphasizing a point, his shadow is caught appearing to make a Fascist salute; and at the end, after the professor expresses doubts that Clerici is at heart really a Fascist, he opens the shutters and Clerici's shadow disappears in the resulting light. In this way, Bertolucci uses the cave image to emphasize both the shadow world of Fascist beliefs, and Clerici's ultimately uneasy relationship with it.

Before moving on there is one more allusion to the cave worth noting. One of the most interesting cinematic portrayals of the cave, once again in the form of a cinema, appears in Stanley Kubrick's *A Clockwork Orange* (1971). Here, the enslaving force is psychological conditioning in the service of the state, part of a future totalitarian government's campaign to clear the prisons of 'mere common criminals'. As a condition for his release from prison, the film's vicious anti-hero Alex (Malcolm Macdowell) is subjected to a kind of cinematic brainwashing. In this cinema, he is strapped to his seat, unable to turn his head away from the screen. Clips on his eyelids mean that he is unable even to close his eyes. Behind him, shadowy, white-coated scientists orchestrate the proceedings. He is shown a string of violent film images, and with the help of drugs is gradually conditioned to feel sick at the very thought of violence. The result is a model citizen, of sorts. This scenario strongly recalls Plato's cave because Alex is literally bound to his seat, unable to look away from the cinematic images; and because when he is brought under the sway of these images his independence is destroyed and his behaviour controlled. However Kubrick also introduces a number of perverse twists that sets it apart from other cinematic representations of the cave. In this cave story, Alex has to go into the cave, to submit to the brainwashing, in order to gain his freedom from imprisonment. Moreover, because he has now become a prisoner in a more profound sense, Kubrick gets us to sympathize with Alex, but it is not at all clear that it would be a good thing for this particular prisoner to escape from his cave.

Descartes, dreams and demons

We have been looking, with the help of some cinematic portrayals, at ways in which Plato's cave image can be used to think about aspects of our social and political existence. We will touch once more on these broader issues of knowledge and society towards the end of the chapter. For now, let us return to matters more directly related to the issue of knowledge. Plato, as we have seen, uses the cave image to illustrate his account of knowledge. In it he throws into question the faith we ordinarily place in our senses. All that our senses reveal to us, he thinks, are mere shadows and illusions, removed from reality. But Plato is not the only thinker to question our faith in the senses. Here it will be helpful to look at the thought of a more recent philosopher, the French philosopher René Descartes (1596–1650). Some two thousand years after Plato, in the seventeenth century, Descartes published his *Meditations on First Philosophy*. And here, he raises issues very similar to those raised by Plato. Like Plato, he wants to question our ordinary reliance on sense experience for our knowledge of the world, and to challenge our complacency, our confidence that what we take to be knowledge really is knowledge. In order to do so, Descartes presents a number of sceptical arguments, which are designed to show that a great deal of what we think we know on the basis of our experience can in fact be called into question – even what seems most obvious. He employs two arguments in particular here, the dream argument and the evil demon argument.

Descartes begins by pointing out that we sometimes go wrong in our judgements about small or distant objects, for example thinking that a distant tower is square when it is in fact round. This is the first kind of sceptical consideration he raises, but as he himself recognizes, this is not enough to radically call into question what our experience tells us about the world. In such cases we can always correct our mistake in the light of further experience, for example by approaching the tower and inspecting it more closely. So it would seem at first glance that we are perfectly capable of distinguishing between the illusory and the real in our ordinary experience. But like Plato, Descartes wants to raise the possibility that our experience might radically mislead us about the world. He proceeds to raise a more radical doubt about what experience tells us, to suggest that he might go wrong even about things which are right before us, for example that he is sitting by the fire, in his dressing gown, holding a piece of paper in his hand. This Descartes does through his famous dream argument. He raises the question: how does he know that he is sitting by the fire, writing, and not asleep, in bed, merely dreaming that he is sitting by the fire, writing? The difficulty in answering this throws into question those beliefs that seem to be based on the evidence of one's immediate experience.

Just as Plato's cave provides a handy model for thinking about the cinema, so too do dreams. It has often been suggested that viewing a film has similarities with dreaming. Speaking of Hollywood as the 'dream factory', and of theatres as 'dream palaces', is not merely to employ a picturesque metaphor. In the cinema as well, we are in a darkened room, our physical activity has been limited, and our visual perception is heightened to compensate for our lack of movement. It has been argued by some that it is precisely because the film viewer's situation is like that of the dreamer that we accept what we see as real, and 'flimsy two-dimensional images have the uncanny substance of real bodies and things' (see Stam et al. 1992, 144). A good deal of film theory based on Freudian psychoanalysis takes its start from this. However, when we come to consider the issue that Descartes poses, of whether it is possible to determine whether we are dreaming or not, it is the differences between films and dreams that come to the fore. As we have already seen in connection with Plato's cave, if the cinematic image is an illusion, it is an illusion that we voluntarily subject ourselves to, and in full awareness of its status as an illusion. So we can easily distinguish between the cinematic 'dream' and reality. With his dream argument, Descartes is suggesting the possibility of a much more radical kind of deception, arising because of the difficulty in determining whether what we see is a dream or reality.

We can however find situations that more fully parallel the dream argument portrayed within films. An updated version of the dream argument appears for example in Total Recall (Paul Verhoeven, 1990). In one scene, a doctor tries to convince the hero Doug Quaid (Arnold Schwarzenegger) that he is not in fact an invincible secret agent, fighting the villains on Mars. Rather, he is a lowly construction worker strapped into a chair back on Earth, and he is merely dreaming that he is an invincible secret agent fighting the villains on Mars. It is all part of a futuristic 'holiday' in which one buys memories of one's trip rather than actually going on the journey. However, the doctor continues, things have gone wrong, they cannot wake Quaid back on Earth, and he is a mere representation sent into Quaid's dream to help him return to reality. All that Quaid has to do is to swallow a little pill, as a 'symbol of his desire to return to reality'. Quaid, of course, has to work out whether the doctor is telling the truth or is in fact in league with the evil forces that Quaid is fighting, and his whole story is really a fabrication designed to trap him. As it happens, he is able to do so. About to swallow the pill, he notices a trickle of sweat running down the doctor's brow, a sign of nervousness that convinces him the doctor is lying.

This might seem like a reasonable enough kind of response to the dream argument – you find some test to determine whether or not you are dreaming, such as some element in your present experience that is inconsistent with your being in a dream. But one of the intriguing things about the dream argument is that it has a way of resisting such easy responses. The problem is that any test we might come up with for determining whether we are dreaming or not, such as pinching ourselves, might itself be part of our dream. In Quaid's case, the trickle of sweat on the doctor's brow, which seems to imply that the doctor is lying and that he, Quaid, is not dreaming, could itself be part of an extended dream. Indeed, all the action in which Quaid finds himself involved could conceivably be part of one long dream, a possibility that is in fact rather teasingly suggested in the film itself. In the final scene Quaid, having defeated the forces of evil, turns to the Girl (Rachel Ticotin) and says 'I've just had a terrible thought – what if this is all a dream'. This possibility is taken much more seriously in eXistenZ (David Cronenberg, 1999) where the relevant illusion-creating device is a futuristic form of video game that plugs into the spine, and allows one to inhabit a complete virtual reality. Towards the end, the central characters Allegra Geller (Jennifer Jason Leigh) and Ted Pikul (Jude Law) seem to escape from the game, only to realize that for all they know they may still be in it. In the final scene, it looks as if they have at last truly escaped. It appears that the game they have been playing, indeed everything that has happened so far in the film, has been part of a game they have been trialling. But just when they seem to have finally, definitively, returned to reality, someone is still able to ask: 'Hey, tell me the truth – are we still in the game?' The film ends here with the issue unresolved. It thus takes seriously the idea that nothing in our experience seems to be able to completely exclude the possibility that everything we currently experience might be an illusion. Anything we care to propose as a test for being awake could itself be part of the dream.

Descartes' dream argument thus raises the possibility that what we presently experience might be a dream, and that what we think is real might not be real at all. However, this is only the second stage in Descartes' series of sceptical arguments. For Descartes, there remain some claims about what the world is like that survive the dream argument. Dreams, he argues, derive their content from waking experience (we dream of people, houses, trees and so on), and so even if we do not know at any particular moment whether what we are experiencing is real or part of a dream, what we experience can still give us a general idea of what the world is like. So Descartes introduces a third sceptical argument, one that seems to throw into doubt all beliefs based on experience. He raises the possibility that there might be an evil demon, an all-powerful being that is able to deceive us completely, causing us to go wrong even in things that we consider absolutely certain. Everything we experience might be an illusion, generated in us by the evil demon. We cannot be sure what the world is like, or even whether there is a world outside us at all. We cannot even be sure of basic mathematical truths, such as 'two plus two equals four'. A more recent version of the evil demon argument is the 'brain in a vat' scenario. How do we know we are not in fact brains floating in a vat, hooked up with various electrodes, with a mad scientist using a computer to feed electronic impulses into us, giving us all the experiences we now have, and making us think that everything is normal? The idea of systematic deception by an all-powerful malevolent being thus raises the possibility that we could be so profoundly manipulated that everything we have ever taken to be reality could be illusory.

With the evil demon, Descartes formulates another haunting philosophical image, to rank with that of Plato's cave. We can gain a sense of just how radical this kind of deception is because many cinematic portrayals of systematic deception fall considerably short. One film that seeks to portray a situation of deliberate, systematic deception is Peter Weir's *The Truman Show* (1998). At the outset of the film at least, the central character Truman (Jim Carrey) is blissfully unaware that the town he has grown up in is in fact a studio set and that his neighbours are actors, and that he is the main character of a show being beamed out live to a huge TV audience. The whole set up is being controlled behind the scenes by the show's all-powerful director Christof (Ed Harris), from a suitably unworldly control room high above the set behind an artificial moon. Despite all this, however, the deception here is far less radical than that portrayed in the evil demon situation. Even when he is thoroughly deceived about the nature of his situation Truman remains at all times in contact with the real world, even if the reality is only that of a television studio set. The situation is similar in *The Game* (David Fincher, 1997). Here Michael Douglas plays the corporate executive Nicholas Van Orton who has been enrolled by his brother in a mysterious live-action game for his birthday. He has no idea of the rules or the aim of the game, but he finds himself caught up in a series of increasingly bizarre episodes. Eventually it becomes impossible for him to tell whether what is happening in his life is really as it seems, or simply part of the game. Yet here also, the deception is not truly radical; the game itself is taking place in Orton's everyday reality, which he never leaves. Even in *Dark City* (Alex Proyas, 1998), where aliens secretly manipulate not only a cityscape but also the memories of its inhabitants, as part of a large-scale experiment to 'see how humans tick', the events in the film still take place within the reality of the characters.

A film that comes significantly closer to the evil demon situation with regard to the depth of the deception that it presents is *The Matrix* (Andy and Larry Wachowski, 1999). The premise of this film is that most of humanity has been enslaved by a race of intelligent machines who use human bodies as power sources. They are however completely unaware of their real situation. Everything seems normal because a supercomputer feeds them a simulated reality ('the matrix'). Only a few rebels have managed to escape this enslavement and are able to offer resistance to the machines. Thus at the outset of the film, before he escapes from the matrix, everything that the central character Neo (Keanu Reeves) experiences and takes to be real is in fact a computer-generated illusion. This is the same kind of updating of the evil demon argument that we find in the brain in the vat scenario. Indeed, as in that scenario, most of humanity in the film is in reality floating in tanks, hooked up with electrodes through which they are fed their simulated reality. *The Matrix* is particularly interesting because it also incorporates some of the other themes we have been discussing. There are multiple references to the issue of dreams, and the possibility that we might be dreaming without knowing it, which Descartes raised in his dream argument. The leader of the rebels, Morpheus (Laurence Fishburne), has the name of the Roman God of dreams and sleep; and when he goes into the matrix to enlist Neo to the resistance cause, he offers our hero the opportunity to 'awaken' from his illusion. The conundrum he poses here is pure Descartes: 'Have you ever had a dream, Neo, that you were so sure was real? What if you were unable to wake from that dream? How would you know the difference between the dream world and the real world?'

Moreover, because the matrix is a collective illusion, with many people sharing the same illusory reality, it is a situation that also resembles Plato's cave. And the film recalls other themes associated with the cave as well. When the traitor amongst the rebels, Cypher (Joe Pantoliano) betrays his comrades because he yearns to escape from harsh reality, to return to the unreal comforts of the matrix, he is like those amongst Plato's prisoners who are bewildered when their illusions are disturbed, and who are happier left in their original state. He is willing to sacrifice truth for a happiness based on illusion. The cave story's linking of illusion and a wider social imprisonment is also touched on, since the matrix is a tool of social control; and those rebels with the courage to face the truth of their situation are fighting against the enslavement perpetuated by the matrix's illusory reality. Overall, the film refers us to a number of the themes we have been considering. At this point however the theme I want to emphasize is the evil demon argument, which the film illustrates well because it invokes both a malevolent, all-powerful agency working behind the scenes, and the possibility of our being completely, systematically, deceived by this agency. Every aspect of peoples' experience is being fabricated here. Descartes' demon argument could easily be restated in terms drawn from *The Matrix* – might it not be the case that everything we experience, everything we have ever experienced, even what we take to be basic logical truths, could be a fabrication generated by some supercomputer? And the effect of such a question is similarly to throw into doubt, in a very radical way, what our experience tells us about the world.

Now it might seem that there would be no way of escaping from the radical kind of doubt that this kind of consideration invokes, no way of ridding ourselves of uncertainty and acquiring certain knowledge. In fact Descartes thinks that we can overcome this doubt, and we'll see what this involves in a moment. But first of all, there is one further aspect of the cinematic experience that allows us to say something about processes of deception. As I mentioned earlier, we the audience are aware that the film we see is an illusion. There is no deception there. However we can still be deceived as to what is going on within that cinematic illusion. Let us examine this more closely. Although characters in a film may suffer from deception or lack of knowledge in various ways, we the audience tend to think of ourselves as being in an epistemically superior position. And it is true that generally speaking, the audience knows more than the fictional agents, because, as George Wilson puts it in *Narration in Light*, the perception of these agents is 'confined within a line of narrative action which they cannot survey' (Wilson 1986, 5). So in *The Truman Show*, for example, we know far earlier than Truman that the world he inhabits is fake. In the opening scene a studio light drops from the 'sky'. To take another example, in Alfred Hitchcock's *North by Northwest* (1959) we know fairly early on that George Kaplan, the man that advertising executive Roger Thornhill (Cary Grant) is searching for in order to clear himself of a murder charge, does not in fact exist, but is the invention of a government agency.

However, we do not always enjoy this privileged epistemic position. That is, the film's director may try to deceive the audience as well, to draw them also into the web of deception, until the moment when the truth is revealed to the audience as well as to the characters. Success here of course depends on the director being able to prevent the audience from guessing the secret prematurely. Thus, in *The Matrix*, we, like Neo initially, have no idea that the world Neo inhabits is an illusion, and we are as disoriented as he is when his real situation is suddenly revealed. Without resorting to the possibilities opened up by virtual reality, this strategy of deception and surprise revelation is also effectively employed by Neil Jordan in his film *The Crying Game* (1992), when both we and the central character Fergus (Stephen Rea) discover that the 'woman' Fergus has fallen for is in fact a man. Once again the revelation is initially disorienting, confounding the beliefs we have built up about what is going on before us. The effect in both cases is to make us suddenly aware of the assumptions we have been making about what we are seeing, suddenly aware of what we have been unthinkingly assuming about the world presented to us; and this gives us a taste of what Descartes seeks to do in raising his sceptical considerations – to challenge our complacency, our confidence that what we take to be knowledge really is knowledge.

Still, both these films present their surprise early on, and in both cases we quickly adjust to the new reality of the situation and acknowledge that our previous understanding was illusory. Are more extreme forms of audience deception possible? How radically can cinema audiences be misled? It is certainly true that entire films can be devoted to systematically misleading their audiences. Bryan Singer's *The Usual Suspects* (1995) begins with the explosion of a docked ship, and consists largely of flashbacks, as one of the survivors, crippled petty criminal 'Verbal' Kint (Kevin Spacey) recounts to a detective the events of the previous six weeks. He tells the story of how he and his colleagues were forced to carry out a raid on the ship by the master criminal Keyser Sose.

Only in the very last moments of the film does it become clear to the detective, and indeed to the audience, that everything that Kint has said, and everything we have been watching in flashback, which is to say, almost the entirety of the film, is a fabrication. These are 'lying flashbacks' and Kint himself is very likely Keyser Sose. This film is particularly appealing in the light of the evil demon argument because the arch-deceiver, Keyser Sose, is suitably ruthless and demonic. And this criminal genius fabricates a logically coherent, plausible world which although completely false passes all the critical scrutiny that the detective, and ideally the audience also, can muster. In addition, the film's use of lying flashbacks confounds our expectation that flashbacks will tell the truth about what has gone on. Alfred Hitchcock used the device in *Stage Fright* (1950), where the opening sequence is a false flashback, an account of events told by the murderer himself which programmes the audience to believe in his innocence. With *The Usual Suspects*, it has become the basis for an entire film.

A similar though less malevolent kind of global deception, without resorting to the lying flashback device, is enacted in Giuseppe Tornatore's *A Pure Formality* (1994). Here Onoff (Gerard Depardieu), a famous writer, is brought to a lonely, isolated police station, without a clear memory of recent events. The film has begun with a gunshot, and Onoff running through the rain until he is stopped and taken into custody by the police. Nearly all the action of the film consists of his relentless interrogation by the police inspector (Roman Polanski) who is trying to find out what has happened. So it seems that we are witnessing a murder investigation. Once again it is only at the very end of the film that it becomes clear, both to the writer and the audience, that everything we have seen is quite other than what it appears – that the murder being investigated is actually the writer's own suicide, and that he is in fact in a kind of other-worldly ante-chamber *en route* to the afterlife. Now films like *The Usual Suspects* and *A Pure Formality* portray characters that are radically deceived by others or because of their circumstances. But the audience is also able to be radically deceived here because the film's director can completely control the kind and range of information that is available to those watching, which opens up the possibility of systematically misleading the audience as to what is going on in the film, manipulating them, bringing them to make false inferences, and so on. So here in fact we have another cinematic parallel for the evil demon scenario, and indeed perhaps one of the best: the director as the arch-deceiver of the watching audience.

Rationalism and empiricism

So far we have seen how both Plato and Descartes seek to call into question the idea that our experience gives us knowledge of the world. Plato suggests that our experience only gives us shadows removed from reality; Descartes, that everything we experience could be a dream, or the fabrication of some evil demon. But this raises the question: how do we attain knowledge of the world as it really is? The cinema-goer can always leave the cinema, escape from its illusions, and emerge into the real world. All of this takes place within the realm of our ordinary experience. And even within the cinema, in cinematic portrayals of radical illusion and deception like *The Matrix*, the real world that the hero escapes into is still a world that can be experienced, a world that remains in important respects familiar to us. But for Plato and Descartes it is the realm of ordinary experience in general that is being called into question, which is being characterized as in some sense an illusion, removed from reality. So how are we to make the radical kind of escape that Plato and Descartes think is required to attain knowledge? How can we go beyond the world of ordinary experience in order to comprehend the world as it really is?

The answer that both Plato and Descartes give is that the senses are not our only source of knowledge. We also have reason (intelligence or understanding) which, once we set aside the distractions of sensory experience, we can use to 'see' with; it is a kind of inner perception or insight. Our senses tell us only about shadows or appearances; the intellect allows us to comprehend the true world underlying those appearances. In this, Plato and Descartes represent a distinctive kind of understanding of knowledge, often called the rationalist approach. This approach typically downplays the role of the senses in the acquisition of knowledge. For rationalists, the senses only give us access to a world of shifting appearances, whereas knowledge has to do with what is unchanging and eternal. Moreover, the senses are too prone to error, illusion and deception to provide reliable information, whereas knowledge has to be certain. For the rationalists, it is our reason or intellect alone that can give us genuine knowledge, knowledge of the world as it really is, the world underlying mere shifting appearances. Only through our reason can we attain knowledge that is certain and cannot be called into question. We can sum up the rationalist position as the idea that by employing certain procedures of reason alone, we can attain at least some important truths about the world.

Plato's cave image embodies his version of the rationalist conception of knowledge. For Plato, we are like the prisoners in the cave to the extent that we rely on sense experience, taking for reality what are merely shifting appearances, distant copies or shadows of reality. Through philosophical training we will be able to escape from our chains, to break away from reliance on sense experience, and learn to use our reason alone. The ascent from the cave stands for the upward journey whereby we come to use our reason alone to comprehend the true nature of things. On Plato's account, the use of reason amounts to a process of recollection, in which we gain knowledge by recalling information that is already present in our minds, acquired prior to birth, but which we have forgotten. And in recalling this information, we come to comprehend the true nature of things, which Plato identifies with what he calls the 'forms'. The forms are the timeless, unchanging essences of things, existing entirely beyond the world of experience. The objects we encounter in our ordinary experience are only imperfect copies, mere shadows, distant echoes, of these perfect forms. For example, the various different chairs we encounter in our ordinary experience are all imperfect copies of an ideal, timeless, unchanging chair, the Platonic form of the chair existing beyond our experience.

In a similar spirit, Descartes, through his sceptical arguments, seeks to wean us away from our ordinary dependence on the senses, to encourage us to start making use of our reason or understanding. His *Meditations* as a whole is a kind of journey through which we turn away from our senses, learn to use our reason alone, and come to comprehend the true nature of reality. We quickly find that although we can doubt everything our senses tell us, there is one thing our reason tells us that we cannot doubt, namely our own existence, because no matter how deceived I might be, I still have to exist in order to be deceived. Hence his famous claim, 'I think, therefore I am'. And it is through our reason or understanding alone, what Descartes calls the 'light of reason', that we are able to establish, on the basis of this first truth, a secure edifice of knowledge concerning ourselves and the world. As the *Meditations* progresses, Descartes establishes not only that he exists but that he exists as a thinking thing, a mind. By inspecting and working with the ideas he finds within himself, he is then able to demonstrate to his satisfaction that God exists. Finally, he is able to establish knowledge of the external world, on the grounds that God, being a good God, is not the kind of being who would wickedly deceive him, which guarantees that the general ideas Descartes has about the nature of the world do in fact correspond to reality. Once again, our reason allows us to comprehend the true nature of reality; and once again, it is a very different world to that revealed by the senses, a world that can only be described in terms of the general ideas we have about the nature of the world, which are mathematical and geometrical in character.

It is possible of course to criticize these rationalist pictures in their details. For example, Descartes thinks that thanks to a benevolent God he can establish knowledge of a wider world, and knowledge of what, in general, this world is like. But not many have found his arguments for the existence of God convincing; and if there is no God to bridge the gap, then we seem to be left with a whole new kind of scepticism, a new kind of uncertainty. The issue, simply stated, is as follows: if all we have direct access to are the ideas in our minds, how can we ever be sure that there is a world external to ourselves? The possibility of this kind of uncertainty is used to great comic effect in John Carpenter's *Dark Star* (1972), which features a band of bored astronauts on a mission to destroy unstable planets that could menace intergalactic colonists. Here, astronaut Doolittle (Brian Narelle) tries to convince one of the intelligent, talking bombs not to explode by convincing it that while it can certainly be sure of its own existence (Bomb: 'I think, therefore I am'; Doolittle: 'That's good!'), it cannot be sure of anything else. The astronaut argues that because all the bomb is really aware of is the electronic impulses in its computer brain, it has no way of knowing what the external world is like, or even if there is any external world at all. As a result, it cannot be sure that it has received a genuine command from outside to explode. It is an ingenious stratagem, but even if it succeeds in preventing the bomb from exploding (and only temporarily, as it turns out), we are still left with the problem of how to escape from the Cartesian self and regain knowledge of the external world.

Such criticisms have to do with the internal details of these rationalist accounts, but there are also those who have criticized the rationalist approach to knowledge as such. Sceptics have suggested that what rationalist philosophers like Plato and Descartes have offered as absolutely certain knowledge of a world beyond ordinary experience is really nothing more than ungrounded speculations on their part, merely personal fantasies dressed up as knowledge. And by presenting their accounts of the world as having been arrived at by some mysterious rational process, they have rendered their positions dogmatic and unverifiable. What is perhaps most problematic for the rationalist position is that almost every view of the real world that has been asserted as absolutely true by one rationalist has been disputed by other rationalists, equally certain of the truth of their own accounts. Partly in reaction to the rationalist approach, we find another influential approach to knowledge in philosophical thinking, known as the empiricist approach. For the empiricists, claims to attain knowledge without reference to sense experience lead inevitably to dogmatic and unverifiable claims about what the world is really like. The empiricist position is that we get our knowledge primarily through the senses, through sense experience and observation.

In other words, the empiricists call into question the rationalists' faith in the power of human reason, and their downplaying of sense experience. For empiricism, it is reason that plays the secondary role. Reason by itself, independently of experience, cannot establish any truths about the world. At best, our reason can determine that certain things are true 'by definition', such as 'all bachelors are unmarried'. But this kind of statement does not tell us anything about the world. It only tells us about the meaning of the words we are using. For the empiricists, the only way to gain knowledge of the world is to go out and actually observe things. All knowledge of the world, they argue, is derived from sense experience and observation. Empiricists tend to dismiss rationalist claims about a world beyond that which we can experience as no more than baseless speculation. They acknowledge the rationalist argument that the sort of knowledge we can acquire on the basis of the senses cannot be absolutely certain, that it is at best merely probable. But they also hold that the rationalist demand for absolute certainty is excessive and unrealistic. It is enough that we are reasonably certain, and we can attain a reasonable degree of certainty to the extent that our claims to knowledge are firmly grounded in sense experience and observation.

Two important advocates of the empiricist way of thinking are the British philosophers John Locke (1632–1704) and David Hume (1711–1776), who came onto the scene shortly after Descartes. In part they were reacting against Descartes' rationalism, but they were also seeking to formulate a conception of how we acquire knowledge that was more in keeping with the new natural sciences. The modern natural sciences emerged during the sixteenth and seventeenth centuries, with figures like Francis Bacon, Galileo Galilei and Isaac Newton in the forefront. What characterized the new natural-scientific approach, according to its advocates, was a reliance on empirical methods, on observation and experiment as the proper avenue for the acquisition of knowledge. And this scientific method seemed to be triumphantly confirmed by the success of Isaac Newton towards the end of the seventeenth century. Newton's comprehensive physics, in which he formulated a number of simple physical laws capable of explaining phenomena as diverse as the tides, the fall of an apple and the movement of planets, represented a decisive vindication of the new natural sciences. Thus the British empiricists, by making experience and observation central to the acquisition of knowledge, were in effect giving a philosophical formulation of the new scientific method.

Is seeing believing?

Empiricism sounds like a much more sensible, down-to-earth way of thinking about knowledge than the rationalist approach. We no longer have to rely on some mysterious rational capacity that discerns ultimate truths about the world independently of ordinary experience. We do not need to depart from ordinary experience in order to gain knowledge of the world. Our knowledge is derived from ordinary experience and observation. However despite its attractions, problems have been raised in connection with this approach as well. One of the most important problems concerns the notion of 'ordinary experience' itself. The empiricist approach puts a great deal of weight on experience, since it is out of experience that knowledge is said to arise. Experience itself is held to be basic, uncontroversial and unproblematic. How can there be any question as to what it is that we directly experience? What we experience is simply 'given' to us, and we can appeal to this to ground and justify our knowledge. At least, so goes the empiricist view. But the question is whether there is ever a straightforward foundation of this sort. It has been argued by a number of commentators that there is no basic experience, prior to knowledge, that we can appeal to. In other words, it is never simply a matter of 'seeing is believing'. Rather, what we experience is always subject to interpretation or judgement of some sort. And if this is so, the argument runs, we can no longer say that knowledge straightforwardly arises out of experience, because what we know, what we believe, influences what it is that we see in the first place.

It certainly seems true that seeing is a more complex process than one might at first think. A trained doctor will be able to see the signs of an acute illness in the x-ray picture, where the layperson will see only blurry shapes. The empiricist might say that the doctor and the layperson have the same perceptual experience, but that they interpret what they see in different ways. On this view there would still be a 'pure' perceptual experience, and a clear distinction between what is directly given to us in perception and our interpretation of it. But how plausible is this distinction? For example, do we only really see the physical properties of someone's behaviour, various movements or changes in shape, and then go on to interpret what is happening as a smile or a wave of greeting? Or do we see a smile or a greeting? What a number of critics of empiricism have argued is that we can never separate out what we really, literally see from our interpretation of it. As far as perception is concerned, the only thing we have direct and immediate contact with are our experiences, and these experiences vary with the knowledge and expectations of the observer (see e.g. Chalmers 1986, 24–8). So on this view, every act of perception involves interpretation. What we perceive is always 'theory-dependent', inescapably shaped or coloured by what we know. Consequently we cannot say with the empiricist that knowledge arises straightforwardly out of experience.

The issue of theory-dependence arises in a very clear way in connection with the cinema. Cinema is primarily a visual medium, showing rather than telling its stories, but this does not mean that it simply presents a story to us in a visual way. How we see what is presented to us is profoundly shaped and manipulated by the film-maker. Film does not merely record events but guides us as to how to see them. As George Wilson argues, film-makers aim most fundamentally to make an envisaged significance visible to the audience, to bring it about that the viewer sees things in a certain way (see Wilson 1986, 7). For example, the director may wish to bring it about that the viewer sees a series of events as causally connected, a character's behaviour as manifesting certain states of mind, or the lives of characters as ordered by chance or social forces. The question then arises as to what is being given to us in perception, and what we 'read into' what we see. Advocates of theory-dependence would argue that it is artificial to suppose there is a basic experience that we then go on to interpret; and that it is probably impossible to draw any strict boundary between perception and interpretation. What is clear is that a great deal goes into shaping how we see events in a film, including the way the action is edited, how scenes are framed and composed, the camera angles and movements employed, and the sound effects and background music. For film-goers to be able to see what is going on in a film they have to bring with them knowledge of the techniques and conventions of film narrative, along with more general beliefs about the nature and operation of the world outside the cinema. Thus, as Perkins puts it, '[i]f we could rid ourselves of knowledge and our customary patterns of thought, we could not make sense of a movie' (Perkins 1972, 72).

Given that the experience of watching a film raises various questions about what the audience actually sees, it is not surprising that some films have directly addressed this issue. One film where the question of what exactly we see comes up in a central way is Alfred Hitchcock's *Rear Window* (1954). Here, L.B. Jefferies

(James Stewart), wheelchair-bound with a broken leg, passes the time by watching the neighbours in his apartment block. His position is like that of the watching cinema audience, for he too is an immobilized spectator, watching unseen in the shadows, isolated from the action he is witnessing. And since the film is shot almost entirely from his point of view, we quickly become voyeurs along with him. In almost all that follows, we see what he sees. With him we become acquainted with the characters who inhabit the block – the aspiring composer, the enticing blonde, 'Miss Lonelyhearts', the newlyweds and Thorwald (Raymond Burr), the travelling salesman across the way with the bedridden wife. Then the bedridden woman disappears one night, and Stewart becomes convinced that what he has witnessed is a murder. But has he? What exactly has he seen? His housekeeper, his girlfriend and his detective friend all offer various theories. New information comes to light (a postcard arrives for Thorwald, apparently from the wife recuperating in the country), which suggests a more innocuous way of interpreting what has been seen. It gradually becomes clear that Jefferies is right and that there has been foul play. But it is not the case that what he has seen across the way straightforwardly allows him to decide the matter. Rather, his expectations and desires shape what he sees, and it is only through the accumulation of facts and the development of theories to make sense of them that he is able to finally decide what he has seen in the first place.

In Hitchcock's film, dramatic tension is built up because of the uncertainty about just what it is that Jefferies, and we in the audience watching along with him, have witnessed. It is not that we cannot see, but that we cannot decide what it is we are seeing. This uncertainty is heightened because so much of the film's running time is devoted to looking. As one commentator has noted, over a third of the film is in fact silent, without dialogue, as we look with Jefferies at his neighbours – an exercise in what Hitchcock called 'pure cinema' (Sharff 1997, 2). So we look intently, and yet we are often not sure what we are seeing. Are the knife and small saw that Thorwald is wrapping over the sink merely household implements or are they murder weapons? Is the trunk that he ties up with heavy rope in the bedroom a piece of luggage or a coffin for his wife? Nothing in what we are experiencing here allows us to establish which is the case, because what we see depends crucially on our theory about what is going on. Hitchcock refuses until close to the end of the film to provide either Jefferies or ourselves with any definitive guidance as to how to see what is before us. Deprived of this guidance for the most part, we become aware of the extent to which interpretation and judgement play a role in what we see in the cinema, the extent to which cinematic seeing is an achievement. In this way, the film also bears out the more general idea that what we see is not simply given to us, that we are actively involved in shaping our perception.

The role of interpretation and judgement in determining what we see is exploited in another way in a number of other films, where the audience is tricked into making perceptual judgements that they later have to question. In Fritz Lang's *You Only Live Once* (1937) circumstances cause the apparently innocent Eddie Taylor (Henry Fonda) to be sent to prison. As Wilson notes, this film repeatedly raises questions about sight and the failure to see. At several points the audience is led into making a mistaken perceptual judge-ment, after which a wider context is revealed and the judgement shown to be wrong. For example, a newspaper in close-up suggests Eddie is innocent until it is revealed as one of a number of possible front pages that have been prepared prior to the outcome of his trial. By doing this, Lang can put a more general question mark over whether Eddie is indeed innocent or guilty, and confound any easy answer to this by reference to 'what we can see before us' (see Wilson 1986, 18). And in *Cabaret* (Bob Fosse, 1972), set in thirties Berlin, an angelic-looking boy sings 'Tomorrow Belongs to Me' until the camera pulls back to reveal his Hitler Youth uniform. We are captivated and seduced until the larger context reveals the real nature of what we are seeing. Here the film alludes to the rising Nazism that provides the larger context for the lives of all the characters in the film, a context that becomes increasingly visible as the film proceeds. Cinema could not achieve these effects if we were not actively involved in constructing the meaning of what we see.

Kant and relativism

If we accept the idea that our experience is unavoidably interpreted in some way, shaped by our background beliefs, then it seems that we cannot accept the basic empiricist position that knowledge is straightforwardly derived from experience. But if so, then how are we to understand knowledge? One possible response might be to move away from empiricism and accept that we have an active role to play in the production of knowledge. This is the kind of answer that is in fact provided by the eighteenth-century German philosopher Immanuel Kant (1724–1804). His work can be seen as a response not only to the British empiricists (particularly Hume), but also to rationalists like Plato and Descartes. Kant accepted the basic empiricist doctrine that all knowledge begins with experience, that experience is necessary for knowledge. But he rejected the empiricist's one-sided emphasis on the contribution of experience alone. He argued that experience by itself is not sufficient to give us knowledge. So what is missing from the empiricist picture? For Kant, it is the contribution of the mind, of reason. Rationalists like Plato and Descartes emphasized this element, of course, but they held that reason alone, independently of the senses, could somehow provide us with knowledge of the world. On Kant's view, rationalism and empiricism are equally one-sided. Knowledge requires both reason and experience, both rationalistic and empiricist elements.

Kant's position as formulated in his *Critique of Pure Reason* is roughly as follows. By itself, sense experience is a meaningless, unintelligible confusion of sensations. We only acquire knowledge when we bring order and intelligibility to our experience, when we actively impose ourselves upon it. We do so by ordering or interpreting our experience in terms of certain organizing principles, certain frameworks of thinking that we have within ourselves. This ordering activity is the work of our minds, of our reason or thought. Kant called these organizing principles 'categories', and he claimed to have identified twelve of them, including the categories of substance, causality and reciprocity. So according to Kant, the reason why the world we experience appears to us as a world of things, interacting with one another, and obeying laws of cause and effect, is that we always interpret our experience in terms of the principles or categories of substance, causality and reciprocity. In general then, for Kant the world we know is the world as it appears to us through the framework of our organizing categories. This view, it is worth noting, also means that we can never know the world as it is 'in itself', but only in terms of the categories through which we interpret it.

Thus on Kant's view, although experience is necessary for knowledge, since it is the 'raw material', it is not enough. In order to attain knowledge, this raw material has to be worked on, organized, interpreted, given a form by our reason or thought. This is a view that acknowledges the contribution we ourselves make to knowledge, the role of our own activity in forming our understanding of the world. In other words, for Kant, we do not simply discover what the world is like. Our view of reality is something that we construct, something we actively organize, in accordance with a framework of categories or principles. However, Kant does not think that this account makes knowledge 'merely subjective', i.e., relative to the principles of interpretation employed by particular individuals. This is because he does not think that different people organize their experience in different ways. Rather, he argues that all human beings, all rational beings, possess the same basic ordering principles, and consequently that each of us orders our experience in the same way. In other words, he holds that there are universal, fundamental forms of human experience. In so doing, he seeks to preserve the idea that knowledge is something that is held in common by people, something that we can all in principle agree on.

Nonetheless, if we reject the idea that we all impose the same categories on our experience, it is not a far step from Kant's view to a radically relativistic kind of account, in which different people organize their experience in different ways and thus have different, but equally legitimate, ways of understanding the world. Here, the Kantian idea that we order and shape the world that we know becomes the idea that since experience is not an independent basis for knowledge, since knowledge involves judgement, it can vary with different frameworks of thinking. And indeed, this has been one development in the theory of knowledge since Kant. It has been argued by a number of people that how we interpret or understand reality depends on the frameworks of thinking, the perspectives, we bring to bear. These perspectives have been variously understood as world-views, conceptual frameworks, forms of knowledge or sets of beliefs, guiding interests and expectations; and the further claim has been made that because these frameworks, forms of knowledge or guiding interests differ amongst different individuals, groups or cultures, these peoples or cultures have fundamentally different but equally legitimate ways of viewing or understanding the world. So we have here the idea of 'cognitive relativism', the idea that knowledge, what can be said to be true, varies relative to individual, social or cultural conditions.

We saw earlier how films can raise questions about what it is that the audience actually sees, because the film-maker is typically concerned to get the audience to see what is going on in a certain way; and that films like Hitchcock's *Rear Window* explicitly explore the role of interpretation in shaping what we see. For the same reason, we can also find films that explore the possibility of there being different but equally valid interpretations of the same events from different points of view. One of the classic examples is Orson Welles's *Citizen Kane* (1941). At the death of newspaper magnate Charles Foster Kane (Orson Welles), a reporter is sent to find the 'real truth' about Kane. Those he interviews, including his best friend Jebediah Leland (Joseph Cotten) and his ex-wife Susan (Dorothy Comingore), offer differing accounts of Kane's life through flashback. For his best friend, he is corrupted by egotism; for his ex-wife, who he tried to turn into an opera star, he is solely concerned with getting his own way. But these are not the lying flashbacks of *The Usual Suspects*. They present us with different Kanes, Kane's life as viewed from different perspectives. When their stories overlap we view the same event from a different perspective. Thus in Leland's account of events, Susan's disastrous operatic debut, portrayed from the point of view of the audience where he is sitting, appears as farce; in Susan's own recollections, the event, now portrayed from the stage, becomes painful and humiliating (see Giannetti 1996, 494). The overall effect of this multiple narration device is that the reporter fails in his task. Who Kane 'really is' remains elusive. The film in fact questions the very possibility of presenting truth 'objectively'.

A more recent film that explores the idea that our perceptions are conditioned by the perspective we bring to bear is *He Said, She Said* (Ken Kwapis, Marisa Silver, 1991). Here, two journalists, Dan (Kevin Bacon) and Laurie (Elizabeth Perkins), are given their own TV show (*He Said, She Said*) in which they give their opposing views on various issues. As they get to know each other, the events in their own relationship are presented twice, from each of their perspectives (once again through flashbacks). What he sees as a romantic first date, she perceives as an awkward accidental encounter. Their different versions of events reflect their different standpoints – male and female, politically conservative and politically liberal, and so on. Similarly, *Hilary and Jackie* (Anand Tucker, 1998) tells the story of Hilary du Pré (Rachel Griffiths) and her famous cellist sister Jacqueline (Emily Watson) from each of their perspectives. This film is distinctive however in that it does not resort to the flashback device to portray the different versions of events, but simply presents Hilary's story, followed by Jackie's. Here the device of presenting the same event in two different ways, such as Hilary's announcement to Jackie that she is getting married, serves to highlight the differences in the sisters' personality and outlook. Overall these films serve to indicate ways in which experience can be coloured by our outlook; and more broadly, they serve to raise the question of whether there can ever be direct access to reality, outside of our particular perspective on what is going on in the world.

Two other films that are often cited as illustrating a relativist position are Akira Kurosawa's *Rashomon* (1951) and Sidney Lumet's *Twelve Angry Men* (1957). However as we will see shortly, this view can in fact be disputed. *Rashomon* tells the story of the rape of a nobleman's bride and his murder by a bandit (Toshiro Mifune), from four different perspectives: that of the bandit, the bride, the nobleman (through a medium) and an eyewitness. Each telling is significantly different. In the bandit's version he is heroic, the woman consents to his advances, and afterwards she insists he and the husband fight to the death so she will be spared disgrace; in the bride's version she is a victim, the bandit runs off afterwards, and she inadvertently kills her unsympathetic husband; in the husband's version he is the victim, his bride wants to run off with the bandit, and when the bandit refuses her request to kill him he kills himself out of shame. The eyewitness's version incorporates elements from all three. It would appear that here the same events are being interpreted in quite different ways, once again suggesting that experience is conditioned by the perspective we are coming from. However, a closer reading of the film suggests that Kurosawa does not want to illustrate the relative character of knowledge but rather is taking a cynical view of the ability of human beings to twist the truth, in order to preserve the idea they have of themselves. While the bandit, the bride and the nobleman all present self-serving accounts of what went on, in which they each appear in the best possible light, Kurosawa also includes a further account by the eyewitness, which seems to represent 'what really went on'. And Kurosawa himself has gone on record to say that his film is about self-deception, our capacity to delude ourselves, rather than relativism (see Jarvie 1987, 306–7).

Similarly, *Twelve Angry Men* (Sidney Lumet, 1957) is sometimes cited in connection with relativism. Here Henry Fonda plays juror #8, the architect, the only person on a jury holding out for a not guilty verdict for a young man accused of murder. By a mixture of argument and cunning, he gradually brings the others around to his point of view. The other jurors bring various perspectives to bear on the issue, for example juror #10, the bigot, whose whole assessment of the case is coloured by his view that 'these people' are born bad, and juror #3, the angry man, whose views are affected by his estrangement from his own son. This film might accordingly be seen as an illustration of the way in which people's beliefs and interests colour their attempts to reconstruct events from a mass of testimony, and thus to imply that the way we understand the world is always coloured by our beliefs and interests. However, as Jarvie points out (Jarvie 1987, 302), the film is probably more accurately seen as one man's heroic stand for the truth, in the face of others whose views are clouded and distorted by interest and prejudice. Fonda is the quiet 'voice of reason', the only juror who remains calm and reasonable throughout. He thus plays the same role as the eyewitness in *Rashomon*. Through his conscientious devotion to the truth, he is able to see past the prejudices of others and identify the clues that make it impossible to convict the young man.

The truth and nothing but

There are two ways of thinking about what is going on in *Rashomon* and *Twelve Angry Men*. We may want to argue that they are falling back into a naive and indefensible notion of unconditioned truth. Since all accounts of the world are conditioned, at least to some degree, by the social and historical circumstances of the knower, any view that pretends to be unconditioned is simply concealing the perspective from which it is coming. Alternatively, the films can be seen as demonstrating the power of truth over views that are clouded by prejudice. And here we have a reassertion of the idea of knowledge or truth as something that is not affected or conditioned by the particular circumstances of the knower, by their pre-existing beliefs, interests or prejudices. This is a view that brings us back to Plato. Plato is one of the earliest and strongest advocates of this strong conception of truth or knowledge. And generally speaking, both the rationalists and the empiricists thought that such knowledge was possible, and in each case their theories of knowledge provided a method for attaining it. For the rationalists, it was to be gained through rational insight, and for the empiricists, by grounding knowledge in basic experiences. For both, any pre-existing beliefs, interests or prejudices we might have could only serve to interfere with the search for truth, and the approaches they proposed for acquiring the truth were intended to free us from their influence. Even Kant, who argued that we needed to bring a pre-existing framework to bear on our experience in order to acquire knowledge, insisted as we have seen that the forms of order we imposed on our experience were universal and independent of our particular interests and circumstances.

This strong view of truth stands in direct opposition to the idea that there is no such thing as unconditioned knowledge, that our understanding of the world is always conditioned in some way by our particular interests and circumstances. For advocates of the strong notion of truth, such views undermine the very possibility of acquiring knowledge, and threaten us with 'cognitive disaster'. In addition, it has been argued that abandoning this strong idea of truth will lead to moral and political problems as well. To see how this might come about, we can once again refer back to Plato. As we saw earlier, Plato's account does not only have to do with knowledge, but also with a certain kind of liberation that can be achieved through knowledge. Others can control and manipulate us by filling our heads with lies, illusion and distortion; by seeing through these illusions and grasping the truth of our circumstances, we can free ourselves from this. Traditionally, lies, illusion and distortion go hand in hand with moral and social corruption, both serving the interests of powerful groups and concealing their activities from view. By the same token, the bright light of truth which reveals the lies, along with the underlying interests they serve, is seen as standing in opposition to evil. However a view which stresses the 'located' character of knowledge seems to undermine this possibility. If there is no such thing as a truth unconditioned by circumstances, if all knowledge in fact serves the requirements and interests of particular individuals and groups, we seem to have lost any standpoint from which to mount such a challenge.

We have already seen, in *Rashomon* and *Twelve Angry Men*, a defence of truth as an antidote to views that are clouded, corrupted and distorted by prejudice or interest. In these films truth also has a clear moral dimension. In *Rashomon*, it stands in opposition to the distorted accounts presented by the bandit, bride and nobleman, who want to present themselves in the best light and to absolve themselves of any wrongdoing. In *Twelve Angry Men*, the advocate of truth is a heroic figure fighting the prejudiced views of the other jurors, prejudices which threaten to bring about a miscarriage of justice. The quintessential cinematic searcher after truth is the detective or private investigator, and here also the moral dimension of truth is usually evident. The detective is traditionally pitted against the evil that hides beneath deception and subterfuge, the evil that cannot bear the light and must hide itself in dark spaces. Uncovering the truth robs evil of its power, and allows the rule of morality and justice to be restored. Even in the moody classics of American forties film noir, *The Maltese Falcon* (John Huston, 1941) and *The Big Sleep* (Howard Hawks, 1946), where society is riddled with corruption and the private investigator himself is also often less than pure, the truth that is eventually uncovered still defeats evil and helps bring justice to the corrupt society.

Yet even if we accept the view that we can have insight into the world that is unconditioned by our circumstances, we may still want to question the idea that this truth has the power to vanquish evil. Certainly, the traditional faith in truth's power to defeat evil has been called into question in some of the more recent detective films. In Jean-Jacques Annaud's *The Name of the Rose* (1986), William of Baskerville (Sean Connery), a Sherlock Holmes-like monk, is sent to investigate a series of murders in a fourteenth-century monastery. He must penetrate the dogma, superstition and fear of the monks, and even contend with the fanaticism of the Inquisitor Bernardo Gui (F. Murray Abraham), in order to eventually reveal the truth behind the murders. Far from being inspired by the Devil, they have a much more human cause. They are, it turns out, the result of attempts to conceal a long-lost work by the Greek philosopher Aristotle, a volume held in the monastery's labyrinthine library. On the face of it, this is a triumph of truth and enlightened reason over fanaticism and superstition. Yet although William solves the mystery and reveals the truth, very little is achieved as a result. The monastery along with the book is destroyed by fire, the Inquisitor rides off, undefeated, and dogma and superstition continue to hold sway.

An even darker and more pessimistic vision is presented in Roman Polanski's *Chinatown* (1974), a film that revives film noir themes but with a significant twist. Here, J.J. Gittes (Jack Nicholson), an LA private eye, takes on the seemingly routine investigation of an errant husband, but soon finds himself confronted with a network of monstrous evil and corruption presided over by the wicked Noah Cross (John Huston). Yet even after uncovering the truth of what is going on, Gittes is powerless to do anything at all about it, the woman he tries to protect from Cross is killed, Cross himself escapes scot-free and monstrous evil triumphs. This absolute failure on the detective's part is more than just a reversal of the standard private eye plot; it is also a reversal of our traditional faith that truth will defeat evil. The victory of evil over truth is complete in David Fincher's *Se7en* (1995). Here the two detectives (Brad Pitt and Morgan Freeman) not only solve the mystery behind a series of murders based on the seven deadly sins, but even manage to take the killer (Kevin Spacey) into custody. Yet far from being defeated, he is still able to carry out one final murder, his own meticulously planned killing at the hands of one of the detectives.

So these recent detective films embody a more cynical view of truth's power to oppose moral and social evil. At the very least they serve to remind us that the forces of truth do not always triumph over corruption, that even when brought into plain view, evil can continue to flourish. And there remains the more fundamental question as to whether we can ever in fact speak of an unconditioned, absolute notion of truth at all, or whether our understanding of the world is always limited and conditioned in some way by our particular interests or social circumstances. The debate between advocates of an absolute notion of truth and those who see truth as conditioned by our circumstances continues in philosophy. It is time for us, however, to turn our attention to other areas of philosophical concern. In this chapter, we have looked at a number of ways in which knowledge has been understood by philosophers. In discussing the role of knowledge in various forms of liberation, we have also moved beyond the issue of knowledge proper and touched on considerations relevant to moral thinking and to social and political philosophy. We will turn to these wider moral, social and political concerns in Chapters 3 and 4. In the next chapter, however, I want to start closer to home and look at philosophical accounts of ourselves, of the self or human nature.

2

ALL OF ME – THE SELF AND PERSONAL IDENTITY

Steve Martin in *All of Me*.
Credit: Universal (Courtesy Kobal)

At one point in Carl Reiner's *All of Me* (1984) a curious sight greets passers-by: the film's hero, lawyer Roger Cobb (Steve Martin), struggling to get from the doorway of his building to the kerbside. What is curious is that he seems to be struggling with himself. Part of him seems to want to go the other way, to go back into the building. We in the audience can hear his thoughts and so we know what is really going on. The personality of heiress Edwina Cutwater (Lily Tomlin) has mysteriously entered his body and now has partial control over his actions. He wants to go, but she wants to stay. As Cutwater's disembodied voice in his head informs him, 'We obviously have mutual control over our body', to which he replies out loud 'Our body? It's my body. I'm not sharing my body with anyone!' Strange though this situation may be, it also presupposes a number of widely held ideas about the nature of the self. We usually think of our self as something within us, as that which is most central to who we are. Moreover, even under quite normal circumstances there are times when we want to say that our behaviour is not expressive of 'who we really are', that we were 'not ourselves' or 'beside ourselves' at the time we were acting. That is, we want to say that not all behaviour expresses our real selves or true nature, only what we would call our 'authentic' behaviour. And third, many have thought of the self as being immaterial or spiritual, as something that is distinct from and even able to separate itself from the physical body, while also inhabiting the body and able to control it in some manner. This idea of the self as immaterial or spiritual is an important part of our idea of the 'soul'. Philosophical theories have abounded as to what counts as our real self or true nature, and what relationship this self might have to the body. To start looking at these accounts, let us turn once again to Plato.

Plato and the parts of the soul

Plato is one of those philosophers who believe in an immaterial self or soul. Once again his views can be found in the *Republic*. His position is that the self or soul is not only immaterial, but also indestructible and immortal. It has existed eternally before birth and will continue to do so after death (see Plato 1974, 608; see also 609–11). We will come back to this idea of the soul as immaterial and immortal in the next section. For now let us focus on another feature of Plato's account of the self: his characterization of the soul as consisting of a number of different parts. Our self is not a simple unity but consists of a number of distinguishable elements. His argument that the soul has parts draws on an experience we all have from time to time, that of inner mental conflict. Plato himself gives the example of someone who is thirsty and wants to drink water, but who also knows that the water is poisoned and for this reason stops themselves from drinking. For Plato, the same self cannot have opposite attributes; it cannot both desire to drink the water and desire not to drink the water. Rather, he argues, there are different parts of the soul in evidence here. There is one part of the soul that wants to drink, and another part that commands the person not to drink. On Plato's account, the first part, which seeks to drink, is the irrational and appetitive part of the soul, and the second, which forbids the drinking because the water is poisoned, is the reasoning part.

Plato spells out his picture of the soul and its parts most fully in Book Four of the *Republic* (435–44). The soul, he thinks, has three parts, reason, desire and spirit. Reason is the part of the soul that knows reality, and which also calculates and makes decisions. Desire is the irrational, appetitive part, composed of the instinctive cravings, urges and appetites. It includes all the physical desires, such as hunger, thirst and sexual desire. And Plato also adds a third part, which he calls the *thumos* or spirited part. It is something like courage or self-assertion. Plato thinks that the existence of this third element in the soul is also demonstrated in certain cases of mental conflict, for example in those cases where a person feels angry and indignant with themselves because they have certain desires. He gives the example of a man who has a morbid desire to look at a pile of corpses, but who is also disgusted with himself for wanting to do so. It is the spirited part that makes itself apparent in feelings like self-disgust, as well as shame, anger, indignation and strength of will. Plato also distinguishes this spirited part from the reasoning part, because children show spirit long before they demonstrate reasoning powers, and because sometimes the reasoning part has to call the spirited part to order.

Along with this tripartite account of the soul, Plato provides us with a conception of how this soul might best function, and in so doing offers an account of what we would now call spiritual or mental health. Plato's view is that spiritual or mental health is achieved when all these parts are in harmonious balance with one another, each playing its proper part in the whole. We have already seen how reason is central to Plato's account of knowledge, and not surprisingly, we now find that it also plays a central role in his picture of the soul. For Plato, the proper role of the rational part is to govern, to rule the other parts of the soul; the spirited part's role is to provide reason with the force it needs to govern; and it is the function of reason, with the aid of spirit, to control and regulate the appetitive part. In another of Plato's works, the Phaedrus, he formulates another memorable image to capture this spiritual organization, comparing reason to a charioteer striving to control the two steeds of spirit and desire (see Plato 1961, 253). For Plato, problems arise if the self becomes unbalanced, if the various parts are not playing their proper role, and in particular if reason is unable to control the appetites. For then the appetites come to rule over us, and we become mere slaves of our desires.

With this, Plato introduces an immensely influential conception of the self or human nature, the view that human existence is fundamentally a struggle between reason and desire, a struggle that reason ought to win. For Plato and many who come after him, reason is the 'higher' part of the human being, and desires are the 'lower' part, primitive, irrational and chaotic. In these accounts, we are usually identified most closely with our reason, our rational side. This is what we most centrally are. Our desires are seen as being less central to us, still part of us but nonetheless in some sense alien to us. They need to be firmly controlled by reason. In other words, we need to exercise temperance and self-control. If the desiring side were allowed to have its way, our 'higher self' would be undermined and we would be at the mercy of our irrational, unruly appetites and passions. This view of human nature reappears in various forms in subsequent thought. Christianity took over the idea of human life as a struggle against desire. For Christianity, desire is always problematic. Particularly in the early Church, it was viewed with deep hostility, as a sign of fundamental corruption, an evil we must struggle against. At best, desire remains a distraction from the higher spiritual concerns, drawing us away from God and the world to come, and keeping us tied to the things of this world. While we remain here we have to rise above desire or keep it under control. Extreme forms of self-discipline, abstinence and austerity were considered worthy exercises from the start, and in the broader history of Christian thought, Christian goodness and virtue have always involved a generous dose of self-denial and privation.

This view of the self or human nature does not disappear with the rise of modern thought. Descartes in the seventeenth century and Kant in the eighteenth century formulate strongly rationalist versions of the account. For Descartes and Kant, the soul or mind is to be identified with reason, which as in Plato's picture plays a central role in our coming to know reality. However, where Plato also included desire, feeling and emotion as part of the soul, even if only as the 'lower' part, these non-rational aspects are now wholly excluded from the self. For Descartes and Kant they belong entirely to the body, which is understood as something distinct from the mind. Insofar as desire, feeling or emotion intrude on the mind they serve only to disorder it, and they must be rigorously excluded if we are to exercise our reason and attain knowledge. For Kant, as we will see in more detail in the next chapter, reason also allows us to determine what is the moral thing to do; and emotion and desire have to be excluded from our moral thinking as well. However, even in these strongly rationalist accounts, we cannot just excise our desires, emotions and feelings. They remain part of our overall make-up, and we have to tame and control them or they will rule over us. For as Kant puts it, 'unless reason takes the reins of government into its own hands, the feelings and inclinations play the master over the man' (Kant, quoted in Dewey and Gould 1970, 190). So once again, human life becomes an endless combat between reason and the passions.

We have, then, an influential conception of human nature as a struggle between reason and desire, one that arises with Plato, is perpetuated through Christianity and reasserted through the rationalist accounts of Descartes and Kant. But while this has certainly been the dominant conception of human nature, an alternative view is provided by, amongst others, the eighteenth-century empiricist philosopher David Hume. For Hume, reason plays a far more modest role in the human make-up. In Book Two, Section Three of his *Treatise of Human Nature* Hume rejects the identification of human beings with reason, and the idea that human beings are a schizophrenic battleground between reason and desire. His view is that desires and passions are an integral and legitimate part of human nature. Indeed we are primarily creatures of desire and feeling. It is desires and emotions that as a matter of fact motivate our behaviour. And there is no conflict at all, Hume argues, between reason and the passions. Reason cannot tell us what is the right thing to do; it cannot provide any kind of motive for human behaviour and so cannot compete with the passions. According to Hume, 'reason is, and ought only to be the slave of the passions' (Hume 1969, 462). That is, reason for Hume can do no more than calculate the best way of realizing our desires. For example the merchant is motivated by a desire or interest in making money, and reason's only role is to allow the merchant to calculate how to best achieve this aim, how to maximize profits and make the most money. To that extent reason can affect behaviour, but without the original desire to make money, reason would have no influence.

As Richard Hanley points out in *The Metaphysics of Star Trek* (1997, 6–7) these two views of human nature are personified at least to some extent in two of the central characters of the original *Star Trek* television show and the various films. The starship *Enterprise*'s science officer Mr Spock (Leonard Nimoy) embodies the first, Platonic view, or perhaps more accurately, this view in its rationalistic, Cartesian or Kantian form. For Spock, reason must always be in charge. In order to acquire his scientific knowledge of the world he must remain strictly rational; and how he is to act in any situation is also to be determined on purely rational or 'logical' grounds. Desire and emotion cannot enter these considerations without confusing matters, and Spock is constantly seeking to control and suppress his emotions. The doctor, Leonard 'Bones' McCoy (DeForest Kelley), is much closer to the Humean type. He indulges freely in emotion, and he reacts emotionally and instinctively to Spock's rationalism. For him, Spock is inhumanly logical, and his refusal to entertain or express emotion makes him cold and unfeeling. For his part, Spock's view of McCoy is typified in *Star Trek: The Wrath of Khan* (Nicholas Meyer, 1982): 'Really, Dr McCoy. You must learn to govern your passions; they will be your undoing. Logic suggests . . . .' Interestingly enough, the *Star Trek* view of things tends to favour the Humean view of human nature. Humanity is identified more closely with the emotional McCoy than the intellectual Spock. Spock is half-alien, half human, and his excessive rationalism is a product of his alien heritage. It is his human side that gives rise to the emotions and feelings that he constantly struggles to suppress within himself.

As Hanley goes on to suggest, neither the Platonic nor the Humean views of human nature are entirely satisfactory. Both are extremes, the one emphasizing reason at the expense of desire, and the other desire at the expense of reason. Part of the appeal of the psychoanalytic conception of human nature, formulated by Sigmund Freud (1856–1939), is that it is an account that seems to combine elements of both these views. Even if we disagree with Freud, it remains undeniable that he has exercised an enormous influence on twentieth-century conceptions of human nature. In the best-known version of his account, developed in his writings of the 1920s such as *The Ego and the Id*, Freud divides the self into three parts: the ego, the rational 'I' which deals with the outside world; the superego or moral conscience, containing social standards of behaviour acquired during childhood; and the id, containing all the instinctual drives that are constantly seeking immediate satisfaction. These instinctual drives are not, as is popularly supposed, confined to sexual desire, but on Freud's account also include aggressive and sadistic impulses. The ego strives to balance the conflicting demands of the id for desire-satisfaction, the moral rules of the superego and the constraints of external reality.

Freud's account of human nature is like Plato's in a number of ways. Both divide the self up into three parts. The ego, with its concern to deal with reality, and the id, as the mass of demanding instinctual impulses, correspond very closely to Plato's reason and desire. The superego is unlike Plato's notion of spirit to the extent that it is a specifically moral phenomenon, a set of moral rules internalized from parents and society, but it does resemble spirit in that it typically helps the ego, or reason, to keep the id, or desire, in check (see Stevenson 1974, 65–6). Freud's account of human nature is also like Plato's to the extent that he takes up the idea that life is a conflict, a struggle to restrain and control the desires. For Freud, the primary conflict is between the super-ego, the moral conscience, allied with the ego, and the desires of the id. Here, Freud makes use of Plato's horse and rider image: 'in its relation to the id [the ego] is like a man on horseback, who has to hold in check the superior strength of the horse; with this difference, that the rider tries to do so with his own strength while the ego uses borrowed forces' (Freud 1986, 450). Where there is extreme conflict between instinctual impulses and moral standards, the denial of instinctual satisfaction demanded by morality is achieved through repression, i.e., by pushing forbidden desires right down into the unconscious portion of the mind. And some such denial is necessary, Freud thinks, if we are going to be able to live and function in an ordered society.

In contrast to Plato however, Freud is much more ambivalent about the repression of desires. Where Plato is authoritarian, demanding strict control of desires, Freud, as Richard Norman notes, 'also recognizes that, beyond a certain point, excessive repression becomes harmful and self-defeating' (Norman 1983, 27). That is to say, Freud's account is also Humean insofar as he considers desire to be a crucial, integral and legitimate part of what we are. As a result, he has a keen sense of the costs of the repression of desire, the denial of instinctual satisfaction required for civilized life. We become civilized, but at the cost of frustration, unhappiness and even various neuroses. For Freud, the desires we have repressed do not disappear but continue to exist in the unconscious, and if the repression is too severe, the denied desires find indirect expression in various neurotic symptoms. Thus as Norman puts it,

> the very control of desires that Plato equates with mental health can, according to Freud, itself be a cause of mental illness, and conversely mental health may actually require the gratification of those instinctual desires which Plato wants to inhibit.
>
> (27–8)

Freud does not think that we can ever do away with all social and moral restraints. Some denial or repression of desire is always necessary. But he does argue that at least some of the frustration and unhappiness that this causes can be alleviated. Excessive demands for restraint can be modified and social life made less 'repressive'.

From our current perspective, coloured as it is by Freud, efforts to suppress or stifle desire, whether Platonic, Christian or rationalist, come across as repressive and unhealthy. A sense of the costs of the Christian hostility towards desire, particularly towards sexual desire, appears in a number of cinematic portrayals of self-denying religious figures. From the zealous reformer played by Walter Huston in Rain (Lewis Milestone, 1932), who strives to save the soul of prostitute Sadie Thompson (Joan Crawford) but eventually surrenders to lust, to the demented preacher (Anthony Perkins) in Crimes of Passion (Ken Russell, 1984), obsessed with reforming prostitute China Blue (Kathleen Turner), we have portrayals of repressed religious figures whose attempts to deny their desiring side have left them tortured and hypocritical. What they condemn and reject they are also tormented and obsessed by, and eventually succumb to. Similarly, for the priests running the 1950s Catholic boys' boarding school in The Devil's Playground (Fred Schepisi, 1976), the school is a hotbed of illicit boyhood desire, to be identified and stamped out wherever possible. Indeed, the whole institution is a mass of repressive rules and constraints, grimly enforced by the priests. But the priests are also the victims of these constraints. Nightly, in their dreams, they are tormented by the demands of their own stifled sexuality.

However, there also remains a feeling that the 'lower desires' cannot simply be given free rein, that they need to be constrained or controlled to some degree. The cinematic vampire, popularized by *Dracula* (Tod Browning, 1931), provides an enduring image of a figure completely given over to its desires, in the form of an all-consuming blood lust. A challenge to morality and civilized order, the vampire has to be hunted down and destroyed. At the same time it has to be said that vampires are usually fairly uncomplicated creatures. They happily pursue their desires and appetites without any trace of inner conflict. The Jekyll and Hyde story, derived from Robert Louis Stevenson's novel and filmed numerous times, offers a more complex understanding of internal make-up, and a more nuanced view of the dangers of giving our desires complete freedom. The two well-known sound versions of *Dr Jekyll and Mr Hyde* are Robert Mamoulian's (1932) and Victor Fleming's (1941). Mamoulian's version opens with Dr Jekyll (Fredric March) giving a lecture on the 'two parts of man', the 'good' side and the 'evil' side. In Fleming's version, Dr Jekyll (Spencer Tracy) presents a similar view at a dinner party, describing human beings as composed of two parts, good and evil, 'chained together in the soul'.

There are clear Christian overtones in this picture of human nature, particularly in its portrayal of desire as 'evil'. Human beings are presented as striving to be good, where this is identified with Christian uprightness; and there is also an evil side, identified particularly with sexual desire, which threatens to undermine our efforts to be good. When Tracy's Jekyll, despite being engaged to Lana Turner, finds himself attracted to a barmaid (Ingrid Bergman), he comments afterwards that it was only a momentary 'attack' from his evil side. In both films we go on to see the dire consequences when the doctor invents a potion to unleash his evil side, and becomes the grotesque, murderous Hyde. So here, desire completely unleashed is hideous, unspeakable and bestial. It is the lower side of human nature, and needs to be controlled or kept in check. It is worth noting that many of these elements can be found, almost unchanged, in as recent a film as *Blue Velvet* (David Lynch, 1986). There, the central character, clean-cut Jeffrey (Kyle MacLachlan) discovers not only the dark, violent underside of his hometown, but also his own base appetites which like Jekyll he must struggle to control. Though involved with the equally clean-cut Sandy (Laura Dern), he finds himself drawn to Dorothy Vallens (Isabella Rossellini) who represents the temptation of illicit, perverse sex. As it happens, Jeffrey draws back from the brink and returns to the side of the good. What he might have become, his Mr Hyde, is represented by the hideous Frank (Dennis Hopper), the sadistic gangster who is terrorizing Dorothy. Frank, like Hyde, personifies bestial desire unleashed.

Nonetheless, even if the Jekyll and Hyde films portray the dangers of unconstrained desire through the figure of Mr Hyde, there is also a clear sense in the Mamoulian and Fleming versions that the so-called 'evil' side remains a legitimate part of our make-up. We are after all said to be composed of two parts; the evil side is there in all of us. The problem does not arise because we have this evil part. It only arises when the two parts come apart, when the good side is lost and the evil side is given free rein. Here it is the influence of Freud, rather than Christianity, that is apparent. Freudian themes are in fact alluded to in both versions of the story. In the Mamoulian version, after Jekyll first takes the potion and falls into delirium, a montage of disapproving faces suggests that the emerging Hyde is in fact Jekyll's id, confronting the constraints of morality and organized social life. Similarly in Victor Fleming's version, as Jekyll turns into Hyde, he experiences a number of revealingly erotic hallucinations which leave no doubt that forbidden instinctual and sexual desires are finding expression. Interestingly, one of the images employed here by Fleming is an image of the horseman and his steeds similar to that invoked by Plato. Jekyll experiences himself as a charioteer whipping two horses along, horses which dissolve before our eyes into two women, the barmaid Jekyll met earlier, and his fiancée. However, this is no longer a Platonic image of reason in control of the other parts of the soul, but seems to be rather a metaphor for the unleashing of Jekyll's desires for sexual possession and domination.

Where these films are most clearly Freudian however is not in their images of unleashed desire but in giving us a strong sense of the costs of suppressing or stifling desire through their characterizations of Dr Jekyll. He is portrayed as a timid, 'repressed' type in the Mamoulian version, and as a vigorous, passionate man frustrated by a repressive social milieu of moral uprightness in Fleming's version. Other film versions of the story make a similar point. In Jean Renoir's version, *The Testament of Dr Cordelier* (1959), with Jean-Louis Barrault in the main role, the Hyde character, M. Opale, is certainly a hideous creature, given over to his base instincts; but the Jekyll character, Dr Cordelier, is a cold fish, constantly professing disgust at other people's expressions of desire, while also not above hypocritically taking advantage of his female patients while they are asleep. In the comic version, *The Nutty Professor* (Jerry Lewis, 1963), Julius Kulp (Lewis) is the college professor who finds a formula to unleash his alter ego, Buddy Love. The brash, piano-playing, womanizing Buddy Love is, if not actually evil, at least profoundly self-centred, concerned wholly with his own pleasure, and indifferent to the feelings of others; but at the same time Kulp is almost pathologically shy and repressed, unable to make any kind of declaration of his affection for his sweetheart Stella (Stella Stevens).

Thus it would seem that neither outright denial of desire nor its uninhibited release is satisfactory. In the end one kind of imbalance or distortion has been replaced by another. We can perhaps leave the last word on this point to the director Luis Buñuel. Many of his films are fierce critiques of religion, taking up the theme of the Church as distorting human existence by trying to hold down our 'instinctual nature'. This theme is well illustrated in a film he made quite late in his career, *Simon of the Desert* (1965). The film is a study of St Simon Stylites, one of the early Christian ascetics or practitioners of extreme self-denial, who spent thirty-seven years on top of a column in the fifth century AD. In the film Simon (Claudio Brook) has ascended the pillar to avoid the world's temptations. Here he also has to resist the various onslaughts of the Devil, in the guise of a beautiful young woman (Silvia Pinal). Of course, Simon is a repressed, foolish figure, denying the emotional and instinctive needs not only of himself but of those around him. He even acts coldly towards his own mother. And yet, as Raymond Durgnat points out (1968, 138), Buñuel is not simply suggesting here that desire should rule without constraint. He also provides a vision of uninhibited hedonism, and it is a special kind of hell. At the end of the film Simon is transported by the Devil to a sixties New York nightclub. While he is on the pillar, the embodiment of the Christian hatred of desire, we tend to sympathize with the Devil. But in the nightclub, surrounded by frenzied pleasure-seekers dancing the latest dance, we find ourselves sympathizing with him.

Descartes and dualism

As mentioned earlier, an important feature of the self or soul, in a number of accounts, is that it is immaterial. That is, it is not bodily or physical in nature, even though it might inhabit the body in some sense; and it could conceivably exist in complete separation from the body, in a disembodied state. The view that the human being is composed of two very different kinds of things, an immaterial soul or mind, and a material body, is known as dualism. For Plato, the soul is the immaterial component of the human organism. It is because the soul is immaterial that it is immortal and indestructible. Bodies, being merely material things, are subject to decay and dissolution, but the immaterial soul is not so afflicted. Plato is one of the main sources of the dualist view, but in modern thought the best-known proponent of this way of understanding ourselves is Descartes.

An important source of Descartes' views is his *Meditations*, which we came across in the previous chapter when looking at his account of knowledge. In the second meditation, as we saw, Descartes establishes that he is essentially a 'thinking thing', a mind. At this stage he cannot be sure that he is any more than this. As the *Meditations* proceeds he satisfies himself that the external world exists and that he himself has a physical body. In the final meditation, Meditation Six, Descartes spells out his views on the dualistic character of the human being. For Descartes, human beings are made up of two kinds of stuff, or 'substance': mental or spiritual substance (minds), and physical or material substance (bodies). These are quite different types of thing. The body is composed of gross physical matter, has mass and occupies space. It is in effect a kind of machine. The mind is a non-physical, ghostly, rather ethereal kind of entity, the seat of consciousness and various mental states. Being non-physical, it does not have any mass or occupy any space. It should be stressed that for Descartes, the mind is completely distinct from anything bodily. This means that it cannot even be identified with the brain, for the brain is still a physical item, still part of the body. The Cartesian mind is something else again. Another important feature of this view is that for Descartes (as for Plato before him), I am essentially my mind, not my body. As a mind, I happen to be attached to a particular body, but I would still be 'me' even if I became separated from my body, or if I became attached to another body.

There is much that is appealing about Descartes' dualist view of the human being. First of all, it fits into the long tradition of thinking of human beings as having an immaterial soul that is able to outlast the body. As we have seen, this view goes right back to Plato; and there is of course the long religious heritage of belief in the immortality of the soul. For Descartes it is perfectly possible for me to continue to exist after the death of my body, or for me to be reincarnated in another body. Both life after death and reincarnation are, at least in principle, possible on this kind of account. But even if we set aside religious considerations, the dualist view seems to be supported by our direct experience of ourselves. If you focus your attention inwards on the contents of your consciousness, on your thoughts, sensations and so on, you do not seem to be dealing with anything physical, anything like electrochemical processes in the brain, but rather with something entirely unphysical, something ethereal and insubstantial. And one further argument that has been invoked in favour of dualism is that we are able to do things, such as engage in reasoning, exercise judgement or even simply have conscious experiences, which seem on the face of it at least to be entirely beyond the capacities of any physical system, any mere machine (see Churchland 1988, 13–14).

As I have mentioned, the dualist view of human beings means that it is possible for the mind to exist separately from its body. The dualist view is thus presupposed in a number of fantasy films where someone's mind becomes separated from their body in some way. This is the understanding of the self's relation to the body behind Carl Reiner's *All of Me*. To fill out some of the details, a guru has been enlisted to transfer the soul of the dying heiress Edwina Cutwater into another woman's body, that of Terri Hoskins (Victoria Tennant); but at the crucial moment something goes wrong with the process and she ends up, as we have seen, in the body of the lawyer Roger Cobb, fighting him for control of it. Eventually she ends up in the body she originally intended to occupy. Now not only does this portray the mind as something that is able to separate from one body and to occupy another, it also brings out the interesting point that there is no reason on the dualist view why there should be only one mind associated with a particular body. Multiple occupancy is entirely possible. Dualism is similarly presupposed in the string of 'mind swap' movies that came out after *All of Me*: movies in which the same mind mysteriously reappears in a different body (*Big*, Penny Marshall, 1988; *Switch*, Blake Edwards, 1991), or two minds swap bodies (*Vice Versa*, Brian Gilbert, 1988). And for all its originality, *Being John Malkovich* (Spike Jonze, 1999), in which filing clerk Craig Schwartz (John Cusack) finds a passageway in his office through which he can enter the mind of the actor John Malkovich, is in the end based on the same dualist premise.

Moreover, there is no reason on the dualist view why the mind or soul needs to be associated with any body at all, why it should not be able to wander around in a completely disembodied form. Dualism is thus a fundamental presupposition of the entire genre of ghost movies, where the person persists in disembodied form after the death of, or in the unexplained absence of, the body. There is a long history of these films, of course, but three of the more recent ghost movies, *Ghost* (Jerry Zucker, 1990), *Casper* (Brad Silberling, 1995) and *The Frighteners* (Peter Jackson, 1996) are particularly interesting in this context. With the aid of sophisticated special effects, they are able to dwell on the various ways in which an ethereal, spiritual entity might interact with the physical world. They show ghosts flying effortlessly through walls and having things pass through them, confirming their ethereal status, but also as intervening in the material world, invisibly moving things around and sometimes being affected by solid objects. How such interaction between the spiritual and the material takes place is an important issue in connection with the dualist view, in which the ghostly mind in effect 'haunts' the material body (dualism has been characterized as the doctrine of the 'ghost in the machine'). The question arises as to how such utterly different things as immaterial minds and physical bodies can affect one another. We will come back to this issue in a moment.

The second general feature of this dualist view to note is that it offers us a particular kind of account of personal identity. I will take up this issue of personal identity in more detail in the next section, but to briefly indicate what is to come, the general question concerning personal identity is: what makes a human being the same person over time? The answer we give to this question depends very much on our conception of the human being. Given his dualist view of the human being, Descartes' answer is clear enough. As noted earlier, for Descartes I am essentially my mind, a spiritual or mental being, and not my body. So what it is essentially to be me, over a period of time, is to have the same mind. This means that I can be the same person if I happen to be reincarnated in a different body, or even if I have no body, if my body has died and has disappeared entirely. Thus in *All of Me*, Lily Tomlin's heiress remains the same person, even though she has come to occupy Roger Cobb's body; and at the end of the film, when she has finally made it into Terri's body, we know that the woman that Roger Cobb is dancing with, although she is physically Terri Hoskins, is 'really' Edwina. Similarly in the case of the other 'mind swap' movies and the various ghost films, persons remain the same even though they may inhabit a radically different body, and continue to be the same individual even after their body has died and disintegrated. On this view it is mind, rather than body, that constitutes who I am and makes me the same person over time.

This view of personal identity might seem reasonable enough, but it has some rather odd consequences. In particular, it makes it very difficult for us to know if a person is the same person over time. Usually we would feel quite confident in claiming that someone is the same person we encountered earlier, because they have the same physical appearance and mannerisms. However on the dualist view, in making judgements of personal identity, i.e., determining that someone is the same person, their having the same body may be a clue, but that is all it is. We can never be sure. Someone is the same person only if they have the same mind or soul, and this is something that another person cannot possibly observe. In *All of Me* and the other dualist movies, these problems do not arise for the audience because we have the advantage of being able to hear the thoughts of the characters in voice-over. In other words, in this situation we have precisely the access to other people's mental operations that we need in order to be sure who we are dealing with. But normally of course, we do not have this access. Thus for all we know, the familiar physical body we see before us, and which we take to be that of our friend, may in fact be occupied by a different mind, and thus be an entirely different individual. Similarly, encountering different bodies in no way allows us to infer that we are dealing with different people. Physical differences may provide a clue that we are dealing with different people, but we have no way of knowing if the same mind has not moved from one body to the other.

This last implication of the dualist view, that having different bodies is essentially irrelevant to the question of whether or not we are dealing with the same person, appears to be a premise of *Suture* (David Siegel, Scott McGehee, 1993). In this film we have a man, Vincent (Michael Harris), who is stalking his supposedly identical half-brother Clay (Dennis Haysbert). Since no one else knows that Vincent has an identical half-brother, he can murder Clay, whose body will be identified as Vincent's. If everyone thinks Vincent is dead, he will get away with murdering his rich father, and be able to disappear with his fortune. The twist here is that the two men do not in fact look alike – for a start, Vincent is white and Clay is black – but everyone else in the movie treats them as if they were indistinguishable. Even the brothers comment on their remarkable resemblance to each other. It seems that only the audience can see they are physically very different. However since another character in the film is the plastic surgeon Renée Descartes (Mel Harris), we begin to suspect that this might be a philosophically self-conscious film; and indeed, if we see the film as alluding to Cartesian dualism, it begins to make more sense. On the Cartesian view, radical physical differences do not imply that we are dealing with different people; it would thus be entirely possible for people to think that two individuals were the same person even if they were physically very different. Seemingly, the film suggests what the world would be like if Cartesian dualism were true.

Yet this world portrayed in *Suture* remains a thoroughly bizarre one, which suggests that we need to carefully consider the philosophical view on which it is based. Let us turn to some of the difficulties with the dualist view. One of the classic difficulties is that if minds and bodies are so utterly different in nature, the one mental substance and the other physical matter, it is difficult to see how they can interact, as they clearly do in everyday life. Ordinarily, I decide to act, and I act; I am wounded and I feel pain. But given the dualist view, how can a non-physical thought in the mind, to lift one's arm, bring about the physical movement of raising one's arm? Similarly, how can a physical injury give rise to a mental perception of pain? We might be inclined here to think of the mind as some kind of energy, perhaps electrical in character, that energizes a body and may in turn be affected by it. That is a view we find for example in Wes Craven's *Shocker* (1989). In the film, an executed criminal manages to live on after death, as an energy capable of 'possessing' bodies and electrical devices and thereby able to cause various kinds of mayhem. But thinking of mind as a kind of energy does not really help, because however insubstantial energy may be, it is still a physical phenomenon, whereas the Cartesian mind is supposed to be something entirely non-physical. So the problem remains: how can a completely immaterial mind affect or interact with a material body?

In his book *Consciousness Explained*, the American philosopher Daniel Dennett discusses this problem of how mind and body can possibly interact in the dualist picture (see Dennett 1991, 35–6). He thinks that the dualist picture is deeply problematic at this point, and indeed that it ultimately fails as a theory because of it. Dualist accounts, he argues, suffer from the following fatal paradox: how can the mind be something wholly non-physical, able to operate in ways that entirely escape the laws of nature, and wholly undetectable by physical means, and yet also be able to cause physical bodies to move? A ghost in a machine, Dennett notes wryly, is of no help to our theories of human nature unless it is a ghost that can move things around. But anything that can move a physical thing is surely itself a physical thing. How can the mind *both* on the one hand elude physical characterization and measurement and on the other, move the body? It is the same paradox, he goes on to observe, that we find in stories featuring the cartoon character Casper the Friendly Ghost. Casper can pass, seemingly unaffected, through physical walls, and yet he is also able to move material objects around, catch falling towels, slam doors and so on.

Movies which feature ghosts, such as *Casper* and *Ghost*, usually have a large number of instances of the paradox that Dennett identifies. In *Casper*, the movie based on the cartoon character, the ghost befriends a young girl (Christina Ricci) who has moved into a house haunted by other, less than friendly ghosts.

In one scene, Casper cooks breakfast for the girl, manipulating pans and cracking eggs open in the process. So here, he can clearly bring about alterations in the physical world. And yet when the girl tries to touch him, her hand goes right through his. In this way his ghostliness is confirmed, but how he was able to handle pans and cook the breakfast a moment ago becomes completely mysterious. The film *Ghost* provides us with another instance of this kind of incoherence. The newly dead Sam Wheat (Patrick Swayze) continually finds himself passing through physical objects, doors, people and so on. In fact, initially at least, he cannot make any impression on the world at all. He has to learn how to interact with and affect material objects – it is apparently a matter of concentrating hard. And yet despite being able to pass ethereally through physical objects, at no stage in the movie does he fall through the floor! The incoherence in these two cases seems obvious when it is pointed out, and it is the same kind of incoherence that we find in the dualist account.

A second kind of problem with the dualist view is the so-called problem of other minds. If the mind is this ghostly, immaterial substance, wholly undetectable by physical means, I may certainly know that I have a mind, that I am conscious, that I have thoughts, feelings and sensations. These are things I am directly, intimately, aware of within myself. But it immediately becomes a big issue how we can know whether other people have minds. I can directly observe other bodies, certainly, but I cannot observe other minds. This problem has already been alluded to in connection with the issue of personal identity. It arose there in the following form: how can I possibly know if someone is the same person as before? That is, how can I ever tell if the body I see before me has the same mind as before? There are further difficulties as well. How can I be sure if the body before me has a mind at all, if it is not in fact some kind of non-conscious robot or automaton? For that matter, how can I be sure that there are any minds at all in existence other than my own? How can I be sure that I am not in fact the only conscious mind in existence, surrounded by robots or automatons?

We might try to deal with this problem by arguing in the following way. In my own case, I know directly when I have certain thoughts, feelings and sensations. I also know that certain of these go together with certain outward behaviours. For example, when I find something funny I laugh, which is to say, I make certain laughing sounds and movements. Therefore, by analogy with my own case, when other people make these same sounds and movements, I can conclude that they are having the same experience of finding something funny that I have when I make these same sounds and movements. The problem with this argument however is that I only have one example to go on, my own, which is a very limited basis for the general kind of claim I want to make about other people; and I can never check whether my conclusions about other people are correct, not even in one other case. It could thus be the case that when other people are laughing, they are really robots that have no feelings, thoughts or sensations accompanying the laughter. Alternatively, it could be the case that they do have feelings, thoughts and sensations that accompany the laughter, but that these are not the same as the ones that I have. They might be for example the feelings that I have when I am feeling anxious and miserable. Whatever the case, the dualist account means that I can never know.

There are thus a number of serious difficulties with the dualist position. And in response many philosophers have sought to formulate some sort of materialist alternative, i.e., to argue that we are wholly physical beings, and that the mental phenomena we encounter are in some way explainable in physical terms. This is not to deny the existence of mind or consciousness, but rather to deny that these mental phenomena are characteristics of immaterial souls. One of the earliest materialist accounts in modern thought comes from the English philosopher Thomas Hobbes (1588–1679), a contemporary of Descartes. He spells out his account in his book *Leviathan*. For Hobbes all human processes, including thought and perception, can be accounted for in terms of interior 'motions'. External stimuli affect our 'vital motions', our basic life-processes, either stimulating them (which we feel as pleasure) or diminishing them (which we feel as pain). These changes in turn bring about inner movements towards the external stimulus (desire) or away from it (aversion), which eventually result in observable bodily movements or actions (see Hobbes 1968, 118–30). This is undoubtedly a crude picture, based on analogies between human beings and the kinds of machines Hobbes was familiar with in the seventeenth century, clocks and watches. But his general programme of reducing all psychology to physiology and ultimately to physics is one that continues to the present day in the form of what is known as 'reductive materialism'. We simply have the advantage of being able to compare human beings to more sophisticated machines, such as the computer.

However, despite the obvious problems of the dualist account, it has one clear advantage. It does seem to account for features of mental phenomena in a way that materialist theories find very hard to do. Any adequate materialist account has to account for our own experience of ourselves, of mental phenomena such as consciousness and thought which seem, to the reflecting observer at least, to be insubstantial and utterly different from physical states and properties. It also has to account for capacities like reasoning, judgement and feeling which seem enormously difficult to explain in 'merely' physical and chemical terms, as mere functions of a mechanical system. There is still no materialist account that has satisfactorily dealt with these issues. This is not to say that a materialist account is impossible in principle. Perhaps it is short sighted to imagine that machines might not be capable of highly sophisticated operations and activities, forms of reasoning and judgement. Machines already exist which can perform logical and mathematical calculations at a rate far faster than any human being. And we certainly seem at a certain level to be able to accept the possibility, portrayed in numerous science fiction films, of computers, robots or androids that are capable of intelligent and even emotional behaviour. It seems much harder however to imagine the converse, that we ourselves are machines, i.e., that the consciousness, thinking and feeling that we are aware of in ourselves through introspection can be understood in physical and chemical terms. A persistent problem with reductive materialist accounts is precisely that they seem to leave out of the picture our own experience of what it is to be conscious, and indeed to leave out consciousness itself.

Locke and personal identity

At this point let us move on to another way of thinking about the nature of the self, through a consideration of the issue of personal identity. What makes us the same person over time? This issue has already come up in the preceding section, in connection with reincarnation in a different body, and life after death. You might want to argue that these are fairly extraordinary kinds of events, and that they may not even occur. But even if we dismiss the possibility of reincarnation or life after death, the question of what makes us the same person over time remains because it arises for other reasons as well. For example, within a normal human life, there will be enormous changes from birth to death, changes in the body and the cells which make up the body (they are replaced every seven years or so), changes in personality and changes in memory. What is it that makes someone the same person despite these physical and mental changes? Moreover, we are sometimes faced with especially puzzling cases, such as cases of multiple personality, personality breakdown and amnesia.

Problems with determining a person's identity are the focus of a number of films. In *The Return of Martin Guerre* (Daniel Vigne, 1983), a man (Gerard Depardieu) arrives in a French village and claims to be Martin Guerre, the husband who left his wife nine years before. There are certainly physical similarities, and he seems to have the appropriate sorts of memories, although there are also some physical changes (he is heavier in build and his skin is more lined) and he has occasional lapses of memory. His wife believes him, although she may be deceiving herself, because even though he might be an impostor he is a much kinder person than the old Martin Guerre. Still, these physical differences, lapses in memory and even personality changes are not sufficient to decide the issue, because people do change, at least to some extent, over time. In *Olivier, Olivier* (Agnieszka Holland, 1992), a boy who disappeared six years previously seemingly returns to his family as a teenager (played by Gregoire Colin), and here also questions arise as to whether this is the same person or a cunning impostor. Again, there are considerable physical changes but also some physical resemblance; and while the mother, Elisabeth, desperately wants to believe her son has returned, she can also point to actual physical evidence in the form of an appendix scar. Her more suspicious daughter Nadine organizes a memory test based on recollection, which he also seems to pass.

In both *Martin Guerre* and *Olivier, Olivier*, the belief that the new arrival is the same person as before is based on physical resemblances and continuity of memory, even though it is recognized that there can be physical changes and changes in memory over time. Of course, physical resemblance can be accidental and memories fabricated, as indeed turns out to be the case in both these films. So we can sometimes go wrong in our identifications. But there are more puzzling cases, cases involving multiple personality and amnesia, which raise profound questions about personal identity. In *The Three Faces of Eve* (Nunnally Johnson, 1957), housewife Eve White (Joanne Woodward) seems to have three distinct personalities, each of which is unaware of the others, and has no memory of what the others have done. Is she then to be counted as three persons or as one? In Hal Hartley's *Amateur* (1994), the sweet-natured amnesiac Thomas (Martin Donovan) cannot remember that he used to be a vicious pornographer, who turned his wife into the world's most notorious porn queen. Without any recollection of his past, is he now a different person? And *Amateur* raises a further issue that questions of personal identity have a bearing on, that of responsibility. Is Thomas responsible for the wicked deeds of his past? It can be morally very important to decide whether a person is the same person as before. Is this frail old man really the same person as the Nazi war criminal of sixty years ago, and is it fair to try him for those crimes?

How we answer these questions about the nature of personal identity will of course depend on what we understand a person to be, what we see as constituting the self or human nature. As we have already seen, one kind of answer is that provided by Descartes. For Descartes, what it is essentially to be me, over a period of time, is to have the same mind, for there to be continuity of spiritual substance. So on this view I can be the same person even if my body changes radically. Indeed, I can be the same person even if I occupy a completely different body, or even if I have no body at all; and it is also possible to imagine the same body being occupied by a number of different selves. However, as we have also seen, there are significant problems with Descartes' dualist view of human beings, not least that it is very difficult to see how mind or spiritual substance can interact with a physical body. Let us turn then to another influential account of personal identity, that of the seventeenth-century British philosopher John Locke. Locke addresses this issue in Book 2, Chapter 27 of his *Essay Concerning Human Understanding*.

Locke refuses to commit himself to the dualistic view of human beings, which is not to say that he denies it either. Rather, he suspends judgement on whether there is a spiritual substance that is distinct from the body. Whether or not this is the case is irrelevant to his views. However he does make a distinction between 'persons' and 'human beings'. For Locke, what makes a person identical over time is not the same thing as what makes a human being identical over time. In the case of a human being, the identity of the same human being is that of the human organism, the biological human being, and the principle that holds it together is its organization as a living unit. In this regard, we are like plants and animals. A sapling growing into an oak tree, despite changes in its matter, size and form, remains the same tree; and the principle that holds it together is its organization as one living unit. Similarly in animals, even though they change in the course of their physical development, identity is provided by their biological organization into a living, functioning whole. And in the case of 'man', i.e., human beings, Locke says: 'This also shows wherein the identity of the same man consists: viz. in nothing but a participation of the same continued life, by constantly fleeting particles of matter, in succession vitally united to the same organized body' (Locke 1997, 299).

What makes a person identical over time is something else again. Personal identity is distinct from the identity of a human being. A person for Locke is a thinking intelligent being, that has reason and reflection, and can consider itself as itself, a thinking thing, in different times and places; which it does only by that consciousness which is inseparable from thinking, and, as it seems to me, essential to it.

(302)

So for Locke, the key elements of personhood are reason, consciousness and self-consciousness. A rational being is conscious, able to think; and self-consciousness is inseparable from thinking, i.e., it is not possible to think, see, hear and so on, without being conscious of ourselves as doing so. And according to Locke, a person has a sense of themselves and of their continuity and identity over time as the same person. Hence, personal identity, the sameness of a rational being, extends as far back in time as this consciousness of ourselves extends. As far back as I can remember being the same person, thinking, experiencing and doing certain things, I am that person. In short, for Locke, memory is the criterion of personal identity. Memory provides the sense of sameness that in Descartes' account is provided by sameness of mental substance.

This, then, is a conception of personal identity that depends on sameness of consciousness or memory, rather than on sameness of mental substance, but in which a distinction can still be made between personal identity and biological or bodily identity. Locke can thus make some of the same points about bodily identity as Descartes, but without having to commit himself to the latter's problematic dualism. On Locke's view, I can be the same person despite significant bodily changes. My body may change radically over the years, my appearance may alter, and so on, but as long as there is a continuity of memory, as long as I can remember being the same person, doing, feeling and thinking certain things, I am still the same person. By the same token, I can also have the same body and yet not be the same person. People with multiple personalities, with different consciousnesses that have no knowledge or memory of the doings of the other personalities, are on this view to be understood as collections of different people. Similarly, amnesiacs who have completely forgotten their past lives are no longer the same persons they were formerly.

The memory criterion for personal identity is presupposed in a number of cinematic portrayals in which different people are associated with the same body, and the same person is associated with a different, or a vastly altered, body. An example of the former is *Total Recall* (Paul Verhoeven, 1990), in which the hero and the villain both turn out to have the same body. The hero Quaid (Arnold Schwarzenegger), has been helping the resistance movement to fight the corrupt administration on Mars. However he learns from a recorded message that he was formerly someone called Hauser, who was in fact an agent in the pay of the very authorities he has been fighting. Quaid himself has no memories whatsoever of his former self. All memories associated with his earlier self have been wiped clean and new ones have been implanted in order for Hauser to become Quaid. It is all part of an elaborate plan to get someone inside the rebel movement and locate its headquarters. Now Hauser wants to be restored ('that's my body you've got there, and I want it back', he tells Quaid in the recorded message), which will entail the destruction of Quaid's memories, indeed of his whole personality. Here, personal identity is tied very closely to memory. On the basis of memory, the heroic Quaid is distinguished sharply from the villainous Hauser. Despite having the same bodies, they are not considered by themselves or those around them to be the same person.

The idea that amnesia about one's past life effectively makes one a different person is put to use in *Angel Heart* (Alan Parker, 1987). New York private detective Harry Angel (Mickey Rourke) is sent to Louisiana to find the elusive Johnny Fortune, who lost his memory during the war and had extensive plastic surgery before disappearing. What he finds is that the person he is looking for is his own former self. Boris Karloff, tracking down a murderer, makes a similar discovery in *Grip of the Strangler* (Robert Day, 1958). For a more playful variation on the theme of memory and personal identity, there is *Rosencrantz and Guildenstern Are Dead* (Tom Stoppard, 1990). The film is based on Stoppard's own play about two minor characters in Shakespeare's *Hamlet*. Having been thrust into the centre of the action, these essentially marginal characters have a very limited sense of who they are, and this is reflected in the limited memories they have of their own experiences and past. At the beginning of the film, they have a great deal of trouble remembering who sent for them, what precisely they have been summoned to do, and even, at times, which of them is Rosencrantz and which Guildenstern. In *Robocop* (Paul Verhoeven, 1987), we have the same person associated with a profoundly altered body. Here, a murdered policeman (Peter Weller) in the Detroit of the near future is transformed into the half-human, half-machine Robocop. Initially his mind is a blank, he has no recollection of his past existence, and he is no longer who he was. Indeed, he no longer seems to be a person at all, to be no more than the strange human-machine hybrid he was designed to be. But little by little he remembers his past life, and in the course of doing so he 'becomes himself' again.

The memory-based understanding of personal identity means not only that the same person can persist despite radical bodily changes, but also that a form of reincarnation is at least theoretically possible. That is, if I find I can remember doing things in a previous life, then I am identical with that earlier person. Locke himself makes this point. He stresses that if I have no memories of a previous life, of previous actions, then I cannot have been that person. But, he continues, 'let him once find himself conscious of any of the actions of Nestor [a Greek king mentioned by Homer], he then finds himself the same person with Nestor' (Locke 1997, 306). Two reincarnation movies that conceive of reincarnation along Lockean lines, i.e., in terms of the reappearance of memories of a former life, are *Chances Are* (Emile Ardolino, 1989), and *Dead Again* (Kenneth Branagh, 1991). In *Chances Are*, a man killed crossing the road is reincarnated. Twenty years later, now a young man, he meets and falls in love with his former self's daughter. When he is invited to his old home, he begins to remember his former life, which naturally raises a few problems for his present relationship. In *Dead Again* a Los Angeles private eye (Kenneth Branagh) is hired to discover the identity of a mute amnesiac (Emma Thompson). Her nightmares derive from a violent past, from which only an old eccentric hypnotist (Derek Jacobi) can free her. The twist is that her flashbacks are to a previous life, when Branagh was a famous female pianist, and Thompson was her famous composer husband, wrongly executed for her murder (the further twist is that Jacobi himself was the real murderer).

There are however some problems with the Lockean view of personal identity. As we have seen, Locke considers that personal identity depends on there being a sameness, a continuity of memory or consciousness. The big difficulty that arises with Locke's view is that there are very often breaks or gaps in consciousness. After all, we forget things that we have done; in addition, we do not necessarily think of things we have done even if we are capable of remembering them; and during sleep, we do not have any consciousness, thoughts or memories at all. So the question is, at these times am I the same person? This issue is of particular significance in connection with questions of moral responsibility. If personal identity is created by sameness of consciousness or memory, that would imply that without memory or consciousness of doing something, it would not be me that did it, but someone else. Thus for example, to blame or to punish me for something that I did in my sleep, while sleepwalking, would be unjust, because since I have no memory or consciousness of it, it was literally not me that did it. Similarly, the sober person is not responsible for what they did when they were drunk, or the sane person for what they did when they were insane. If I am 'not myself' or 'beside myself' in these ways, then I am literally not the same person.

This is certainly taken to be the case in *Total Recall*. Quaid and his former self Hauser are presented as very different moral agents. Quaid is 'good' and Hauser is 'bad'; and Quaid is not held to be responsible for the wicked deeds of Hauser. In *Angel Heart*, Harry Angel is made to pay for the deeds of his former self, but this is only after he has 'found himself', which is to say, when he starts to remember having carried out these deeds in the final moments of the film (whereupon his employer, who turns out to be the Devil, sends him to Hell). We may certainly be willing to accept that Quaid, who has no recollection whatsoever of being Hauser, is not to blame for Hauser's misdeeds; and that the appropriate moment to punish Angel is when he finally remembers his wicked deeds. Nonetheless, Locke's view of moral responsibility has some puzzling implications. If, for example, I cannot remember crashing my car because I was completely drunk at the time, does this really mean I am not responsible for crashing it? And do we really want to say that the old man who cannot remember having committed various atrocities in the Second World War is not responsible for them? Under normal circumstances at least, Locke's claim that if I do not remember doing something then I am not responsible for it seems rather implausible. If it is something I did a very long time ago indeed, when I had a very different character, then perhaps the claim that my present self is not responsible becomes more plausible. Yet even here we may still want to ask: is this because it was actually not me, my present self, who performed the earlier action, or simply because I am not responsible for all actions that can truly be called mine?

Kant, personhood and moral worth

There are a number of moral issues attached to the issue of personal identity, and to what it is to be a person. We have already seen how questions of responsibility and blame arise in this connection. In this final section, we turn to another moral issue associated with personhood. Recall Locke's definition of a person:

> a thinking, intelligent being, that has reason and reflection, and
> can consider itself as itself, the same thinking thing, in different

times and places; which it does by that consciousness which is inseparable from thinking, and, as it seems to me, essential to it.

Remember also that for Locke, a person is to be distinguished from a biological human being. This idea of personhood is an important one in modern philosophical and ethical thought. It is widely held that persons have a special value, and that they deserve particular moral respect. For example, only persons, it is sometimes claimed, have a right to life. And since being a person is distinguishable from being biologically human, this means that being human, i.e., being a member of the species *homo sapiens*, does not automatically qualify one for the special kind of moral respect due to persons.

An influential formulation of the idea that persons have a special value and are deserving of a special kind of respect comes from the eighteenth-century philosopher Immanuel Kant. Kant shares Locke's view that persons are primarily characterized by their rationality. In Kant's case, persons are essentially rational agents, capable of deciding for themselves the shape and goals of their existence. And according to Kant, this capacity for rational self-determination makes persons uniquely valuable. We should always treat persons as 'ends in themselves', and never simply as means to an end. That is, since persons have their own rationally determined goals and projects, we should treat them with these goals in view and not merely as the instruments or means for the realization of our own projects. In short we should never treat them as 'mere things'. Mere things have value only insofar as they serve human purposes, but persons, as Kant puts it, have 'an intrinsic value – that is, *dignity*', which makes them valuable 'above all price' (Kant 1964, 102–3). Since Kant, there have been many reformulations of the notion of personhood, and various additional criteria for personhood have been proposed, such as self-consciousness, the capacity to have mental states and the ability to use language. Nonetheless, these accounts usually preserve as central the criterion of rationality emphasized by both Locke and Kant. And however personhood is understood, there remains the idea that persons have a special moral status of some sort, and that they should not be treated as mere things.

Kant also follows Locke in distinguishing a person from a human being, and this is another important feature of the concept of the person, one that is shared by most views on personhood. This point needs to be emphasized. Moral claims about personhood are often expressed as claims about human beings, but the two terms are not in fact identical. The former usually refers to a rational, conscious being of some sort, while the latter merely designates a biological category, membership of the species *homo sapiens*. Consequently not all human beings are persons, for they do not have the required rationality or consciousness; and those considered not to be persons may be accorded less moral respect. For example, they may not be thought to have certain rights such as the right to life. Such judgements are always controversial of course, but on many standard views of personhood, human beings who are not persons would include human foetuses and those in irreversible comas. By the same token, there can also be persons, conscious rational beings, who are not human beings, such as intelligent aliens, androids, gods, spirits or angels. And it follows that these beings should be accorded the same moral respect that we give to human persons. In both cases then, it would seem, simply being human, a member of the human species, is not what is of moral importance.

Notions of personhood and respect for persons often emerge in science fiction contexts, particularly in connection with the idea that it is possible for there to be persons who are not biological human beings. The science fiction world is full of intelligent aliens, androids, robots and computers, for whom the question of personhood arises. It arises for example for the android Data (Brent Spiner), Mr Spock's successor in the *Star Trek: The Next Generation* television series and films. The question of personhood is posed most explicitly for Data not in the films but in an episode of the television series entitled 'The Measure of a Man'. This episode revolves around a court case in which the issue is precisely Data's moral status. The question to be decided is whether the android is a mere thing, property, which can thus be dismantled for use in research and experimentation, or a person, with the right to refuse consent to such treatment. The prosecution argues that he is simply a machine, but his defending counsel, Captain Jean-Luc Picard (Patrick Stewart) counters that being a machine is not relevant to the question of the android's personhood. In the course of his own argument Picard invokes three criteria for personhood: intelligence, consciousness and self-awareness. The outcome of the trial is that the fact that Data is not biologically a human being, that he is a machine, does not count against him. He meets the above-mentioned criteria for personhood and is thus entitled the moral respect due to all persons.

Outside of science fiction, the issue of personhood is sometimes invoked in connection with the refusal to acknowledge the personhood of certain human beings, individuals who may be intellectually, emotionally or physically damaged in some way. This comes across with particular force in Werner

Herzog's *The Enigma of Kaspar Hauser* (1974), which deals with the discovery and fate of Kaspar Hauser (Bruno S.). Chained up in isolation for most of his life, Hauser is left in a village square where he is discovered by the townspeople. Some, like the kindly professor Daumer (Walter Ladengast) treat him as a person, to be accorded respect and kindness; others in the town see him as a freak, an oddity, or most chillingly, as a scientific specimen they look forward keenly to dissecting. Similar issues emerge in David Lynch's *Elephant Man* (1980), a film about the deformed nineteenth-century 'elephant man' John Merrick (John Hurt). The object of hideous abuse in childhood, and treated as an inhuman freak for most of his life, he is gradually coaxed by a kindly doctor (Anthony Hopkins) into revealing a refined personality. In his memorable declaration, 'I am not an animal; I am a man!', he lays claim to the status of personhood. As often happens, the claim of personhood is expressed in terms of a claim to be a man, a human being; but the issue is not Merrick's status as a biological human being, which he obviously is, but as a person, a morally significant being, who deserves to be treated with respect.

Now the *Star Trek: The Next Generation* television episode mentioned earlier, like many science fiction stories, relies in the end on the familiar rationality-centred understanding of personhood; but it also takes pains to 'humanize' Data by making him capable of feeling emotions like pride, and of having emotional attachments to other crew members. This is significant, because in recent years questions have been raised in philosophy about the traditional tendency to emphasize reason and intelligence in our understanding of personhood. Apart from anything else, this kind of view means that all non-human animals tend to be regarded as mere things, having value only insofar as they are useful for human purposes. This means that they can be treated in any way we please, and indeed, that there is nothing intrinsically wrong with mistreating or even torturing them. Kant himself found this a troubling implication of his account, but his understanding of personhood commits him unavoidably to the view that mere animals have no moral importance at all. Some contemporary philosophers, such as Mary Midgley, have argued that social and emotional complexity, and the capacity to enter into enduring, emotionally rich relationships, should play a role in determining what counts as a person, a morally significant other. Such an understanding of personhood would allow it to be applicable to some animals, such as the higher apes, or dolphins (see Midgley 1985, 60–1).

The idea that intelligence is not everything, that emotionality and sociability might also play an important role in defining personhood, is evident in Ridley

Scott's *Blade Runner* (1982). Here, a future society has been infiltrated by four laboratory-created 'replicants', human-like androids created for manual labour. They are the slaves of the future, without any rights or intrinsic value, merely instruments for the exploration and colonization of other planets; but now some of them have escaped and have returned to earth. As 'faulty machinery' they have to be tracked down and destroyed by the 'Blade Runner' Deckard (Harrison Ford). However, the androids come across as much more than mere things. The film humanizes or 'personalizes' them, and it does so most of all by giving them an emotional life. Their manufacturer, the Tyrell corporation (whose motto is 'more human than human') has started to produce androids with memories, a past, allowing them to think that they are human. But what really humanizes them is not these implanted memories but their anguish at the thought that their memories may not be their own. It is at the moment in Deckard's apartment when replicant Rachel (Sean Young) expresses her despair at this prospect that Deckard first starts to see her as more than a mere android, and the two begin to have a relationship. That same capacity for complex emotional response humanizes the replicants that Deckard is pursuing. They have feelings for each other, and for other living things; and in the climactic battle, replicant Batty (Rutger Hauer) almost kills Deckard but generously decides to let him live. Throughout the film, the line between the humans and the replicants is constantly called into question; indeed it is suggested at a number of points that Deckard himself might be a replicant.

An emotion-based conception of personhood also seems implicit in *Invasion of the Body Snatchers* (Don Siegel, 1956), where aliens gradually take over the bodies of the inhabitants of a small Californian town, turning them into 'pod-people'. As the townspeople are taken over, they become depersonalized, and this is manifested above all in their becoming blank and unemotional. It is emotionality that marks the difference between 'us' and 'them'. Thus at the beginning of the film, the film's hero Dr Miles Bennell (Kevin McCarthy) returns from an out-of-town conference to find his patients complaining that their relatives are 'impostors', because unlike the people they once knew, these individuals lack all traces of emotion. Later on, he refuses the pod-people's offer to join them because it would mean giving up his ability to love and to have feelings; and as he and his girlfriend Becky (Dana Wynter) try to escape from the town by passing themselves off as pod-persons, it is Becky's show of feeling (she screams when a dog is almost run over) that gives them away. *Invasion of the Body Snatchers* is often seen as reflecting the Cold War anxiety of fifties America over totalitarian communism, and the nightmare prospect of individuals being reduced to mere instruments, dehumanized cogs in a larger, impersonal social whole (see for example Biskind 1983, 141). Here, then, the question of personhood is no longer simply an individual matter but has been linked up with wider social and political concerns.

The spectre of depersonalization through the deadening of emotion and feeling has also been invoked in connection with the effects of modern technological society, for example in Stanley Kubrick's 2001: *A Space Odyssey* (1968). In the film, two astronauts on a mission to Jupiter have to battle the ship's computer HAL for control of the ship. The astronauts are depersonalized and unemotional, little more than appendages of the sophisticated technology around them. They converse without feeling, make logical decisions and always agree; and Frank Poole (Gary Lockwood) receives a birthday message from his parents with disturbing indifference. Only when finally forced into action by their misbehaving computer do they show signs of being something more than depersonalized functionaries. For his part, HAL is anxious about how he comes across, proud of his record for accuracy and concerned about the mission. It seems that it is because he is forced by his programming to lie about the true purpose of the mission that he has his breakdown and begins his murderous rampage. In other words, it is in HAL that we find those traits of feeling and emotionality that are arguably most important for person-hood. There is a nice twist here, another of Kubrick's perverse renderings of familiar themes. In this film, it is the humans, the astronauts, who are inhuman, dispassionate automatons; and it is the neurotic, emotional computer HAL who, ironically, emerges as the most 'human' character in the film.

We will continue to discuss the issue of the self, taking into account the social and political setting, in Chapter 4, and the theme of modern technology as depersonalizing or dehumanizing will be further explored in Chapter 5. But in this chapter, having begun with issues about the nature of the self or human nature, we have gradually moved into a consideration of the moral implications of our notions of selfhood. And in the next chapter, Chapter 3, our focus will be on moral philosophy.

3

CRIMES AND MISDEMEANORS –
MORAL PHILOSOPHY

Woody Allen and Martin Landau in *Crimes and Misdemeanors*.
Credit: Orion (Courtesy Kobal)

At the end of *Crimes and Misdemeanors* (Woody Allen, 1989), the distinguished doctor Judah Rosenthal (Martin Landau) meets film-maker Cliff Stern (Allen) at a wedding and tells him he has a story that would make a great movie plot. The story is of a successful man whose mistress is threatening to reveal the affair and ruin his marriage and career. He decides he has no choice but to have her killed. After the deed is done he feels terrible guilt, and imagines that he has sinned in the eyes of God. He is an inch away from confessing all to the police. But then one morning he awakens and the crisis has passed; he is no longer guilt-stricken, and as the months pass he finds he is not punished, but in fact prospers. Now, his life is completely back to normal. It is the perfect murder. To Stern's misgivings about this tale he replies 'well, I said it was a chilling story, didn't I?' In fact, we in the audience know that it is more than just a good story for a film, that what he is relating has actually happened, and that the man in the story is the doctor himself. The question being raised here is not just whether the doctor did the morally right thing in the circumstances (most of us, of course, would think he did not). A deeper question is being asked: why should we be moral in the first place? Why should we do the right thing if we can do the wrong thing and get away with it? This calls on us to think about the very nature of morality, about the role it plays and its importance in our lives. So let us consider this question of why we should be moral, which will in turn lead us to a consideration of some of the more important philosophical accounts of morality.

The ring of Gyges

We can begin by stating the issue clearly. Suppose I find myself able to acquire something I desperately want, provided I lie, steal or perhaps kill someone. We are all familiar with those moments when we find ourselves wanting to do something even though we know we shouldn't, or not wanting to do something even though we feel that we ought. We are torn between getting what we want, and sticking to moral principles. The tension here is sometimes characterized as being one between self-interest and morality, between acting purely to satisfy my own interests regardless of others, and doing the right thing. In such cases it might be thought that the moral considerations are the ones that ought to win out, and that in a morally good person they will. Surely, we imagine, even those who profess to be concerned only with pursuing their own interests will recognize the force of moral considerations. Perhaps they have been made cynical by circumstances, but when it counts they will come good. So we are not surprised for example when Humphrey Bogart's character Rick, the night-club owner in *Casablanca* (Michael Curtiz, 1942), initially someone whose only concern is to look out for his own interests, who 'sticks his neck out for nobody', turns into a supporter of the Resistance, willing to sacrifice much for the cause, even the woman he loves. Indeed, remarks by the police prefect Captain Renault (Claude Rains) make it clear early on that Rick was an idealist in the past, a supporter of anti-Fascist struggles, and that it is only circumstances that have made him bitter and cynical. We are sure that he will eventually return to the fight.

This kind of transformation, from someone who for whatever reason is only concerned to 'get by' even if it means being complicit with great evil, into a person of moral integrity, willing to make a stand, is a familiar cinematic theme. In *On the Waterfront* (Elia Kazan, 1954) Terry Molloy (Marlon Brando) is transformed from a washed-up boxer who runs errands for the corrupt waterfront union boss into someone willing to stand up against the corruption. In *Fahrenheit 451* (François Truffaut, 1966) Montag (Oskar Werner), the 'fireman' who burns books in a future totalitarian society, turns from obediently serving the state to questioning and ultimately opposing it. In *Schindler's List* (Steven Spielberg, 1993), World War Two businessman Oskar Schindler (Liam Neeson) evolves from an opportunist and profiteer into a man of conscience, saving Jews from the concentration camps by bringing them to work in his factory. In each case, it is very much in the interests of the individuals involved to stay quiet, to co-operate; the path they decide to take puts them at considerable risk, and yet they find they cannot do otherwise. All these films embody the reassuring view that moral considerations have a certain force, that such considerations should take precedence over those to do with one's immediate comfort, desire and self-interest, and that even if they don't always do so, in good people at least they will eventually prevail.

And yet the question remains: why should one be moral? Why should moral considerations take precedence over, say, considerations of self-interest? People do not always act in a moral way; and if it is going to cost someone dearly if they do the right thing, or if they stand to gain a great deal of benefit from immoral actions, what sort of reason could there be for their continuing to abide by moral standards? What are we to say to someone who thinks that self-interest is the only realistic guide to conduct, and who regards anyone constrained by moral considerations as a fool? This is the view presented for example by Gordon Gekko (Michael Douglas), the ruthless, predatory corporate raider in Oliver Stone's *Wall Street* (1987). *Wall Street* is one of a number of films that criticized the rampant consumerism and acquisitiveness so prevalent in the West in the 1980s (Mike Leigh's 1988 *High Hopes* is another). In the film, Gekko sums up the attitude of unapologetic self-interest in his 'greed is good' speech, delivered to a group of stockholders. According to Gekko, not only is greed nothing to apologize for; greed in its many forms, for life, love, wealth and knowledge, is nothing less than the driving force of human evolution and progress. His contempt for those like his protégé Bud Fox (Charlie Sheen), who find themselves bound by ethical standards, is palpable. Now we might want to dismiss Gekko's views because he is so obviously the villain of the film; but this fails to address what he has to say. His claim is that self-interest is, and indeed should be, the major factor guiding our conduct. What are we to say to this?

To further explore this issue, we can turn once again to Plato. Plato is in fact the first philosopher to raise the question of why one should be moral. He does this in Book 2 of the *Republic* (1974, 358–68), by way of a fable about the Ring of Gyges. Gyges, a poor shepherd from Lydia, found a ring that had the power to make the wearer invisible. Using this ring, he seduced the Lydian queen, plotted with her to kill the king, and, taking over his position, became wealthy and powerful. So here, Plato raises the question of why we should be moral in a very strong way, because he removes even the motivation to be good that might come from the fear of being caught and punished. The ring means that Gyges can get away with anything he likes. And through this story, a certain view of morality and human nature is also being put forward for consideration, a view that Gekko would surely approve of. In the last analysis, it is implied, we only do the right thing because if we don't we will be caught and punished; and if we could in fact do whatever we wanted, without fear of being found out, we would abandon all ethical standards and set about pursuing our self-interest. Moreover, it is being suggested, we would be perfectly rational in doing so. Only a fool would continue to do what is right under such circumstances.

An updated version of the Gyges story appears in *Groundhog Day* (Harold Ramis, 1993). Here Phil (Bill Murray), a cynical weatherman, finds himself waking up on the same day, over and over again. This means that he can do anything he wishes and get away with it, because his actions have no lasting consequences; tomorrow, whatever he has done will be erased and the day will begin again. Realizing this, his initial response to his situation is very Gyges-like. He proclaims 'I'm not going to live by their rules any more', i.e., the rules of ordinary, well-behaved citizens. So saying, he embarks on a night of automotive mayhem. Where this tale differs from Plato's story is that, since *Groundhog Day* is a conventional Hollywood film, there is a more comforting outcome. As the film progresses, our hero travels the standard path of development from amoral cynic into a morally decent person. Hollywood remains fond of the happy ending in which the moral world is reassuringly confirmed; and where those who do wrong, if they fail to improve, are at least found out and punished. Even in quite unconventional portrayals of evil such as David Lynch's *Blue Velvet* (1986), and Peter Greenaway's *The Cook, The Thief, His Wife and Her Lover* (1989), evil has still been properly punished by the end. Both *Blue Velvet*'s crazed gangster Frank Booth (Dennis Hopper) and Michael Gambon's brutal Thief end up being killed by those they have tormented and abused. However there are some movies whose interest lies precisely in reminding us that in the 'real world' it is not always so, that evil in fact quite often goes unpunished. In so doing, they pose the question of why one should be moral with renewed force.

Take for example Roman Polanski's *Chinatown* (1974), the noirish detective story mentioned towards the end of Chapter 1. The film is striking in its willingness to allow wickedness to triumph. Although private eye Gittes uncovers a network of graft, murder and incest, neither he nor the police have the power to do anything about it. And it is a similarly uncompromising treatment of this theme that we find in *Crimes and Misdemeanors*. The doctor has his mistress killed when she threatens to expose their affair and ruin his life, and, quite simply, he gets away with it. This film is particularly interesting in the present context because along the way, as the doctor agonizes over what to do about his mistress, various views are put forward as to why one should be moral. We will have an opportunity to look at these in a moment. For now, one aspect worth noting is that the film also manages to comment on the conventional Hollywood resolution, in which good prevails and evil deeds are paid for. In the final scene of the film, when as we've seen the murderous doctor meets Allen's film-maker at the wedding and recounts his story in the guise of a film plot, Allen replies that it would be a better story if the murderer were driven by guilt to give himself up. The doctor's reply is that this is what happens in the movies, not in real life: 'If you want a happy ending, you should go see a Hollywood movie.' Robert Altman's satirical *The Player* (1992) similarly mocks the Hollywood taste for happy endings by providing one for the villain; when a studio executive (Tim Robbins) kills a writer he thinks (wrongly) has been sending him death threats, not only does he get away with it, but he ends up happily married to the dead writer's girlfriend, in the most idyllic of circumstances.

If we are going to be realistic, we need to acknowledge that wrongdoing is not always found out and punished, that people can and do get away with evil. So we need to ask whether there is any reason for behaving morally if we can get away with being immoral. Is it true that the only reason people adhere to ethical standards is because of fear of being caught and punished if they do not? Or can we give a better answer to the question of why we should be moral? One response might be that even if we can avoid external punishment, we will suffer at our own hands for evil deeds, through guilt or remorse. On this view it is our conscience that keeps us on the 'straight and narrow'. However conscience is not as strong a force as one might think. Given some of the things people do, it is clear that not everyone is constrained by their consciences. Even those who think they are may be less constrained than they imagine, once they find that their acts go undiscovered and unpunished. This is what the murderous doctor of *Crimes and Misdemeanors* discovers. While recounting his tale, he indicates that although he suffered deep-seated guilt at first, to the point where he was close to a mental collapse and on the verge of confessing to the police, the guilt diminished as time went by, and even if he occasionally has a bad moment he has learnt to live with it. As he goes on to point out, people learn to live with all sorts of terrible sins. And over and above these considerations, even if conscience does prod us, a simple appeal to the force of conscience does not tell us why we should obey it, what justifies the belief that we ought to do so. We need to go more deeply into the issue.

Plato and inner balance

We have seen how Plato's Ring of Gyges story poses the question of why we should be moral in a very strong way. Plato himself invokes the Ring of Gyges story because he wants to reject the view of morality and human nature it implies, the view that the only reason to abide by ethical standards is to avoid being caught and punished, and that if we could do whatever we wanted, without fear of punishment, we would abandon all morality and pursue our self-interest. The rest of the *Republic* is in effect his answer to the question of why we should be moral even if we can get away with being immoral; and in the course of this, he puts forward his own view of morality.

Plato's response to the question of why one should be moral is to argue that self-interest is not really in conflict with morality. The apparent conflict between morality and self-interest is really only a conflict between morality and a *false* notion of self-interest. This false notion of self-interest in turn rests on a false notion of the self, in which the self is identified with one's immediate desires alone (see Irwin 1989, 102). Plato's position thus turns on his conception of the self. As we saw in Chapter 2, Plato understands the self or soul as being composed of three parts, a rational part, a desiring element and a spirited part. Each has its proper function in the whole. In a properly balanced soul, the rational part rules. With the help of the spirited part, reason governs and directs the non-rational desires. By themselves, the non-rational desires cannot be trusted to pursue my real interests. I may have a desire to drink the water, but the rational part, which knows that the water is poisoned, is able to judge what is good for me as a whole and prevent me from drinking. The rational part looks at the overall picture, at what is good for the self as a whole and for each part. So if I am really self-interested, I must be ruled by the rational part; I must have a properly balanced soul, and for Plato, having this inner balance is what it is to be moral.

Plato's answer, then, to the question of why one should be moral – spelt out in Book Four of the *Republic* – is that being moral, far from being opposed to self-interest, in fact benefits the soul. Being moral means having a harmonious, well-ordered soul, in which the various parts are organized by the rational part for the good of each part and for the good of the whole. Moral goodness thus amounts to a kind of mental health or well-being, and mental health in general is clearly something that benefits the possessor. Moreover it is a state that we not only need to be in for our own good but which we also enjoy being in, and so Plato can argue that the moral life is not only desirable but also happy. In this well-ordered, harmonious condition, Plato argues, we have the additional virtues of courage, temperance and wisdom. We are wise because the ruling element possesses knowledge of what is advantageous for each part and for the whole; temperate, or self-controlled, because spirit and desire are subordinate to the ruling part, and there is no rebellion against it; and brave because the spirited part allows us to pursue the precepts of reason, and to overcome the distractions of pain and pleasure (see Plato 1974, 436–44).

If we were not morally good in this sense of being well-balanced we could not pursue our own interests. We would not do what is good for us overall, but would instead be subject to the tyrannical demands of our desires, desires that have grown out of all proportion, have lost touch with reality and are out of control. Other people would suffer as well, for the pressure of our desires would distort our relations with others. Driven by our obsessive desires, we would no longer respond to the wants and needs of others, no longer treat them as persons in their own right. We would be driven to satisfy ourselves at their expense, for example to seek unlimited sexual pleasure through force or deception. The immoral person is thus unbalanced, at the mercy of their desires, and the thoroughly immoral person is close to being a madman. On this view Mr Hyde becomes the very model of evil, the evil that results when desire escapes from rational control and gains ascendancy. The cinematic vampire is another figure of evil that is in the grip of uncontrollable, bestial desire. And the idea that extreme wickedness implies an unbalanced, obsessive, out-of-control personality is evident in a whole line of monstrous criminals, from Peter Lorre's child murderer Hans Beckert in M (Fritz Lang, 1931), who 'cannot help what he does' and has no control over 'this evil thing that's inside of me', to the raging, uncontrollable Frank Booth in Lynch's Blue Velvet, consumed by libidinal desire and aggression.

Plato's account of morality is bound up not only with his conception of the self but also with his account of knowledge. As we saw in the first chapter, for Plato, to comprehend the true nature of things is to have knowledge of the forms, the timeless, unchanging essences of things that exist beyond the shifting world of sense experience. Now these include the forms of moral ideals and virtues, wisdom, courage, temperance and, above all, the form of the good. What Plato is saying is that there is one universal, objective form of the good life, which we can discover through our reason. Accordingly, discovering the good life is a rational task, like determining the principles of mathematics. It is through this knowledge that the rational part knows how to live well, what is good for the person overall. Moreover, although Plato's moral theory seems to be based on a notion of self-fulfilment or self-realization, on achieving the kind of balance that is proper to ourselves, we can only fulfil ourselves through knowledge of these timeless forms, and above all, through knowledge of the good. Individual harmony and order thus mirrors the larger order of the world of forms. So in the last analysis, the basis of morality for Plato is not to be found in human nature but in his conception of ultimate, objective reality, the world of the forms.

Plato's view of morality involves the emphasis on reason that we have already seen in his views on knowledge and the self. And many have found his moral account too intellectualistic and rationalistic. Can we know what the right thing to do is, in the way that we can have mathematical or scientific knowledge? Is establishing the right thing to do, or the proper life to lead, anything like gaining knowledge of the world? Equally, is there really only one correct answer to what it is to lead the good life, which reason can discover, as Plato seems to imply? Might there not be a variety of ways in which one can be good? Furthermore, as we saw in the previous chapter, Plato's emphasis on reason means that his notion of mental harmony is a rather repressive, authoritarian one, marked by suspicion and hostility towards desire. What this means for morality is that being moral, living the good life, requires firmly controlling and restraining the desires. It is an ascetic morality, a morality of stern self-denial. And as has already been suggested, this kind of moral authoritarianism might be less a recipe for mental health than itself a source of disharmony and illness. The virtuous but repressed Dr Jekyll is not a particularly appealing alternative to the evil Mr Hyde. The Platonic hostility towards desire was also taken up in the Christian conception of moral life, as a struggle between the aspiration to the good and the distractions of worldly desire. This is another austere moral picture that identifies virtue with self-denial and privation, and which we may want to question for just that reason.

We will come to a more sustained discussion of Christian ethics in a moment, but two other aspects of Plato's account are worth commenting on. First, Plato equates being morally good with having a well-ordered self, and moral evil with internal disorder. Yet it might be argued against Plato that one might be utterly dedicated to evil yet still have a well-ordered, disciplined, harmonious soul. There is nothing in self-mastery itself that implies one has to be morally good. To put this objection in a slightly different way, what Plato's account seems to value most of all is self-mastery and temperance, but these are not in themselves moral values. Someone could have a harmonious self and yet not necessarily be morally good. The theory makes single-mindedness the central virtue, but couldn't there be a person who single-mindedly pursued moral evil? Indeed, the greatest crimes would surely be impossible without such single-mindedness and self-mastery. This is why Amon Goeth (Ralph Fiennes), the Nazi concentration camp commandant in *Schindler's List*, does not quite ring true as a symbol of Nazi evil. He is monstrous, ruled by sadistic impulses, close to being insane; but the Holocaust is a crime that required sober self-discipline and single-mindedness to carry out. The combination of self-mastery and enormous evil is precisely what makes some other recent cinematic monsters so intriguing: figures like Anthony Hopkins' Dr Hannibal Lecter in *The Silence of the Lambs* (Jonathon Demme, 1991), the refined cannibal who kills and mutilates his victims to the music of Bach; and Kevin Spacey's serial killer in *Se7en* (David Fincher, 1995), whose meticulously planned murders are based on the seven deadly sins. These monsters are intelligent, single-minded and fully in control of themselves; indeed, their particular crimes would not be possible without an almost superhuman self-discipline.

Second, Plato presumes that if we acquire the appropriate knowledge, and develop virtuous habits based on reason, we will lead the good life. Immorality is primarily due to ignorance. But this may be an over-optimistic picture, one that is too confident of the power of reason. People who have lived a moral life can still come to do immoral things. They do these things even if they know what is right, even if they know that what they are doing is wrong. In these cases, we might say that they suffer from weakness of will, an inability to resist temptation; but this also means that their rationality does not seem to have given them sufficient incentive to be good. In a cinematic context the male hero's inability to resist the woman he knows to be 'dangerous' or 'forbidden' is a recurring theme in film noir and has reappeared in a number of more recent films. *Sea of Love* (Harold Becker, 1989) and *Basic Instinct* (Paul Verhoeven, 1992) feature cynical, hard-boiled detectives (Al Pacino and Michael Douglas, respectively) who become attracted, despite their better judgement, to murder suspects. Male anxiety and paranoia over this loss of control reach fever pitch in *Fatal Attraction* (Adrian Lyne, 1987) where a married man (Michael Douglas) falls for a book editor (Glenn Close) and gets more than he bargained for when he tries to end it; his transgression calls forth a vengeful monster who terrorizes him and his family. Plato has no room in his account for those who choose a path at odds with what they know to be good or right. However, that we can know the good and yet choose not to abide

CRIMES AND MISDEMEANORS — MORAL PHILOSOPHY

by it is something that is acknowledged in the Christian conception of morality, and it's to this that we now turn.

Religion and morality

With the coming of Christianity a new view of morality emerged, a religious conception of morality that was to dominate Western thinking throughout the medieval period. Even today there are many for whom morality is impossible without a religious basis. This is the view expressed by Ivan in Dostoevsky's novel *The Brothers Karamazov*, when he proclaims that 'if God does not exist, everything is permissible'; and repeated by Sonia (Diane Keaton) in Woody Allen's Russian novel parody *Love and Death* (1975), when she tells her cousin Boris (Allen): 'Let's say that there is no God and each man is free to do exactly as he chooses; well, what prevents you from murdering someone?' Behind such claims is a profoundly God-centred understanding of the world and morality, one that emerged out of both the Jewish and Christian traditions. In these traditions God is presented as the law-giver who has fashioned the world and us for a purpose. That purpose is revealed to us, at least to some extent, through the Scriptures and the Church. According to these sources, in order to guide us in the right way of living God has formulated certain rules, certain duties we are to obey. We are not compelled to obey them, for we have been created as free agents, and so we can know the good and choose not to abide by it. It is up to us to decide whether to accept or reject these rules. Nonetheless, these rules tell us how we ought to live.

So on this religious view of morality, moral rules are God's laws, his commandments. This line of thinking has been spelt out by some theologians as the 'divine command' theory of morality. Morally right means that which is commanded by God; and morally wrong means that which is forbidden by God. Whereas for Plato being moral was a matter of achieving a certain kind of virtuous, internally balanced character, righteous living now becomes a matter of obedience to the divine commandments. To be moral is to be the obedient child of God. And Christian ethics offers us a new kind of reason for being moral, for following the rules of morality rather than simply pursuing our own interests. If moral rules are the commandments of God, and immorality means disobeying God, then on the day of final reckoning we will be held accountable for what we have done. This theistic perspective appears in *Crimes and Misdemeanors*, in the course of the doctor's reflections on whether he should have his mistress killed, as the main alternative to the view that being immoral is alright if you can get away with it. It is represented by the doctor's patient and friend, rabbi Ben (Sam Waterston), and by his father, who appears in flashbacks. God sees everything, says his father, and those who are righteous will be rewarded while those who are wicked will be punished for eternity. The rabbi echoes this view, and adds that we need a God-given moral law, for if there is no higher power, or moral structure with real meaning, then all we have is an empty, valueless world.

The idea that moral rules are an expression of God's will is not however without its problems. This view of morality depends, of course, on a belief in God and the validity of the Scriptures. If this belief is questioned, it is undermined. But even if we accept the religious position, it is not clear how we are to establish what God's will actually is, what God in fact commands. The scriptures are not always consistent and are open to considerable interpretation, as are miracles, dreams and other signs that might be invoked. The problem becomes acute if the will of God is invoked in order to justify what to ordinary observers seem to be evil, cruel or in other ways questionable acts. How do we know that those who invoke it are not simply mistaken or deluded, or perhaps rationalizing what they do? The ferocious inquisitor Bernardo Gui (F. Murray Abraham) in The Name of the Rose may claim theological justification for his acts of torture and killing, but how can we be certain that he is doing the will of God? How can we be sure that there is any real difference between him and the ignorant, hysterical witch-hunters of seventeenth-century Salem portrayed so effectively in The Crucible (Nicholas Hytner, 1996)? They also are convinced they are acting in the name of God. Similarly, when the papal official in The Mission (Roland Joffé, 1986) informs the South American Indians that it is the 'will of God' that they be turned out of the Jesuit mission and left to the mercy of the Portuguese slave-traders, we, like the Indians' leader, want to ask: 'How does he know he knows God's will?'

A second problem with the divine command view of morality is that it only works if we accept that God is good. And if we consider the existence of worldly evils such as violence, cruelty and premature death, this seems to raise questions about the unqualified goodness of God. This is one of the issues raised in the film The Rapture (Michael Tolkin, 1991). Here, bored telephone operator Sharon (Mimi Rogers) finds religion and, after the murder of her husband, hears God's call to go out into the desert to await the second coming. Once there, she murders her daughter to send her more quickly to heaven. What makes this film interesting is that it does not dismiss the central character as a deluded fanatic, but instead accepts fundamentalist religious premises. The issue now is that the woman finds herself unable to be reconciled with a God who could let her kill her child, and who allows 'so much suffering, so much pain on the earth he created'. God may forgive us, she says, but who is to forgive God? A similar problem arises in Ingmar Bergman's medieval tale *The Virgin Spring* (1959), in which Tore (Max von Sydow) takes brutal revenge on shepherds who raped and killed his daughter. Afterwards, he wonders how God could have allowed him to do such a terrible thing. As it happens, the film ends with a miracle (a spring appears at the site where the daughter was murdered) which seems to indicate divine forgiveness for his actions. So here, in contrast to *The Rapture*, God is reconciled with the evil he seems to allow. The problem is not really resolved though, because this reconciliation is only made possible at the cost of God becoming an utterly mysterious, inscrutable figure (as he so often is in Bergman's films). And such a view of God is also cold comfort for the divine command theory, since it makes the issue of how we can know God's will even more problematic.

These difficulties caused by the presence of worldly evil are part of a more general difficulty, the so-called problem of evil, which is the problem of reconciling the idea of a good, all-powerful God with the cruelty, pain, disease and suffering that afflicts us in this world. If God is good and all-powerful he could surely spare us from these evils. For some, the presence of such evil represents an argument against the very existence of God. Others have tried to argue in various ways that God and worldly evil are reconcilable (the part of theology that tries to do this is known as theodicy). One way of trying to reconcile the two is by holding that what seems evil is 'for the better' in the longer term, perhaps because it allows us to perfect our souls, and so it is all part of God's plan. In *The Rapture*, this is how the central character first tries to come to terms with evil, when her husband is murdered. Another way of trying to reconcile God and worldly evil is to argue that since God created human beings with free will, it is people, not God, who choose to bring evil into the world. However both these responses have had their critics, for whatever story we tell about evil, we can still ask why a benevolent, all-powerful God allows so much evil, and does not intervene to at least lessen it. Yet another way out here might be to argue that God is not good, but is in fact a malevolent deity. But this means that a significant aspect of the Christian notion of God has to be abandoned; and of course it would cause severe problems for the divine command theory of morality, which as we've seen depends on God being good.

There is one further problem with the divine command theory, which as James Rachels points out (1993, 47–50), has to do with how it formulates the very notions of 'good' and 'evil'. On this account, there is no reason why God cannot command what seem to us to be hideously evil acts like murder. We cannot say that a good God would never command such an evil act, because it is God's will that determines whether an act is good or bad. Thus, if God commanded us to murder, murder would be the right thing to do. But this also means that God's commands are entirely arbitrary. He has no more reason to command an action than to forbid it. Moreover, the very idea that God is good is destroyed on this view. If good and bad are determined by God's will, then to say that God's commands are good is only to say that God's commands are commanded by God, which is an empty statement. One way of dealing with this problem might be to drop the idea that an action is right because God commands it, and to hold instead that God commands an action because it is right. God has the infinite wisdom to know what is right and what is wrong, and in the light of this knowledge commands the right conduct. However this approach has its own difficulties because it seems to make a religion-based conception of morality unnecessary. God is no longer required in order to make an action right or wrong. There are standards of right and wrong independent of God's will, which God himself has to adhere to. Thus, what is distinctively theological about this account of morality seems to disappear. The eighteenth-century philosopher Kant certainly held that God himself has to obey moral principles determined independently of the divine will, so let us look at Kant's moral theory.

Kant: doing one's duty

If the Christian world-view was dominant during the medieval period, the modern period has seen the increasing undermining of traditional religious belief. Religion has not disappeared, of course. It continues to exert an influence, and to provide a moral perspective. But it is a distinguishing mark of our modernity that we no longer appeal so readily to religious authority to back up our guiding principles. And despite the claims of Dostoevsky and others that God is the only basis for morality, and that if we abandon God all will be permitted, there are post-religious ways of thinking about and justifying morality, forms of moral thinking that sit more comfortably with the modern outlook. This is an outlook in which human beings have replaced

God as the centre of reference; and morality now turns to various conceptions of human nature for its basis.

One such account is provided by Kant. In his *Groundwork* he provides us with an account of morality that no longer looks to God as the law-giver who provides us with rules. Instead, Kant looks to reason, or more precisely, to human beings understood primarily as rational beings. Morality is no longer obedience to God, but to our own rational conscience. We ourselves are the law-givers who establish the moral rules. That is, we, through our rationality, legislate moral rules for ourselves. This is not however a return to Plato's kind of rationalist morality. It is true that for Plato the moral person is the one who obeys the commands of reason, but Plato located the ultimate basis for morality in objective ideals, the forms, that reason is able to comprehend. For Kant, the basis for moral authority is not objective forms outside of us, but human beings themselves insofar as they are rational beings. We saw in Chapter 1 how for Kant, human reason provides the organizing forms or categories in terms of which we organize our experience and acquire knowledge of the world. His moral theory follows on from this, insofar as reason also determines the forms or principles in terms of which we are to organize our practical conduct, and live the moral life. So on Kant's view, moral rules are rational laws, the commands of one's own reason – what Kant calls 'the moral law within'. And with this account, we have another answer to the question 'why be moral?' The reason we should be moral, rather than pursuing our immediate wants and desires, is that only in doing so are we living up to our proper status as rational beings. There is a lot going on here, so we need to explore Kant's account in more detail.

In the *Groundwork*, Kant starts with the familiar idea that moral considerations have a special force, and that they should outweigh other considerations. For Kant, however, the moral is typically experienced in the form of the stern voice of duty, commanding us to put pleasure or personal interest aside, and to do the right thing whatever the consequences. He sees it as a matter of our ordinary moral experience that we distinguish between duty and personal interest or desire, and that we generally consider that doing our duty, doing what is right, should take precedence over merely personal interest, desires and inclinations. Whether or not ordinary moral experience is always like this, we certainly get a taste of this idea of morality in *High Noon* (Fred Zimmerman, 1952). Here town marshal Will Kane (Gary Cooper) waits for the return of an outlaw, who once terrorized the town, on the midday train. It was Kane who arrested him and sent him to prison, and now he is coming back to take his revenge. Kane cannot leave, even though he has been deserted by his new bride and by the townspeople he has served for years, and has been left to confront the killer alone. He stays in order to do his duty as town marshall, to uphold the law. He is heroic, but it is not the desire for glory that motivates him. When his bride Amy (Grace Kelly) asks him whether he is trying to be a hero, he replies: 'I'm not trying to be a hero. If you think I like this, you're crazy.' He simply has to stay, to do his duty, putting aside all other considerations including his own wishes and feelings. Other films can be interpreted in these terms as well, particularly if they involve an element of stern self-denial. For example, we could see *Casablanca* as portraying the triumph of duty over desire, when Rick gives up the woman most dear to him for the sake of the higher cause, the struggle against Fascism.

Kant seeks in his moral theory to analyse, explain and defend this notion of duty as something that outweighs all other considerations. He argues first of all that the consequences of our acts have no bearing on the moral worth of our actions, only the motivations behind them. This is not implausible. To go back to *High Noon*, in the end Kane succeeds in killing the outlaw he has been waiting for, but even if he himself had been killed, his actions would presumably still be worthy of moral praise. What is praiseworthy is the stand he takes, regardless of the consequences of doing so, regardless of whether he succeeds or fails. Second, Kant argues that only those actions that are motivated by a sense of duty, that are done 'for duty's sake', are moral actions. Again, this is not implausible. Certainly in *High Noon*, Kane's actions seem particularly moral and worthy because he does what he does simply because it is the 'right thing to do'. We don't feel the same way about Kane's friend and deputy Harvey Pell (Lloyd Bridges), when he offers to stand by Kane provided Kane gets him the job as the next marshall (Kane's reply: 'I want you to stick – but I'm not buying it. It's got to be up to you'). However we may not want to go quite as far as Kant in this regard. For Kant, it is not only actions done out of self-interest, desire or inclination that are to be excluded from the realm of the moral. Even an action done out of love or compassion, while it may be praiseworthy, is not a moral action. We will return to this issue in a moment.

Kant goes on to argue that when we are acting out of a sense of duty, when we are obligated by moral laws, we are acting in accordance with our rationality. For Kant, reason is capable of formulating these laws or principles of conduct, of generating rules for living; which is also to say that moral principles are rational in character. So how does reason establish moral principles?

To be moral, for Kant, is to act in accordance with principles that are binding not just on me but also on all rational beings. After all, something cannot be rational for me and not for you. So in order to act morally we need to determine that the principle we are thinking of acting on is universalizable, i.e., that it could consistently be followed by all agents in relevantly similar situations. In the Groundwork he gives the example of promise-keeping. Is it moral to break a promise when it suits me? That is, can I make the principle 'I may always break a promise when it's in my interest to do so' into a universal law? No, Kant argues, because if everyone did so, no one would believe promises people made in the first place, and the whole practice of promising would break down. So Kant provides us with a procedure by which reason can establish whether a principle is moral; and along with this, he gives us a general formula for what it is to be moral: act only on that principle that could be turned into a universal law.

So why, according to Kant, do we see moral demands, the demands of duty, as outweighing other considerations such as personal interest, desire or inclination? And why does he think we have to rigorously exclude all desire and inclination from the realm of the moral? His answer reflects his conception of human nature. As we saw in the previous chapter, Kant is amongst those who take up the Platonic conception of human nature, which tends to identify human beings most closely with their 'higher' rational side, and sees them as engaged in a constant struggle to control their 'lower', desiring side. He shares with Plato and also Christian moral thinking a hostility towards desire. In Kant's version of this picture, our reason constitutes the deepest and most valuable part of us. It is what raises us above nature and makes us unique. Everything else in nature is moved blindly, by mechanical forces. Even animals behave in this mechanical way. Human beings are partly like this, for they have a non-rational, natural side to their make-up, namely their desires, inclinations and emotions. But this is their lower side, which they share with the rest of nature. They are also, and more importantly, rational beings. Only rational beings have the capacity to act consciously in accordance with principles they formulate for themselves. This is something higher, something which sets us apart from the rest of nature.

Given this view of human nature it follows that rational agents ought to determine their actions in this way. As Charles Taylor puts it, 'the fundamental principle underlying Kant's whole ethical theory is something of this form: live up to what you really are – rational agents' (Taylor 1985, 324). To be moved to act by our desires, emotions and inclinations, to become just another thing conforming to mechanical necessity, is to break faith with our rational nature, to fall below our proper status. It is only when we are behaving rationally, in accordance with moral laws we formulate for ourselves, that we are living up to our true status as rational beings. Moreover the special value of rationality is something we ourselves recognize. We experience our rationality as being something 'higher'. This is why Kant thinks we experience moral commands, the demands of duty, as being more important than other considerations such as personal interest, desire or inclination. At the same time, because we are not purely rational beings, we do not effortlessly do what is rational, what is morally right. We are sometimes swayed by desire and inclination. So being moral is a constant struggle to rise above, suppress and control our desires and inclinations; and this is why, according to Kant, we experience moral laws as duties, as things we recognize that we ought to do even if we don't always manage to do them.

These are the main features, then, of Kant's moral theory. There are two further aspects worth noting. First of all, the idea that rationality is something higher than nature, that it has a special value, gives him another way of characterizing what it is in general to be moral. We have already seen one formulation: act only on that principle that could be turned into a universal law. Kant gives another, this time in terms of how we should treat rational beings. Everything else in nature can be used as instruments for our own goals and projects, but rational agents have their own goals and should be treated with these goals in view. Hence we should always treat rational agents, ourselves and others, never simply as means but always also as ends in themselves. In other words, we should respect them as beings with their own goals, capable of forming goals and acting in accordance with principles they have formulated for themselves. This is Kant's notion of respect for persons, which we looked at in Chapter 2. His moral theory leads us directly to the idea that persons, or rational agents, have a special value and are deserving of moral respect. Thus, to revisit an earlier example, it is because *Star Trek: The Next Generation*'s android Data is a rational agent that he should not be treated as a mere means, taken apart in order to be used to further scientific research, but has his own goals and his own preferences in the matter, which ought to be taken into account.

A second feature of the Kantian conception of morality to note is that it is bound up with a powerful notion of freedom. For Kant, being moral certainly involves obeying laws, but these are laws that we as rational beings formulate for ourselves. So when we are being moral we are determining ourselves, obeying only the dictates of our own rationality. By the same token, we are free from external influences, not only the influences of external nature, including our own desires and inclinations, but also the dictates of external moral authorities, other people, a church or whatever. Morality for Kant is thus bound up with freedom, which he calls 'autonomy', understood as my determining for myself the principles I live by, giving shape and direction to my own existence, rather than being determined by external influences. Equally, if I am subject to external influences, in a state of 'heteronomy' as Kant puts it, I cannot be said to be acting morally. This interlinking of morality and freedom is evident in *A Clockwork Orange*, in which, as we've seen, the film's anti-hero Alex is subjected to aversion therapy to cure him of his violent tendencies. He is thus transformed into a 'good' person, one who is unable to do any wrong without feeling physical distress. But it can be argued that he is not really morally good in this state, that he is not a moral agent at all, because these acts are not the result of self-determination but of the influence of external forces. This indeed is the view of the prison chaplain who complains that the conditioned Alex may have ceased to be a wrongdoer, but he has also ceased to be a 'creature capable of moral choice'.

Kant's vision of morality as arising out of human reason, insofar as rational agents formulate moral rules for themselves, and give shape and direction to their lives, has been immensely influential. However, numerous questions have also been raised about Kant's formulation of this ideal. Some of these questions involve the role of reason in his picture. Doubts have arisen as to whether reason as Kant presents it is capable of generating the moral rules we need. Is the rather abstract process of determining whether a principle can be consistently made a universal law sufficient to establish all moral principles? Moreover, Kant's emphasis on reason means that being moral requires the exclusion of all desire, inclination, emotion and feeling from the scene, so that we can be motivated purely by rational considerations. The result is a rather cold, austere conception of morality, in which we are required to act purely out of a sense of duty, and where feelings like love and compassion have no place. Instead we have to constantly struggle to suppress, control and discipline all feelings and desires, to prevent them from intruding on our moral thinking. As with the Platonic and Christian pictures, we may find this repressive, self-denying conception of the moral life rather unpalatable. Indeed, although Kant is willing to hold that we could be moral beings without any feelings of love and compassion, it might be argued that an absence of love or compassion in our moral behaviour itself amounts to a moral failure.

A further area of concern is Kant's insistence that the consequences of our acts are morally irrelevant. It is certainly possible for actions to be morally praiseworthy if done from good intentions, even if these actions lead to unfortunate results. As noted earlier, Kane's stance in *High Noon* would surely be morally worthy, even if he ended up being killed. To that extent, Kant's view seems plausible. But can we go as far as to say that consequences have no bearing at all, as Kant seems to want to? For example, would it be morally praiseworthy never to break a promise, even if doing so would save thousands of people from a terrible death? There is some question, also, whether Kant himself entirely avoids smuggling in a consideration of consequences into his moral conclusions. After all, when considering the universalizability of a principle like promise-keeping he looks to the consequences of not keeping promises. So perhaps we cannot simply exclude consideration of the consequences of our actions from moral reflection, as Kant suggests. There is however another distinctively modern moral theory in which the consequences of our actions play a central role, utilitarianism, and it is to this that we now turn.

Utilitarianism

Utilitarianism was first formulated by the English philosopher Jeremy Bentham (1748–1832) towards the end of the eighteenth century and refined by his successor John Stuart Mill (1806–1873) in the nineteenth century. Like Kantian moral theory, utilitarianism is a modern conception of morality in that it does not rely on God to provide us with moral rules, but grounds morality in human nature. Unlike Kant's theory however, utilitarianism does not view human beings primarily as rational beings, beings who should obey the austere, pleasureless dictates of their rationality. It rejects the whole tradition, going back to Plato, of viewing human nature as a battleground between reason and desire. Its view of human nature is much more in the Humean tradition, in which human beings are primarily motivated by desire and passion, and reason is the servant of the passions. Human beings, for utilitarianism, are primarily creatures that feel, creatures that seek to maximize pleasure and avoid pain. The role of reason is now to calculate what we can do to best bring about pleasure and avoid pain. And morality is now a matter of the consequences of our acts, of doing whatever will maximize the amount of pleasure, of happiness, in the world.

The notion of human beings as primarily creatures that seek pleasure and seek to avoid pain is the starting point for Bentham's pioneering formulation of utilitarianism, in his *Introduction to the Principles of Morals and Legislation*. Pleasure and pain govern life, Bentham holds, and they point not only to what people in fact do, but also what they ought to do. People in practice always act so as to maximize their pleasure, which Bentham identifies with happiness, and to minimize their pain, their misery or unhappiness. And all we mean by calling an act good or right, Bentham thinks, is that it promotes pleasure. When we say that we ought to do something, we mean that the act in question is useful in bringing about pleasure or happiness. On this basis he formulates the general utilitarian position. The moral character of an act derives from its consequences, from how much pleasure or happiness it produces. We ought to live and act in such a way as to promote the greatest happiness for all those who are in any way affected by the action. An action is right insofar as it tends to create the greatest happiness for the greatest number of people.

Utilitarianism is certainly a very appealing moral theory. Morality on this view is no less than the attempt to bring as much happiness into the world as possible. This is a morality that seeks to improve the world, to reform our personal and social practices. This makes being moral a very attractive option; and now the question of why we should be moral, why we should do the right thing, can be answered by saying that we should be moral because human beings seek pleasure, they value happiness, and moral acts are those that promote this happiness. Of course, the utilitarian argues that moral acts are those that produce the greatest happiness not just for the individual who acts but for the greatest number, and you might ask why should we seek to produce the greatest happiness for as many people as possible, rather than simply maximize our own individual happiness? In fact, Bentham is not entirely clear on this point. In pursuing our own happiness, he believes, we should seek the general happiness of society as well, but it is not quite clear why. Even if I must always seek to maximize my own happiness, I am surely not obliged to take the happiness of other people into account, except insofar as it serves to increase my happiness; and there are also clearly times when my happiness requires that other people be deprived of theirs. Bentham does not address these considerations.

Nonetheless, it might still be said, who could argue with the general proposition that we should oppose suffering and promote happiness? Well, let us leave this issue aside for the moment and look at some of the other positive features of utilitarianism. One attractive feature is that it appears to make it possible to calculate with certainty what is the right thing to do. For the utilitarian, we are not aiming to produce something other-worldly or mysterious, but rather an actual effect on the world, concrete differences in people's lives; and these are effects which can be measured in some way. In deciding what to do, we simply have to determine which course of action will produce the greatest amount of happiness for all those affected by the action. An action may have a number of consequences, of course. It may produce both happiness and unhappiness. But for utilitarianism, an action can be good if it produces some unhappiness, as long as, on balance, it produces the most happiness in comparison with other actions. So utilitarianism opens morality up to rational debate and resolution. And not only can we establish the right thing to do once and for all. This also means that there are no longer any moral dilemmas, at least in principle. Take for example the terrible dilemma faced by concentration-camp survivor Sophie (Meryl Streep) in *Sophie's Choice* (Alan Pakula, 1982), where she is forced by the Nazis to choose which of her two children is to live and which is to die. For utilitarianism, there is no fundamental problem here. This is in essence a matter of calculation, of working out how much happiness and unhappiness each alternative will produce, and choosing the one that produces the most overall happiness.

However, this process of calculation is not as straightforward as it might sound. To begin with, there can be practical difficulties in calculating the consequences of our actions, in determining how much overall happiness they are going to produce. Clearly, it would be very difficult in practice to establish which choice is going to produce the most overall happiness in the above example. To take another wartime example, in *Saving Private Ryan* (Steven Spielberg, 1998) Captain John Miller (Tom Hanks) leads a squad of soldiers into Normandy after D-Day to bring home a soldier whose brothers have all been killed. As they proceed the soldiers find themselves resenting having to risk their lives for someone they do not know, and who surely has no more right to live than they do. At one point Miller wonders what it would take to make the mission worthwhile: 'This Ryan had better be worth it. He'd better go home and cure some disease or invent a longer-lasting light bulb or something.' The thinking here is entirely utilitarian. If Ryan ends up doing something wonderful for humanity, then despite all the risks and suffering involved in the mission, saving him will be justified because it will produce more overall happiness than not saving him. So if Ryan produces sufficient happiness on his return we will be able to say that the mission was the right thing to do. But once again there are practical difficulties in making this kind of calculation. How do we measure the overall effect Ryan will have on the world? Also, how far into the future do we measure? Do we take into account the effects he will have on those who are alive now, or on future generations as well?

Apart from practical difficulties in calculating the consequences of actions, there is also the question of how we are to measure the happiness that results. In order to determine that one course of action is preferable to another, we need to be able to compare happinesses, to say that one act produces more overall pleasure or happiness than another. However, happiness takes many forms, and if very different kinds of happiness are produced, it is not clear how we are to compare them. For example, suppose saving one soldier will result in his mother feeling profound happiness at his safe return, while saving another will result in a widespread, though rather pedestrian, happiness, when he goes on to invent a longer-lasting light bulb. Can we say that one action produces greater or less happiness than the other? In fact they seem to be qualitatively different kinds of happiness, so different in character that they cannot really be compared. Bentham himself thought that pleasures differed only in quantity, and that by using various scales – intensity, duration, likelihood of recurrence, etc. – it would be possible to measure the overall amount of pleasure in each instance. But it is not clear that we could ever arrive at precise figures for these measurements. Overall, Bentham's proposal looks rather implausible.

A second set of problems for the utilitarian picture has to do with the identification of happiness with pleasure. Early on, critics of utilitarianism seized on Bentham's claim that all things being equal, pushpin (a party game) is as good as poetry. For Bentham, happiness is to be understood in terms of pleasure, and pleasures differ only in quantity, so if different activities produce the same amount of pleasure there is nothing to distinguish one as better than the other. But critics labelled utilitarianism a 'pig philosophy' as a result. Surely, it was argued, pleasures like those associated with poetry were 'higher' or more refined than others, such as the pleasures of party games. In his book *Utilitarianism*, Bentham's successor John Stuart Mill sought to refine the utilitarian position by arguing that for human beings there were indeed 'higher' and 'lower' pleasures, and that we should aim to maximize the higher ones. As Mill famously put it, 'better to be a Socrates dissatisfied than a pig satisfied' (Mill 1987, 281). The higher pleasures here are intellectual or spiritual pleasures like literary or artistic enjoyment, and the lower pleasures are physical pleasures, the carnal and corporeal pleasures that the lower orders so delighted in. Mill is not simply saying that we ought to cultivate these higher pleasures; he thinks we will not be truly satisfied, fully happy, if we do not. Of course some might respond that they are perfectly happy pursuing trivial physical pleasures, and that Mill's talk of higher pleasures reflects intellectual snobbery or class prejudice. Mill's answer is that the higher pleasures can be said to be superior because human beings really prefer them; if people are faced with a choice between higher and lower pleasures, having properly experienced both, they will always opt for the higher ones.

The idea that some pleasures are higher than others, and that we tend to prefer the higher to the lower, is taken up in a number of films. In My Fair Lady (George Cukor, 1964), based on George Bernard Shaw's play Pygmalion, the working-class flower-seller (Audrey Hepburn) is introduced to the higher pleasures of Professor Higgins and his circle. Having experienced the higher pleasures of elevated society, she finds she can no longer go back to her old working-class life, where only the lower pleasures are possible. Similarly, in another Pygmalion story, Educating Rita (Lewis Gilbert, 1983), a working-class hairdresser (Julie Walters) who tries to better herself by studying at university finds that she now prefers the higher pleasures of literature and can no longer be content with the simple pleasures she once enjoyed (singing in the pub and so on). However, what is Mill to say to someone who, having tasted the higher pleasures, turns their back on them? In Dangerous Liaisons (Stephen Frears, 1988), a professional philanderer (John Malkovich) and a sadistic aristocrat (Glenn Close) take this path, deriving their pleasures from ruining the lives of innocents through sexual deceit and betrayal. And if people do indeed prefer the lower pleasures to the higher, what right, it might be argued, has anyone to label these pleasures inferior? Mill acknowledges that some who have been able to appreciate the higher pleasures subsequently turn back to the lower, but he thinks that these are cases of degeneration, explainable in social and psychological terms. At this point however, Mill is in danger of abandoning the very criterion of personal preference he earlier relied on; and thus leaving himself open once again to the accusation of intellectual or class snobbery.

A further problem that arises with utilitarianism is that all kinds of questionable acts, including gross injustice and premeditated murder, appear to be justifiable on utilitarian grounds, given the right circumstances. A number of films provide illustrations of this. In Breaker Morant (Bruce Beresford, 1980) an unjust court-martial is allowed to go ahead, and three Australian soldiers are sacrificed, in order to serve the greater good by preventing the Germans from entering the Boer war. In The Last Supper (Stacey Title, 1996), a group of liberal American students decide to do away with obnoxious right-wing types by inviting them over to dinner and poisoning them. They justify their actions on the utilitarian grounds that these people cause all kinds of misery, and their murder will make the world a happier place. As one of the characters, Marc (Jonathan Penner), puts it, wouldn't anyone murder Hitler in cold blood if they were able to return to a time before he rose to power, knowing all that he was going to do? Similar thinking can be used to justify some very harsh social policies. The brainwashing of prisoners like Alex in *A Clockwork Orange* is justified by the government on the utilitarian grounds that it will reduce crime and relieve the overcrowding in prisons. *Harrison Bergeron* (Bruce Pittman, 1995) depicts another future society, one which holds televised public executions on the grounds that this serves as a deterrent. While this may seem extreme, it is a standard utilitarian argument for capital punishment that it has a deterrent effect on serious crime, any distress to the executed criminal being outweighed by the benefits to the general public; and televising executions is quite consistent with such a viewpoint.

So utilitarianism has a disturbing capacity to justify all kinds of questionable acts, because of their good consequences. In response, one might want to argue that certain acts are simply unacceptable, and should never be permitted, no matter how beneficial the consequences might be. This is in fact the Kantian position. Although, as we saw, the Kantian position itself seems problematic to the extent that it excludes all consideration of consequences from moral consideration, it does provide an alternative to the utilitarian perspective for which anything is justifiable if it has good consequences. The conflict between the two perspectives in this regard is evident for example in the mock-philosophical discussion in *Love and Death*, where Boris and Sonia, now married, consider whether to go to Moscow to kill Napoleon. If we don't kill Napoleon, says Boris, he will lay waste to all of Europe; but this utilitarian argument is immediately countered with a Kantian one, as Boris wonders if murder doesn't carry with it what he calls a 'moral imperative', i.e., whether there is something inherently wrong with killing someone, whatever good might come of it. Similarly, in *Quiz Show* (Robert Redford, 1994), the producers of a fifties American television quiz show try to convince academic Charles Van Doren (Ralph Fiennes) to accept having the answers beforehand, because if he does well on the show he will promote education (they tell him he will be an 'intellectual Joe DiMaggio'); but Van Doren's reply, 'I'm just trying to imagine what Kant would make of that', implies he is aware that a different moral perspective on the situation is possible, that cheating is intrinsically bad, whatever the consequences. For the moment at least, he rejects their offer.

Existentialism: absurdity, freedom and bad faith

Although we can point to problems with both the Kantian and utilitarian approaches, these accounts remain the two most significant and influential modern moral theories. Utilitarianism in particular has proved surprisingly resilient. Numerous arguments have been raised against it, but it has been modified rather than abandoned. There is one further account of morality we can consider here, an account very much of the twentieth century – existentialism. While there are significant precursors in Friedrich Nietzsche (1844–1900) and Søren Kierkegaard (1813–1855), existentialism proper flourished in the 1940s and 1950s. It is linked in particular with a number of French thinkers who became well known after the Second World War: Jean-Paul Sartre (1905–1980), Simone de Beauvoir (1908–1986) and Albert Camus (1913–1960). Of these perhaps Sartre is the most representative. His book *Being and Nothingness* contains the definitive formulation of existentialism, and the account of existentialism given here will be largely his.

Existentialism is distinctive in holding that there is either nothing outside of or within ourselves that we can appeal to in order to justify our values and moral rules. There is no God to give us guidance as to how to live; reason is unable to provide us with rules for living, as Kant thought; and nor can we appeal to human happiness as our goal, in the utilitarian spirit. Existentialism shares with Kantianism and utilitarianism the view that human beings are the basis of morality; but for existentialism, if there are moral rules or values of any sort, it is because we have freely chosen them, and nothing can guide us in these choices. It is entirely up to us to give our existence its values and goals. Thus from the existentialist perspective, Kane's decision in *High Noon* to stay in town and face the returning outlaw is a free choice which cannot be justified in any way whatsoever. Rick's choice in *Casablanca* to sacrifice Ilsa for the sake of a better future for humanity, Terry's decision to take a stand against the corrupt waterfront union boss in *On the Waterfront*, Montag's decision to rebel against the state in *Fahrenheit 451*, Schindler's decision to help the Jews in *Schindler's List* – all these are free choices, for which they must bear full responsibility. So why on this view should we be moral, rather than non-moral, self-sacrificing rather than opportunistic, rebellious rather than complicit? There is no answer to that. It is up to us to choose which way to go, and whatever we choose is ultimately without support or justification. To explore existentialism further, it is helpful to look at a number of the specific themes it explores: absurdity, the death of God, freedom, authenticity and bad faith.

For existentialism, the world is 'absurd'. That is, there is no reason for the way the world is, for what happens in it, and human beings in particular have no reason or justification for existing. Life is essentially meaningless, and the only thing that awaits us is death. This feeling of absurdity arises partly because for the existentialists, 'God is dead'. This slogan, first articulated by Nietzsche (see Nietzsche 1974, 181–2), refers to the gradual erosion of religious belief that has taken place over the last three hundred years. As a result, the existentialists argue, there is no longer any God-given order or grand plan which we can appeal to in order to give point and purpose to our existence; and this means that the world is a bleak, meaningless place. For some, we need religion precisely to keep such meaninglessness at bay. This is the position of the rabbi in *Crimes and Misdemeanors*, that we must believe in a God-given moral structure or there is no point in going on; and also of the main character in *The Rapture*, whose turn to religion allows her to escape from an empty life, and to believe that even the murder of her husband is somehow meaningful, part of some larger plan. But for existentialism, recourse to God is no longer an option. To resort to belief in God is, as Camus puts it in his book *The Myth of Sisyphus*, to commit 'philosophical suicide' – to try to evade absurdity at the cost of denying thought and sacrificing our critical faculties.

Moreover, the existentialists no longer believe that we can replace God with human nature as the reference point; they reject the idea that either reason or happiness can provide our lives with guidance or purpose. They no longer agree with Kant that reason can establish values or goals for us. For them, his attempts to found morality on some purely rational procedure only mean that his thinking has become lost in an ethereal world of philosophical abstraction. But what about the more down-to-earth notion of human happiness, and the utilitarian ideal of working for the common good? The individual's capacity to contribute to the happiness of others is sometimes put forward as a reason for thinking that life is meaningful. This is the view for example in *It's a Wonderful Life* (Frank Capra, 1946). George Bailey (James Stewart), the director of a small town savings and loans association on the verge of bankruptcy, thinks that he is a failure and is on the verge of suicide. An angel (Henry Travers) convinces him that his life is worth living by showing him how much worse things would have been if he hadn't existed.

By living he has brought much happiness to those around him, to his family, friends and those he has helped through his savings and loans association. But the existentialists reject the very idea that happiness, for oneself or for those around one, is a worthy goal. They tend to identify happiness with unthinking contentment, a state which like religious belief can only be achieved through philosophical suicide, the sacrifice of one's critical faculties. As long as we are more than unconscious brutes, we can never be truly content. We could only become happy by ceasing to be human.

This existentialist sense of the meaninglessness of life was undoubtedly intensified by the horrors of the Second World War, and a sense that the traditional and familiar moral and social values had collapsed. As Max Charlesworth puts it, 'Post-war European man found himself in a desolate and featureless landscape without any signs to guide him, without any hope that he could by his efforts bring about a better world' (Charlesworth 1974, 2). Hence the appeal of existentialism in the forties and fifties. This disenchantment with traditional values and the sense of the absurdity of existence was also fed by the ensuing Cold War and its threat of a nuclear catastrophe that could wipe out all human achievements in an instant. A number of films of the period reflect this concern, notably *On the Beach* (Stanley Kramer, 1959), which portrays the last people left alive after the third world war. They have taken refuge in Australia and as they await their death from the radioactive clouds spreading around the globe, they try to cope with their seemingly pointless existence in various ways. Some turn to religion, to philosophical suicide; others, to the real thing. Ingmar Bergman's *The Seventh Seal* (1957) also takes up this theme, dealing with it in the form of a historical allegory. In fourteenth-century Sweden, the knight Antonius Block (Max von Sydow) and his squire return from the Crusades to find the Black Death rife in the land. Faced with the threat of mass death, people are questioning all moral and religious values. God himself seems to have abandoned humanity, and the dominant question raised by the film's characters is whether life has any meaning at all. At the time the film was being made, Bergman indicated that for him the atom bomb corresponded to a modern plague (see Cowie 1982, 141).

For philosophical and historical reasons, then, the existentialists argue that the world is absurd, that there are no pre-existing standards or values human beings can appeal to in order to justify their existence or actions. The other side of this, however, is that human beings are free to give their lives whatever goal or purpose they choose. If God does not exist and all prevailing values are in question, then everything is indeed permitted. Indeed, human freedom is the most central theme of the existentialist account. For the existentialists, human beings are above all free subjects; our freedom is what sets us apart from everything else in nature, and makes us distinctively human. This is freedom understood as a capacity for self-determination, independently of all external forces. It is a version of the Kantian notion of autonomy, only without Kant's faith that reason will provide us with guidance as to how to act. Without any guidance whatsoever we freely choose our values and goals, and in doing so give our existence meaning and purpose. To try to evade our responsibility, to pretend that our goals and values are in some way imposed on us, is the great existentialist sin; it is what Sartre calls 'bad faith', the cowardly evasion of our freedom. Of course, it is certainly attractive to try to evade acknowledgement of our freedom. To be wholly responsible for all our values is a terrible burden, which we experience, according to Sartre, as 'anguish'. That is, I experience a fundamental anxiety before the necessity of having to choose, to be totally responsible for my existence. By denying my freedom I can find contentment and happiness. Nonetheless, to take refuge in the belief that my values and goals are simply imposed on me by God, society or nature, and that I have no choice but to do what I do, is to deny the very freedom that makes us human. It is to be 'inauthentic'.

Out of this is born the image of the existential hero, who heroically refuses to rely on external props, to appeal to pre-existing values and standards, but instead shoulders the heavy burden of responsibility for their existence. Camus summed it up in his image of the Greek hero Sisyphus, condemned by the Gods to endlessly roll a stone up a hill only to have it roll down again – a pointless, absurd task that he nonetheless embraces defiantly, even joyfully (see Camus 1975, 109–11). In the American cinema of the fifties and sixties, the existential rebel was linked with alienated youth, and incorporated into the growing countercultural movement. A number of films of the period focus on what we might call instinctively rebellious individuals, unable to accept the stifling values of middle-class society and striking out on a path of their own. The classic figure here is Marlon Brando's Johnny in *The Wild One* (Laslo Benedek, 1954), leader of the bikers' gang who invade a small town. His protest is summed up in the famous exchange with the girl he's dancing with in the bar: 'What are you rebelling against, Johnny?' Johnny: 'What've you got?' Closely following in Johnny's footsteps is James Dean's troubled youth in *Rebel Without a Cause* (Nicholas Ray, 1955), alienated from the world and the values of the adults around him; Dennis Hopper and Peter Fonda on the road in *Easy Rider* (Dennis Hopper, 1969), rejecting not only conventional values but also those of the sixties counterculture; and Jack Nicholson's Bobby Dupea, on the run from both his upper-middle-class musical career and his alternative working-class life as an oil rigger in *Five Easy Pieces* (Bob Rafelson, 1970). These are all heroic figures to the extent that they refuse to fall into unthinking conformity with conventional values and the expectations of those around them, who strike out on their own path, even though this means being unhappy, troubled and lost.

No doubt these films provide a fairly romantic view of the existential rebel. The individual alienated from conventional social values and adrift without a reference point can be a much less appealing figure, as for example in Wim Wenders' film of existential alienation *The Goalkeeper's Fear of the Penalty* (1971). Here, goalkeeper Joseph Bloch (Arthur Brauss) walks out of a football game, wanders aimlessly through the city, and arbitrarily commits a murder. He does not seem to have any real idea where he is going or why he acts, and the film reinforces this by refusing to offer any kind of explanation for his actions. He comes across not as a heroic figure but as a disturbed loner. Still, alienation is only part of the existentialist story. For the existentialists, we may no longer be able to appeal to conventional or God-given values, but this also means that we ourselves take centre stage in giving our lives meaning and value. This is the individual's defiant self-affirmation in the face of an absurd world cele-brated by Camus in his image of Sisyphus. A film closer to this spirit is Woody Allen's *Hannah and Her Sisters* (1986). Here Hannah's ex-husband Mickey (Allen) suffers a cancer scare and starts wondering if life has any point, since we are all destined to die. He finds that he is unable to take refuge in religion, to commit philosophical suicide, and is close to actual suicide when he comes to the realization that even if there is no God, and death turns out to be the end, he should stop worrying and enjoy life while it lasts. In best Sisyphean fashion, the recognition of life's absurdity is combined here with a defiant decision to embrace it and go on regardless.

The opposite of the existential hero is the person who tries to avoid confronting the absurdity of existence, to hide from the burden of taking responsibility for their life through philosophical suicide or bad faith. We are in bad faith, for example, if we believe there is a God or a human nature that provides us with an ultimate purpose or direction, that we had no choice but to 'follow orders', that our actions are determined by social conditioning, unconscious drives or physical causes. These are all ways in which we pretend to ourselves that we are not free, and thus try to evade responsibility for what we do. Thus in *Quiz Show*, even when Van Doren is confessing to his father that he cheated on the television quiz show, he offers self-justifying accounts of his actions ('what was I supposed to do, disillusion the whole country?'). As his father points out, he makes it sound as if he had no choice in the matter. Similarly, to claim as Peter Lorre's child-killer does in M that he 'cannot help what he does', is, for the existentialists, to take refuge in self-deception. Even that most driven of characters, the cinematic vampire, is susceptible these days to existentialist criticism. In *Interview with a Vampire* (Neil Jordan, 1994), the vampire Louis (Brad Pitt) refuses to accept that he is destined to be evil. Though his mentor Lestat (Tom Cruise) tells him that it is now his nature to kill, he struggles to find a different purpose for his existence. Compare this with *The Addiction* (Abel Ferrera, 1995), where Kathleen (Lili Taylor), an idealistic philosophy student appalled by a world that could allow evils like the Holocaust, is turned into a vampire and becomes everything she hates. There are copious references to Sartre and other existentialists (her thesis is on existentialist philosophy), but the film puts forward the entirely unexistentialist view that in the end Kathleen has no choice but to accept her fate, and indeed that all human beings have an innate predisposition towards evil.

Self-deception is a common enough tendency in human life, but we may want to question the existentialist tendency to see it primarily in terms of an attempt to avoid the burden of our freedom. Often, what seems to motivate the misrepresentation of events to ourselves is that we are trying to preserve a certain conception of who we are, a certain self-image. To return to Kurosawa's *Rashomon*, which we looked at in Chapter 1, as the story is retold from a number of different perspectives, it becomes clear that the events are being presented in such a way that whoever is telling the story appears in the best possible light. This kind of self-deception is also evident in *Judgement at Nuremberg* (Stanley Kramer, 1961), where Ernst Janning (Burt Lancaster), a senior German judge on trial at Nuremberg after the war, deludes himself that he only went along with the Third Reich to lessen its harshness, to prevent a worse man taking his place. And in *Mephisto* (Istvan Szabo, 1981) the actor Hendrik Hofgen (Klaus Maria Brandauer) who sells his soul to the Nazis in exchange for fame and fortune imagines that he is exploiting them in order to further his art, but in the end it becomes clear that he has deeply deceived himself, that he was never anything more than a tool of the Nazi regime, caught like a fly in its web. It is not entirely clear how these cases of self-deception can be incorporated into the existentialist model of denial of freedom and responsibility.

But perhaps a more significant problem that arises with the existentialist account concerns its notion of freedom itself. It has been argued by many that in its stress on human freedom as absolute, existentialists like Sartre fail to properly take into account the influence of our situation or circumstances, not only our physical being but also social and historical context. Not that existentialism simply ignores our situation. Sartre in particular argues that we always exist in a specific situation, with a certain past, in certain social and historical circumstances. Indeed, he argues, we can only be free in a specific situation, that being in a situation is a necessary condition for freedom. But he also wants to say that this situatedness does not limit my freedom in any way, that I remain absolutely free. My freedom manifests itself in my capacity to choose goals or possibilities that go beyond my present situation, and nothing in my situation can determine what possibilities I choose. For example, my situation does not compel me in any way to join a revolution; I choose revolution, and it is in fact only in the light of my free choice that my situation appears to me as 'intolerable'. So understood, my factual situation is indeed a necessary condition for my freedom, but only in the sense that I require it in order to be able to look beyond it, to envisage alternatives to it.

Nonetheless, we may still wonder whether Sartre has not underestimated the force of circumstances, the influence of our social and historical situation on how we choose. We may wonder whether freedom can be understood purely in terms of a rejection, a revolt against one's circumstances and past. The existentialist belief that we can escape radically from our circumstances in this way is called into question in *Breathless* (Jean-Luc Godard, 1959). Michel (Jean-Paul Belmondo), a petty criminal, guns down a policeman and hides out in the Paris apartment of a young American student Patricia (Jean Seberg), who eventually betrays him to the police. Along the way, Michel sees himself very much as the existential hero. He seems to be an anarchic free spirit, the master of his own fate, and the film itself has an unconventional, improvisational look that seems to reflect this freedom. But as David Sterrit points out (1999, 56–60), it gradually becomes clear that Michel is considerably influenced by his culture. Many of his rather theatrical mannerisms and gestures are in fact borrowed from the movies (especially Bogart movies). Michel and Patricia certainly make choices, but these choices are very much limited by their social situation and the options that it makes available. In the end, they both play out roles that existed long before they came on the scene – killer, lover, and in the end, squealer.

More recently, the idea of freedom as repudiation of one's past and circumstances in order to make oneself anew has been questioned in *Three Colours: Blue* (Krzysztof Kieslowski, 1993), the first of Kieslowski's 'three colours' series. After the death of her husband and daughter in a car crash, Julie (Juliette Binoche) tries to leave behind all vestiges of her former existence, to withdraw from the world, in order to live a completely autonomous life. She burns her composer husband's compositions, puts her mother in a home, and moves into a Paris apartment where no one knows her. As she tells her mother, 'I want no belongings, no memories, no friends, no love.' It is the perfect recipe for the existentialist rebel, who heroically distances him- or herself from conventional expectations and rejects all familiar reference points. But Julie finds that in practice she cannot escape from her past or from human relationships and commitments, and that she is unable to live without belief or hope. Bit by bit she becomes involved in the life of her neighbours, people from her past track her down, and she is eventually moved to provide a home for her husband's mistress, pregnant with his child. Gradually she is drawn back into the stream of life. Radical freedom and independence turn out to be an impossible dream.

Sartre himself, in his later writings, came to question the core existentialist notion of the radically free individual, capable of standing apart from all external circumstances and choosing itself in complete freedom, that he had formerly championed. He came to pay more attention to the situation we find ourselves in. Without abandoning his commitment to freedom, he came to argue for an account which acknowledges that human beings are profoundly influenced and constrained by their social, political and historical circumstances. His thinking thus began to turn in the direction of social and political philosophy. In this chapter, we have focused on moral philosophy, on why individuals should be moral and what being moral might involve. It is now time for this discussion also to move on to wider social and political concerns, to social and political philosophy; and this will be the topic of the next chapter.

4

ANTZ – SOCIAL AND POLITICAL PHILOSOPHY

Antz.
Credit: Dreamworks (Courtesy The Ronald Grant Archive)

The animated film *Antz* (Eric Darnell, Tim Johnson, 1999) opens in the heart of the ant colony, with the central character Z-4195 (voiced by Woody Allen) lying on a couch in a psychiatrist's office. Z is finding it difficult to adjust to his role as a worker in ant society: 'It's this whole gung-ho super-organism thing I can't get . . . I'm supposed to do everything for the colony, and what about my needs? . . . The whole system makes me feel insignificant.' To which his psychiatrist replies: 'Excellent. You've made a real breakthrough. You *are* insignificant!' Z offers one kind of perspective on the relationship between the individual and society, a perspective that we also find in the existentialist picture we have just been looking at. On this view, individuals stand essentially in opposition to society. Social demands and constraints are threats to the individual's freedom, to their very identity. To succumb to them, to conform to social expectations, is to lose one's individuality, to become part of the herd, to disappear into the faceless crowd. The proper role of society is to be the backdrop against which heroic individuals can stand out, rebel and assert their individuality. This tendency to see the individual as having priority over society is a distinctively modern view of social and political existence, one that has a powerful hold on our thinking: the view that we are first of all individuals, and only secondarily members of society. But before saying any more about this, it will be helpful to look at a view in which it is society that comes first, and the individual a distant second.

Plato's ants

This brings us back once again to Plato's *Republic*. Here, as we saw in the previous chapter, Plato argues for a view of the moral person as the well-ordered self, in which the different parts, reason, spirit and desire, each play their proper role in the whole. To be moral is thus to be free of inner disharmony and conflict, to attain a state of mental well-being which is both beneficial and enjoyable. But the *Republic* is also an argument about what constitutes a moral or just society. At the social level also, the ideal situation is one of balance, in which the various parts play their proper role. The result will be a state of harmonious social well-being, free of discord, violence and dissent, a state that is both beneficial to the people as a whole, and conducive to their happiness. The different parts of society are the guardians or rulers, corresponding to the rational part of the self; the auxiliaries or soldiers, corresponding to the spirited part; and the workers, the general rabble, corresponding to the desires. Society is well-ordered and harmonious when the guardians, who have knowledge of what is in society's best interests, rule the workers, assisted in this task by the spirited auxiliaries. Plato also thinks that different people have different natures, suiting them to different social roles. Some are born to rule, others to fight, others to work. Society is happiest when each individual does the job that their nature has best equipped them for; and each person should stick to what they are fitted for.

Plato's vision of a just society is liable to strike us as rather oppressive and anti-individualistic. It is certainly authoritarian. As Richard Norman (1983, 27) points out, the authoritarianism that is already present in his account of the self, in which reason needs to firmly control the desires, has been turned into a political authoritarianism, an argument for the complete subordination of the population to a ruling intellectual élite. There is no room here to question the rulers or the overall social order they enforce. This does not trouble Plato. For him it is self-evident that one should obey those who speak with the authority of knowledge. The rulers have knowledge of the best social arrangements and the interests of society as a whole, and should be obeyed. Others don't have knowledge and need to have virtue imposed upon them. If they do not obey, they may well do the wrong thing. We however are less willing to accept that governments can or should determine what is the good life for us, or what our well-being or happiness consists in. Moreover, this is a picture on which individuals are thoroughly subordinated to their role in the social order. For Plato what is above all important is the unity of the state, in which each individual plays his or her proper role. Each individual is fitted out by nature to play a certain role in the social division of labour, whether guardian, auxiliary or worker, and they should stick to what they are fitted for. To do otherwise is to bring disharmony and discord into the society.

118

There is no room here for individual expression or non-conformity, no value whatsoever accorded to individuality. We however are less willing to accept that the unity of the state should take absolute precedence over the individual and individual freedom.

Plato explicitly compares his ideal society to a beehive (Plato 1974, 520), and the metaphor of an insect colony, with its rigid division of labour and complete subordination of the individual to the requirements of the collective, is particularly apt. And we can find numerous echoes of the Platonic vision of society in *Antz*, as well as some of the misgivings that this vision is likely to provoke when viewed from a more individualistic perspective. In this film the ant society, like Plato's, is divided rigidly into three classes, in this case aristocrats, soldiers and workers. 'Everyone has their place', the queen ant tells the princess, 'you, the soldiers, the workers', and each must perform their proper role without question. The proper social role for each ant is determined by its nature, and we see the ants being identified at birth as belonging to one of the three groups. In this society, the individual is insignificant. What is important is the 'team', the colony, and individuals are only important insofar as they contribute to the overall good of the colony. As we saw at the beginning of the chapter, individualistic misgivings about such a society are given voice by the central character Z, who just doesn't understand 'this whole gung-ho superorganism thing'. Z is the ant who questions the conformism of his fellow ants ('mindless zombies capitulating to an oppressive system'), who refuses simply to accept the role imposed on him, and who wants to choose his own path in the world. Through Z the film stands up for the individual, and for the struggle to make society respect the individual's choices as to how to live.

Our misgivings about the Platonic vision of the state as a superorganism or superentity are no doubt intensified by the appeal to such notions in twentieth-century totalitarianism, as for example in Stalinist Russia and Nazi Germany. The peculiar horror of individuality being swallowed up in some faceless social whole has been portrayed in a number of films that refer to the modern totalitarian experience, including *Invasion of the Body Snatchers* (Don Siegel, 1956), and *Nineteen Eighty-Four* (Michael Radford, 1984). In *Invasion of the Body Snatchers*, which as mentioned in Chapter 2 has been widely interpreted as a Cold War anti-communist allegory, townsfolk are gradually taken over and turned into 'pod-people', dehumanized, emotionless servants of an invading alien intelligence. The result is a kind of collectivist utopia in which all the citizens contribute, and in which 'everyone is the same'. In *Nineteen Eighty-Four*, which portrays the police state of George Orwell's anti-Stalinist novel with grim effectiveness, the tone is set in the opening scene. In a cinema showing a patriotic newsreel, anonymous, black-clad citizens rise from their seats in unison to praise their leader Big Brother. Later in the film, it is made clear that the government considers each individual to be no more than a 'cell' in the great organism of the state. In both films, preserving one's individuality requires a courageous rejection of social conformity, whatever the benefits falling in line might bring. In *Invasion of the Body Snatchers*, the town doctor Miles (Kevin McCarthy) refuses the pod-people's offer of life amongst them, a life that he is assured will be without pain, fear or worries. In *Nineteen Eighty-Four*, Winston Smith (John Hurt) has a secure if lowly place in the party hierarchy, but nonetheless feels compelled to start a personal diary and enter into an illicit sexual relationship.

Now although individuality is being promoted here in the face of conformity to society, we would presumably not want to go so far as to say that society ought to be dispensed with altogether, that we can do entirely without organized social life. Collective, organized activity is necessary if we are to enjoy the benefits of civilization. *Antz* stands up for the individual against the group, but even here it is clear that the colony is only able to enjoy a reasonable standard of living through its collective activity; and it is only saved from disaster in the end by the concerted action of its inhabitants. But it is a widely held view that human beings are individuals first and only secondarily members of society, that society is there to serve the needs of individuals, and that individuals should be as free as possible in society to live their own lives. Here we are far distant from the kind of social and political order envisaged by Plato. We are also distant in our thinking from most pre-modern Western societies. In Greek and Roman society, and in medieval Europe, individuals were seen first of all as part of a social organism, a structured community. The overriding concern was with a social and cosmic balance, or a larger, God-given order, that transcended individuals and determined their duties. The individual-centred form of thinking we are more familiar with only began to emerge in the course of the seventeenth and eighteenth centuries. As in modern moral thinking, so too in modern social and political thinking, human beings, individuals, become the starting point. And it is to the modern, individual-centred form of social and political thinking, known as liberalism, that we now turn.

Liberalism: the heroic individual

Liberalism is not only a social and political theory. It is also a way of thinking about society, an outlook, which is widespread in contemporary Western societies. Amongst its earliest proponents we find the seventeenth-century English thinkers Thomas Hobbes and John Locke. So what then does liberal social and political thinking involve? Most fundamentally, it makes the individual the central concern, and the starting point for all thinking about social life. For liberalism human beings are first of all individuals, and only secondarily members of society. They thus need to be protected from society. Liberals in general hold that, as far as possible, governments and laws should not encroach on what individuals want to do, that individuals should be as free as possible to pursue their needs and interests. This is not to say that individuals ought to be completely unhindered. There needs to be some kind of central government, some social and legal constraints on what individuals may do. But for liberalism these restrictions are a necessary evil. Even if some constraints are necessary, they should be as minimal as possible. Individuals should still be as free as possible, free to pursue their individual wants, desires and interests without interference.

Why, according to liberal thinking, do individuals need to submit to some degree of government control and social authority? The answer is that if all social authority were removed, things would be very unpleasant indeed. The earliest thinkers in the liberal tradition, Hobbes and Locke, envisaged what they called the 'state of nature', a time before the invention of society, when human beings lived quite separately and alone. Whether such a state of nature ever actually existed is debatable, but we can also think of this proposal as a kind of thought experiment: what would happen if all forms of social authority were suddenly withdrawn? In the state of nature there would be no governments, no laws, courts or police. Individuals would be free to do whatever they want. And under these circumstances, the liberal argument goes, the first thing individuals would want to do would be to get out. If people were completely free to do whatever they wanted to do, they would constantly interfere with one another in the pursuit of their wants, resulting in a chaotic situation in which no one would be able to satisfy even their most basic needs; that, or the strong would satisfy themselves at the expense of the weak. Each individual would be at the mercy of others, and everyone would be under constant threat of violent death. This is the bleak vision of life in the state of nature that Hobbes presents, in his major work *Leviathan*. In

Hobbes's memorable words, it would be a 'war of all against all' and life would be 'solitary, poor, nasty, brutish and short' (Hobbes 1968, 186).

The idea that without some kind of organized social life human beings would descend into chaos and savagery is the central theme of *The Lord of the Flies* (Peter Brook, 1963), based on William Golding's book. In this well-known tale, rendered in stark, documentary-style terms by Brook, a group of English schoolchildren find themselves shipwrecked on an island. Liberated from adult authority, they descend into vicious, bloodthirsty violence and warfare. Life becomes a competition for power and status, and those who get in the way are tormented and killed without remorse. Shortly before he is killed, Piggy (Hugh Edwards) still tries to make the case for civilized social order ('which is better, to have rules and agree, or to hunt and kill?'), but the others are past listening by this stage. The idea that society or civilization is a veneer, a thin barrier standing in the way of chaos and violence, resurfaces in post-nuclear-apocalypse films like *Mad Max* (George Miller, 1979). *Mad Max* portrays, if not a state of nature, at least a society perilously close to ruin, perhaps after a nuclear war. Only motorcycle cops like Max (Mel Gibson) stand in the way of complete chaos. They struggle to control the marauding bikie gangs that terrorize the highways. It is important to note however that Hobbes' claim is not that there is some underlying, innate predisposition to evil in human beings. It is not that people are 'bad', but rather that our ordinary desires, when not held in check by society, will lead to chaos. For Hobbes, as for Bentham, human beings are primarily creatures of desire who seek to maximize their pleasure and minimize their pain. In Hobbes' account, human beings are utterly egoistic, completely driven by self-interest, motivated by selfish desires which require satisfaction if they are to be happy. Hence, Hobbes argues, conflicts will inevitably break out between people as they try to satisfy themselves at the expense of others. And in the state of nature there is no limit to what we are free to do in order to satisfy our wants, up to and including killing other people.

While the picture that Hobbes' successor Locke paints of the state of nature is less bleak than Hobbes', the essential idea remains, that in the state of nature individuals will conflict with one another in the pursuit of their wants, and in doing so will get in the way of one another's satisfaction. And so for both these thinkers it is in the long-term interests of individuals, in their rational self-interest, to escape from the state of nature, to join together to form an ordered society. It is indeed better, as Piggy put it, to 'have rules and agree'. And how is this transition to come about? For the early liberal thinkers, to escape from the state of nature is to enter into a kind of contract, a 'social contract'. Once again, this need not be seen as a historical event; we can think of this as a contract that everyone implicitly accepts in participating in society. In this contract, everyone agrees to give up some of their freedom, to submit to a central authority, a ruler or ruling body. The central authority will keep the peace, make laws to regulate relations between individuals and administer justice. The benefit of this is that the central authority will protect individuals from interference by other individuals. So on the liberal view, a degree of state power is justified; the area of individual freedom must be limited by law. In addition to explaining the purpose of the state, the social contract theory also gives us another way of thinking about the nature of morality. Morality here is understood as a set of rules to regulate social relations amongst basically self-interested individuals. So we have another kind of answer to the question: 'why be moral?': we need to obey moral rules in order to avoid the problems of the state of nature.

There are two points that need to be made about the social contract account. First, it is an account in which political authority is based firmly on the consent of those being governed, those who agree to submit to the central authority. Hobbes, it is true, argues for a 'great Leviathan', an absolute monarch with sweeping powers, in order to bring the terrible state of nature to an end. In his emphasis on strong social authority he is rather unliberal. But the authority of Hobbes' sovereign still derives ultimately from the people, who authorize the sovereign to declare and enforce the rules by which they are to live. In his *Second Treatise of Government* Locke similarly holds that political authority must be grounded in the consent of the governed, but he differs from Hobbes in arguing that a representative, democratic form of political authority is what is required. He does not think that Hobbes' absolute monarch would in fact solve the problems of the state of nature, because the people would now be threatened by the whims of this powerful sovereign. Locke emphasizes that the government is appointed by the people, representing their will, and is therefore responsible to them. It is entrusted by the people with certain powers, but these powers are never entirely relinquished, merely delegated. If the government violates the limits of the power given to it, it may be removed immediately from office. Thus it is Locke, rather than Hobbes, who is the primary architect of modern liberal-democratic thinking.

Second, while liberal thinkers generally argue for a degree of state power over individuals, they also insist that there must always exist a certain minimum area of personal freedom that should never be violated. Without it, individuals would have no opportunity at all to pursue their wants. The space that is allowed varies, depending on the thinker one consults. Hobbes thought that individuals needed to be strictly controlled by an absolute monarch if a return to the state of nature were to be avoided; Locke, more optimistically, thought that social harmony and order was consistent with leaving quite a large area of individual life free from state interference (see Berlin 1969, 126). But whatever the case, some area of individual existence must remain independent of social control. In other words a distinction must be drawn between the realm of public life, where the state's authority rightly prevails, and private life, on which the state may not legitimately encroach. Otherwise, the power of the state will become oppressive and threaten to crush the individual. Such is the case for example in the totalitarian world of *Nineteen Eighty-Four*, where no part of individual existence is outside of state control, no private realm whatsoever is recognized. Even in their homes, people are kept under surveillance through the ubiquitous telescreens. It is the other side of the individual's absorption into a faceless whole; the state reaches into the heart of individual existence. This is also why the political rebellion of Winston Smith (John Hurt) can take the form of keeping a diary, or an illicit sexual liaison. In this society, even the most intimate personal or sexual act is a concern of the state, and can thus become an act of political rebellion.

In liberal thinking, the area of non-interference is typically drawn in terms of 'rights', defining those areas of human life that are immune from governmental interference. For Locke, the individual has certain 'natural rights', rights which exist before and regardless of social arrangements: the right to life, the right to property (which is needed to maintain life) and the right to go about one's business unmolested. This doctrine of individual rights found its way into European political life in the course of the eighteenth century, where it played an important role in various struggles against entrenched royal power through which modern liberal democracies were established. It appears in the 1793 French Declaration of the Rights of Man concerning equality, liberty, security and property; and also in the Bill of Rights in the American constitution, which states that the government does not have the power to limit certain kinds of conduct, such as the freedom to speak, or to worship as one pleases (see Popkin and Stroll 1986, 79). And the language of rights is regularly invoked in the defence of individual freedom against what is perceived to be excessive state interference. It is the American constitutional amendment on freedom of speech that is invoked for example in *The People vs Larry Flynt* (1996), Milos Forman's portrayal of *Hustler* magazine publisher Larry Flynt. When he publishes material that some deem to be pornographic, and there are calls for censorship, Flynt (played by Woody Harrelson) successfully defends his right to freedom of speech in a series of court cases. In the trial scenes, the 'freedom to speak one's mind' is explicitly defended as a central aspect of individual liberty.

In this film Flynt is portrayed as a champion of individual liberty, a heroically eccentric individual fighting against a society that threatens to stifle this spirit (Forman's American films, *One Flew Over the Cuckoo's Nest* and *Amadeus* amongst them, have often portrayed such eccentric individualism). But *The People vs Larry Flynt* also calls attention to another feature of rights, as they are traditionally understood in liberal thinking – they are negative in character. That is, classic liberal rights or 'civil liberties' define areas in which one should be able to act without external interference. Within those areas, the liberal view has it, one should be able to do as one pleases, however questionable what one is doing might seem to others. Forman's film brings this point home, because his heroic individual is by no means a likeable or admirable character. Even his lawyer finds Flynt's activities questionable, but he is concerned with defending his client's right to speak or publish what he wants without interference. It is, he says while summing up during the first trial, a matter of defending freedom itself. And we can say in general that for liberalism, freedom is understood primarily in negative terms, as 'freedom from', the freedom of the individual from external interference, particularly from governments and their laws. In its starkest form, which goes back to Hobbes, this is all that freedom is. For Hobbes, freedom is no more than the absence of external physical or legal obstacles to what we want to do, whatever it is that we want to do. In other words, Hobbes is not concerned about the nature of our wants themselves, only that there be nothing preventing their satisfaction.

But at this point we may ask, is it adequate to think of freedom in these purely negative terms? Amongst other things, such a view fails to acknowledge that constraints upon us may not just be obvious external ones – laws, and threats of punishment if we break the law. There may be more subtle, more insidious constraints on what we want to do. As suggested in Chapter 1, an important way in which people can be controlled and manipulated is by filling their heads with false images of the world. Our very wants may be manipulated, by advertising, propaganda, brainwashing and the like, so that we end up wanting what others want us to want. And, it might be argued, this kind of coercion is far more profound, and far more effective, than crude external constraints. Such is the ultimate victory of the regime over Winston Smith in *Nineteen Eighty-Four*. After his illicit sexual liaison he is imprisoned, tortured and brainwashed by the party official O'Brien (Richard Burton). The regime's victory is complete because Smith is not simply made to confess his crime, to betray his lover or to profess loyalty to the party, but because in the end his very perceptions and feelings are being dictated; he has come to *love* Big Brother. So we have the idea here of a profound kind of coercion, one that strikes at the very soul of the victim. Through it, society wins an absolute victory over the individual. It is the same kind of insidious coercion we see in the Cold War classic *The Manchurian Candidate* (John Frankenheimer, 1962). Here, American sergeant Raymond Shaw (Laurence Harvey) returns from the Korean war a hero, but it turns out that he and his entire platoon were captured and brainwashed by the communists to think that he was a hero, and that he has been programmed to perform a political assassination on his return. And it features in Kubrick's *A Clockwork Orange* (1971), in which brainwashing is part of government policy to recondition certain types of criminals, to reprogramme them to be 'good' so that they can be returned to society as 'free' individuals.

In these films, the culprits conveniently enough are totalitarian or authoritarian states seeking total power over the individual. However, such insidious coercion is in fact entirely compatible with liberal societies, in which there is an ostensibly democratic government, minimum legal restrictions and extensive civil rights. Indeed, this is a kind of manipulation that is ideally suited to this context because it makes overt political coercion unnecessary. Evil totalitarians can thus give way to pernicious influences closer to home. Voters may be influenced to 'freely' support a political figure or party. The satirical *Bob Roberts* (Tim Robbins, 1992) suggests that manipulative campaigning can seduce uncritical voters into supporting a reactionary political candidate. On the campaign trail, American senatorial candidate Bob Roberts (Tim Robbins) wins wide popularity for his ultra-conservative views by packaging them in sixties-style protest songs. The equally satirical *Wag the Dog* (Barry Levinson, 1997) goes further in portraying the manipulation of public opinion for political purposes. Here, professional image-makers, called in by a US administration to deal with a political scandal, manufacture a bogus war to distract the media and the public. The film points to the role of the modern mass media in shaping public perceptions, and the possibility of manipulating the news and entertainment media to mobilize support for a government. Both these films are constructed around the premise that overt physical and legal constraints are not the only way in which people can be coerced.

It would seem then that a purely negative view of individual freedom, one that fails to take these more insidious forms of coercion into account, is inadequate. However this is not the only way freedom has been understood in the liberal tradition. Even if liberalism begins with, and has often embraced, a purely negative Hobbesian notion of freedom, there are also more 'positive' understandings of individual freedom in the tradition. Here liberal thinking has been able to draw on Immanuel Kant and John Stuart Mill, both of whom move away from the crude, Hobbesian view of individual freedom. For both Kant and Mill, freedom is not just a matter of there being no external obstacles to what we want to do; it also matters what it is that we want to do. And both thinkers base their position on a notion of human being as something more than Hobbes' creature of desire. Turning to Kant first: Kant as we have seen formulates the idea of individual freedom as a matter not only of independence from external influences but also of self-determination, of acting in accordance with those wants or goals that we have rationally formulated for ourselves. Moreover, Kant argues, this capacity for rational self-determination is uniquely and intrinsically valuable. It is crucial to our personhood, fundamental to a properly human life. We need some degree of autonomy in order, as Isaiah Berlin puts it, to be 'a subject, not an object . . . somebody, not nobody; a doer – deciding not being decided for' (Berlin 1969, 131). With this, Kant provides an important formulation of the liberal ideal, with a strong justification for its defence of the individual from external interference. On Kant's account, self-determination is fundamental to human dignity, and individuals should be respected as the originators of their own life-plan.

Mill similarly provides a defence of the individual and self-determination, in his book *On Liberty*. We have already seen how Mill distinguishes between higher and lower pleasures. For Mill, the quality of one's satisfactions is what matters. The full development of human capacities involves moving away from crude, material desires to the higher wants, and this is Mill's ideal – that we should exert and develop all our capacities. The proper goal of each person is self-realization or self-fulfilment, the harmonious development of all our powers to a complete and consistent whole. Moreover, there is no universal form of self-realization. For Mill, 'each person's form of self-realization is original to him/her, and can therefore only be worked out independently'

(Taylor 1985, 212). In short, for Mill, self-determination is a matter of self-realization, of realizing ourselves in accordance with our own pattern. With this, Mill provides another powerful formulation of the liberal ideal, another justification for the liberal defence of freedom as individual independence. In Mill's case, his defence has a utilitarian basis. The principle of maximizing happiness, Mill argues, demands that every individual be free to develop their powers according to their own will and judgement, because as he puts it, 'the free development of individuality is one of the principal ingredients of human happiness' (Mill 1975, 70). For Mill the only constraint that can legitimately be imposed on an individual's freedom is if their actions bring harm to others.

The common idea being put forward here is that individual freedom is not just negative, a matter of being able to realize our wants without external interference, whatever those wants might be. It is also positive; a matter of being free to live a certain kind of life, a life which I myself rationally dictate, or one in which I can fulfil or realize who I am. And this more full-blooded conception of freedom allows us to take into account the possibility of more insidious, more invasive kinds of coercion and constraint, the kind exerted on Winston Smith in *Nineteen Eighty-Four*, Alex in *A Clockwork Orange*, or the public in general in *Wag the Dog*, in which our wants themselves are manipulated. Given this kind of view, we can distinguish, at least in principle, between those wants, decisions or projects which are authentic, which come from me, which reflect who I am, my 'real interests', and those which are alien, imposed from outside, not truly mine. For Kant, my real wants are those that originate from me as an autonomous, rational individual; for Mill, they are those through which I fulfil or realize myself. So by invoking a more substantive notion of individual freedom we can respond to one line of criticism of the liberal picture. However there are further problems that arise in connection with liberalism, and in considering them we will have the opportunity to examine some of the alternatives to liberal thinking.

Marxism: the social individual

There are two crucial presuppositions in the liberal picture, and both of these can be questioned. The first of these is that liberalism presupposes that human beings are essentially pre-social. That is, on the liberal view, human beings are first of all isolated individuals, with certain natural needs and wants, able to exist fully formed in a pre-social state of nature; and only secondarily members of a society, which is formed by the coming together of these already-formed individuals. Yet we may wonder whether individuals could indeed exist fully formed outside of society, even in principle.

Living outside of society is arguably more likely to leave us in the state of chronic underdevelopment portrayed in François Truffaut's The Wild Child (1970). The film tells the story of a boy (Jean-Pierre Cagnol) who is found running wild in the forest, having been abandoned by his parents many years earlier. The savage, bewildered child comes close to being consigned to an asylum before being rescued by scientist Jean Itard (Truffaut) who tries to domesticate him and teach him to speak. Perhaps this relative lack of socialization and training has left the child 'innocent', untainted by society, reason and science, but the key point to note is that it has also left him severely stunted in development. Truffaut's own position seems to be that any loss of 'primitive freedom' is outweighed by the value of the child's learning to use language and communicate. A similar story is told in The Enigma of Kaspar Hauser (Werner Herzog, 1974), in which the mysterious Kaspar Hauser (Bruno S.) is discovered standing mutely in a town square, after having spent much of his life alone, chained in a cellar. He is not a child but an adult who has somehow escaped all socialization, and it falls to the kindly Professor Daumer (Walter Ladengast) to try to civilize him. This film differs from Truffaut's in that Herzog seems primarily concerned to portray Hauser as the natural man untainted by civilization, whose spirit is increasingly crushed the more civilized he becomes; and through him to show up a repressed and repressive society. Yet it remains the case that lack of socialization has left Hauser's development significantly impaired. When he is first found he has no social skills and indeed can barely speak.

So it is questionable that human beings could ever live outside of social relationships, in a state of nature. In addition, it is not clear that we can give an account of social relationships simply in terms of the will and intentions of individuals, the decisions of individuals to relate to one another in certain ways. We as individuals find ourselves caught up in an already-existing framework of social relations in which we decide and act. We all play roles in various kinds of social relationships with one another, as husbands and wives, teachers and students, employers and employees, and so on, in which we are required to act in certain ways, and our actions are subject to certain conditions, expectations and constraints. In films a sharp distinction is often made between the hero, a strong autonomous individual, a law unto themselves, such as Rick in Casablanca or Kane in High Noon, and the ordinary members of the community, mere 'types' who play predictable roles (see

Schirato and Yell 1996, 143–4). Yet as *Breathless* suggests, even those like Michel and Patricia who think themselves anarchic free spirits can be seen to be playing out roles that existed long before they came on the scene. To accept that we all play social roles of various kinds need not imply that we could never transform these roles or change these relations; if we could not, no social change would be possible. But it does suggest that we need to take into account more than just the decisions of individuals in understanding our social existence. Overall, what these considerations suggest is that, in contrast to the liberal account which sees society as a collection of individuals, it is more realistic to see human beings as social creatures, creatures who exist in a framework of social relations, and who are shaped and conditioned by those relations.

Second, there is a tendency in the liberal picture to think that the primary social reality that individuals have to contend with is society's political organization, in which a central governing body imposes laws on the population. For Hobbes for example, this is really all there is to organized social life. And if we take this view of society, the primary concern for individuals is that governments do not exceed their proper limits, become despotic and impose repressive laws that violate individual rights. By the same token, on this view, as long as there is a relatively liberal form of government, which respects individual rights, people will be free from oppression. However it can be argued that there is a lot more to society than just its political organization, that to understand our social circumstances we need to look beyond the political order. There are important relations in society other than those between a government and its citizens, such as the economic relations that exist between the rich and the poor, between employers and employees. If this is so, then it is not enough to be concerned that governments and their laws do not exceed their proper limits. It is quite possible that there might be a liberal political order whilst other forms of oppression, such as forms of economic oppression and exploitation, remain in force. And a liberal understanding of social and political life will not recognize these further forms of oppression.

The critique of these liberal presuppositions is the starting point for Marxist social and political thinking, the tradition which begins with the work of the nineteenth-century philosopher Karl Marx (1818–1883). Marx departs from liberal thinking in two important ways. First of all, in his account of society he shifts attention from the individual to the social relations in which individuals exist. Individuals are seen as necessarily part of a community.

They cannot develop their capacities except through contact with each other. Moreover, they live and act in the context of a framework of social relations that conditions and constrains their activities. Their very wants and capacities are conditioned by their social and historical circumstances. Second, Marx shifts the focus from the political to the economic. For Marx, to understand our social existence is primarily to understand its economic structure. By our social and historical circumstances, Marx principally means the way that our productive, labouring activity is organized, the division of labour allotting different roles to different people, through which they produce the goods that sustain them. So for Marx the economic dimension of society is fundamental, and it is in terms of the economic that the rest of society, including the system of political power, the state, is to be understood. The role of the state now is to defend and maintain the power of the economically dominant class. For Marx, the individuals who asserted their rights in the course of the eighteenth century were primarily members of the emerging capitalist class; and the role of the modern liberal state, even though it presents itself as representing the interests of all, is to defend and maintain capitalist economic domination and exploitation.

Marx pays particular attention to analysing the modern, capitalist form of economic organization, which began to emerge in the sixteenth and seventeenth centuries. In the capitalist form of production, the bulk of humanity, the labourers, work under the direction of their capitalist employers, in order to produce the commodities which the capitalists can then sell for a profit. Marx argues that the capitalist order involves deeply exploitative relations. Workers live and work under the direction of an owner, in the context of a division of labour governed by the need to maximize profit rather than a concern for workers and their conditions. Considerations of profitability require that the employer get the maximum amount of labour out of the workers for the least possible wage. According to Marx, the conditions under which people work under capitalism prevent them from satisfying their needs in a number of ways. The workers are separated from their fellow workers, with whom they must compete for jobs, as well as from the capitalists who are exploiting them. They are also separated from the products of their labour, which are made for sale on the market rather than for the benefit of, or direct consumption by, the workers themselves. Above all they are denied control over their own productive activity, their labour, which is owned, controlled and used by the capitalist. To use Marx's term, under these conditions the workers are 'alienated', cut off from what is rightfully theirs; they are separated from one another, from the products of their labour, from control over their lives (see Marx 1967, 287–301).

Marx formulates his account against the background of the harshly exploitative working conditions of the nineteenth century. Something of the harshness of unchecked capitalism is captured in a more recent context in *Matewan* (John Sayles, 1987), the story of labour struggles in the coal-mining industry in Matewan, West Virginia during the 1920s. Here, the miners work under conditions of extreme exploitation. Their control over their situation is minimal. The Stone Mountain Coal company owns not only their labour but also their land and homes. The company's drive to maximize its profits means that the workers are paid the minimum amount possible, and live in abject poverty; and also means that considerations of profit take precedence over decent working conditions and the welfare of the workers. The mine is unsafe, and many have died in mine explosions and cave-ins; and the company will not spray the walls to get rid of inflammable coal dust, because it costs too much. The pressure to continually increase profits drives the company to pay less and less for the coal the miners dig up, which eventually drives them to the strike action which is the focus of the film. The workers are set against each other because the Italian immigrant workers continue to work, and the company brings in black miners as well. As the union organizer (Chris Cooper) tells the workers, 'they [the company owners] have got you fighting each other – white against coloured, native against foreign'. Indeed, the strike does not have any real effect until the three factions come together and the workers organize themselves into a collective force. In the end, however, the challenge to the company's authority is put down through force, and throughout *Matewan*, the threat of outright violence remains as a means of maintaining control.

Over and above overt forms of economic exploitation and oppression, Marx also argues that social control is effected by shaping people's understanding of their situation and hence their very wants and desires, so that they feel content with their situation. We have already come across this more profound form of social control, as a possible form of manipulation that is not always recognized within the liberal tradition. It plays a much more central role in Marxist thinking, where it appears under the labels of 'ideology' or 'false consciousness'. Education, the mass media, even film and popular culture have been seen as promoters of a distorted, ideological view of the world. Given the possibility of this kind of manipulation, it is not relevant to the claim that workers are alienated that they themselves say they are content with their situation, their place in the scheme of things. For it can be argued that the same system that denies their needs and interests also produces in them a false understanding of what their needs and interests are. For example, to the extent that individuals, through education, the mass media and so on, are brought to believe that a certain economic order is the best possible system, or the only possible way of organizing things, this influences what they might even consider wanting. And by bringing workers to accept their situation, this kind of manipulation serves to maintain their subordination and perpetuate the existing state of affairs. In *Matewan*, false consciousness takes the form of the racism that divides the workers and helps maintain the *status quo*, until they see through this and realize their common interests as workers.

Thus for Marxism, the capitalist economic order not only prevents workers from satisfying their wants and interests but also distorts and falsifies their wants themselves. Now this claim presupposes some notion of what our needs truly are, some notion of our 'real interests', and Marx's position here is derived from his underlying notion of human nature, his notion of what we most essentially are. Although he stresses the way in which our wants and capacities are conditioned by our social and historical situation, he also argues that there are aspects of human existence that remain invariant or unchanging. Above all, he sees human beings as creatures who have a fundamental need to express and develop themselves through labour or productive activity; as essentially communal creatures who seek to produce collectively; and as rational creatures who ideally should be able to organize their collective productive activity for themselves. So our real interests lie in collectively controlling our labouring activity. This picture is in fact a descendant of Kant's vision of freedom. We have already seen how Kant's ideal of freedom as rational self-determination, living in accordance with rules that one has formulated for oneself, is a powerful formulation of the liberal ideal of individual freedom. But this conception of human beings as able to generate the forms they live by out of their own activity has also gone beyond liberalism to inspire Marx's vision of collective liberation, the ideal of collectively organizing our social existence for ourselves.

For Marx then, it is only when we can determine our existence in this way that we are living a fully human life; and it is above all this fully human life that Marx thinks is being denied under capitalism. Here is a situation in which workers are unable to control their productive activity, which is owned and controlled by the capitalist overseer. Instead of exercising collective control over their activities, instead of working for their collective benefit, workers are separated from one another and required to produce for the profit of others. Humanity's nature or essence is not realized under these social and economic arrangements. Rather, what exists is an alienated and deformed form of human being. By the same token, the ideal of a fully human life becomes the basis and goal of progressive social change, the revolutionary overcoming of these oppressive conditions. This requires that the workers rise up against their political and economic masters, wrest control of the work process from their capitalist overseers, and bring it under collective control. In this way human beings will be in control of their social existence; they will have realized their essential capacity for autonomous, collective labour.

The relatively few Hollywood films dealing with labour relations, like *Matewan*, along with *Salt of the Earth* (Herbert Bibermann, 1953) and *Norma Rae* (Martin Ritt, 1979), have tended to focus on worker resistance in the form of unionism and strike action. These films stand out not only because of their subject matter but also because they celebrate collective action. This is in sharp contrast to the more familiar Hollywood scenario in which social change comes, if at all, from a few courageous individuals acting more or less in isolation to set society straight (see Schirato and Yell 1996, 144). That is a view more in keeping with the liberal perspective, with its celebration of the individual. This individualistic perspective even appears in the midst of films that feature unions. In *On the Waterfront* (Elia Kazan, 1954), Terry Molloy (Marlon Brando) has to decide whether to tell a government investigator (Leif Erickson) the truth about corruption in the waterfront union; something he eventually does do. This is very much a film about what one courageous individual, willing to take a stand, can do. As Terry Christensen notes, the film praises individual action at the expense of collective struggle: 'It never occurs to Terry, for example, to rally the troops and reform the union from within; collective action simply is not an option' (Christensen 1987, 93–4). In films like *Matewan* however, there are no individual heroes. It is the collective activity of the union that is celebrated, the union that is the hero, even if in the end the strike is crushed.

However, the kind of collective activity called for by Marxism goes beyond union struggles. For Marxism, unions may serve to limit the exploitation of workers, but they ultimately remain within the capitalist system, and can themselves become corrupted by it. This possibility emerges in *Blue Collar* (Paul Schrader, 1978), which features a corrupt Detroit auto worker union whose complicity in maintaining the *status quo* is gradually revealed. In this film it is the union, not the company, that sets the workers against one another along racial lines. Some have seen *Blue Collar* simply as an anti-union film, but as Schrader himself points out, the film comes to a 'very specific Marxist conclusion' about the limitations of unionism (see Schrader 1985, 206–7). On the Marxist account it is necessary to go beyond unionism, to raise political demands and eventually to engage in revolutionary struggle. The Marxist vision of full-scale revolutionary transformation receives its most emphatic cinematic expression in *October* (Sergei Eisenstein, 1927), a propagandistic celebration of the 1917 October Revolution in Russia. The film ends with the old Czarist order finally overturned, and filled with hope for the socialist future that lies ahead. What it shares with the previously-mentioned workers' films is the sense that only collective effort on the part of the people can bring about progressive social change and liberation. Indeed, individual actions and motives are almost entirely neglected in Eisenstein's depiction, in favour of the collective. Through his editing it is the people *en masse* who come to the fore, pouring into the squares, surging through the streets, streaming into the Czar's winter palace. We are given the impression of the people as an irresistible tide of humanity, of the revolution as a great historical transformation.

History, of course, was not to bear out the hopes of the October Revolution. Let us turn at this point to some of the possible problems with the Marxist account. One set of problems arises from the Marxist conception of real interests, the interests that are said to be denied under capitalism. It is a conception of real interests that arises in the end from a philosophical view of human nature, of what counts as a properly human life. To that extent, what these interests are can be decided on independently of whatever people themselves – workers or labourers in this case – may claim to want. And it is certainly an advantage not to have to rely on the expressed preferences of workers themselves. After all, they may be subject to ideological manipulation, their wants and preferences falsified by the very system that denies their real interests. However one difficulty with philosophical notions of human nature is that it is very difficult to verify them. We have already come across many different views of human nature in the course of this book. Even within the Marxist tradition itself there have been different views about what our real interests are. How then do we decide between different philosophical conceptions of what human nature is? How do we know that a theorist's vision of what counts as a real interest or a properly human life is not in fact an arbitrary ideal or prejudice on the part of the theorist? Marx himself, it is true, could point to evidence for his view in the form of worker suffering and dissatisfaction under nineteenth-century work conditions, which was expressed in various forms of resistance, strikes, machine-breaking and the like. However his conception of human nature goes beyond what could be justified on this basis alone.

A further problem with philosophical conceptions of our real interests or essential nature is that they may themselves play a role in forms of political oppression. Amongst others, the philosopher Isaiah Berlin has argued that such notions need to be rejected because they can all too easily justify oppression of the individual. If the individual's real interests or essential nature is identified with something wider than the individual, with a communal entity like a race, a church, a state, then this entity is entitled to impose its will on individuals. It is only by conforming to the dictates of the larger entity that individuals can follow their real interests and thus be free. Should they resist, should their actual wishes and interests be quite different to those being imposed on them, it can be argued that they are simply ignorant and deluded about what their real interests are. So on this view, Berlin (1969, 132–4) argues, it becomes possible to ignore the actual wishes of individuals, to bully, oppress, torture them, even to forcibly 're-educate' them, all in the name of their supposed real interests and higher freedom. Such is the fate of Winston Smith at the end of *Nineteen Eighty-Four*. Having been subjected to torture and brainwashing, he now regards his former rebellion as the result of mental derangement; he has been 'cured', and now asks only that he be shot while his 'mind is still clean'. That such total subordination to the state could ever be identified with liberation is at the heart of Berlin's concerns. Writing in the Cold War context of the fifties, he associates this kind of 'freedom' with what he sees as the totalitarian Marxist regimes of the Eastern Bloc. But he also identifies a problem with any position which claims that people's real interests and preferences are different to those they currently experience, for it then becomes legitimate to coerce them in the name of their supposed freedom.

A second set of problems has to do with the Marxist emphasis on the economic dimension of society. As we have seen, Marxism goes beyond the liberal account, which tends to see society only in political terms, because it also acknowledges the economic relationships between rich and poor, employer and employee. Indeed what defines Marxism as a theory of society is that it is committed to making economic processes the basis for social explanation. All other aspects of society have to be understood either directly or indirectly in terms of the economic. However we may wonder if this permits an adequate explanation of the non-economic aspects of society. It is not clear, for example, that the state or other social institutions can be fully understood as no more than servants of the dominant economic class. For example, in its crudest, most reductive interpretation, religion is just another social institution that supports the economically powerful. In *Aguirre, Wrath of God* (Werner Herzog, 1973) which follows Spanish conquistadors down the Amazon basin in search of the gold of El Dorado, the monk Gaspar de Carvajal (Del Negro) says bluntly that 'the Church was always on the side of the strong'. But more complex accounts are possible. In *The Mission* (Roland Joffé, 1986), the Vatican representative certainly sides with the Portuguese colonialists who seek to make inroads into the South American wilderness and enslave the Indians; but the Jesuit missionaries, led by Jeremy Irons, try to protect the Indians from the Portuguese. Indeed, the Portuguese ambassador complains bitterly that 'the work of the missions is the work of the devil – they teach contempt for property and lawful profit, and they are disobedient to the king's authority'. Similarly in *Matewan*, the older preacher (played by the director himself) is loyal to the company and portrays union action as inspired by the devil ('The prince of darkness is in the land . . . his name is bolshevist, socialist, union man, communist'), but the boy preacher Danny (Will Oldham) is able to provide biblical justification for the strikers.

Various attempts have been made within the Marxist tradition to avoid an overly reductive or 'economistic' view of society, but such attempts to give a degree of autonomy to non-economic realms always come into conflict with the requirement of any Marxist theory, that the economic realm is the key to understanding the social system as a whole. The emphasis on the economic means there is a danger that non-economic social relations and forms of oppression will not be properly addressed. Take for example, gender relations, relations between men and women. Feminist approaches generally share with Marxism the view that we are first of all social creatures, existing in the midst of social relations that condition and shape what we are able to do. Forms of gender oppression are not so much a matter of particular men and women deciding to treat one another in certain ways, but rather of systematic relations of oppression in which men and women play characteristic social roles of domination and subordination. This is the kind of point made for example in Marleen Gorris' *A Question of Silence* (1982), the story of the trial of three women for the murder of an inoffensive male shop clerk. Though unacquainted, they spontaneously co-operate in killing him after he catches one of them shoplifting. Looked at simply in terms of the actions of individuals, this is a cruel, unjustified act, perhaps the result of a momentary fit of group madness. But as the trial unfolds it becomes clear that the murder was in fact motivated by intolerable male oppression of various kinds. Each woman suffers some form of it, from domestic slavery to discrimination and abuse in the workplace. The murder is thus an act of political protest, not against the shop clerk but against systematic male violence, and in the end this is what is on trial in the film.

But while feminism largely shares Marxism's move away from an individualistic perspective, there are also tensions between Marxism and feminism. It is not clear that forms of gender-based oppression can easily be accounted for in Marxist terms, as a function of workplace relations or relations between rich and poor. We find such oppression not only within the workplace, where women have often been confined to lowly paid jobs, but also in areas far removed from the workplace, in family, domestic and sexual relations; we find it going on at all economic levels of society, regardless of social position; and we find it throughout history, regardless of the way the economy is organized. Within Marxism itself, it has to be said, the issue of gender oppression has been largely neglected. For Marx, the workers are the victims of capitalist domination, but he fails to note that the workers themselves practised their own kinds of oppression over their wives and children in the family home. Issues of women's and children's oppression continued to be sidelined in subsequent Marxist political thinking, where feminism was sometimes even condemned as a capitalist ploy to split the workers' movement. In the end it is quite telling that, while the workers in *Matewan* struggle heroically to improve their working conditions, their wives remain obedient, supportive domestic slaves throughout.

Three faces of power

In both liberal and Marxist political thinking, the notion of power plays a central role. Liberal thinking concerns itself with political power, its justification and limits. Marxism focuses on forms of economic domination and exploitation in the workplace. In general, we cannot go very far into any sort of social or political inquiry, indeed any sort of reflection on our social and political circumstances, without raising the issue of power. In this final section we will look in more detail at how power is being understood in these accounts, the assumptions involved in various traditional notions of power. This will allow us to consider some more recent developments in social and political thinking, in which the notion of power has undergone significant reformulation.

So far we have come across two ways of thinking about power. First of all, power is understood as that which prevents us from doing what we want to do, either by imposing limitations on what we are able to do, or by coercing us into doing things other than what we want to do. In the liberal picture, power is primarily a matter of these overt constraints, constraints imposed on us by the government through its laws, backed up by the threat of force and imprisonment if we do not comply. Second, we have a more radical conception of power, in which people are prevented from doing what they want to do because their very wants are manipulated, because their perceptions of their situation are controlled so as to influence what they might even consider wanting. So we may be able to do what we want to do, to pursue our wants, but it is our wants themselves that have been manipulated. They are the products of a system that works against our real interests. Here, power seems much more invasive, much more insidious and absolute. It is the view of power that inner party member O'Brien presents in *Nineteen Eighty-Four*, while he is torturing Winston Smith. We do not destroy the heretic, he says; we make him one of ourselves before we kill him. Power is a matter of 'tearing human minds apart and putting them together again in shapes of your own choosing'. And in the end, as we have seen, Smith's wants, desires and feelings have come to be determined by the state. The triumph of the state is absolute. A variety of Marxist thinkers in particular have taken up this notion of power, in terms of notions like false consciousness or ideological manipulation through which individuals are reconciled to their place in the capitalist system.

The difference between these two conceptions of power however is largely a matter of degree. In both cases, power is understood in negative terms. That is, it is what prevents you from doing what you want, from pursuing your real interests. It stands in the way of your self-determination, your self-realization, the proper expression of your nature, a properly human form of existence. This is achieved either through overt constraint or, in the more radical account, through falsification, i.e., power prevents you from pursuing your real interests or nature by producing a mistaken understanding of what your needs are, a false view of your self or nature. So on this negative view, to discover and assert our true self or nature is to stand in opposition to power. However in recent years this whole way of thinking about power has been called into question, and alternative accounts of the way power operates in society have emerged. In particular, the French philosopher Michel Foucault (1926–1984) has argued that power needs to be seen primarily in positive terms. It does not work to curb or crush individuals, but rather to develop their capacities in certain directions and thus to turn them into certain kinds of individuals; it is not bound up with falsification but with knowledge; and notions of our true self or real nature, far from being opposed to power, are in fact key elements in its operation.

Before exploring Foucault's conception of power further, we need to put his views in context. Like Marxism, Foucault wants to break away from the liberal focus on the political, on the state. He similarly wants to argue that in order to fully understand the society that confronts us, we need to look beyond the government and the legal order it imposes on the population. However, unlike Marxism, Foucault does not focus on the economic realm, and argue that all other social and political phenomena can be explained in terms of it. For Foucault, productive activity is certainly an important dimension of social existence, but he does not automatically assume it to be fundamental to other areas of society, such as education, medicine, child-rearing, the military, legal processes or the state. The relationships between these various spheres, Foucault argues, should not be pre-judged; they need to be worked out in each case. What Foucault does want to claim, in his book *Discipline and Punish*, is that from around the seventeenth century onwards, new forms of power, new techniques of social control, have emerged and have been implemented in a whole range of social institutions and practices. They have been taken up in the productive process, but also in other areas, in schools, hospitals, the family, armies, prisons and the state. Let us look in more detail at these distinctively modern techniques of control and regulation that Foucault describes.

Foucault calls these new techniques of social regulation 'disciplinary' techniques. They are techniques for controlling individuals and populations, ways of organizing, supervising and training them in a detailed, continuous way. These techniques include (1) the division of work spaces, classrooms and other institutional spaces so that each individual has their proper place, and the breaking up of activities into distinct stages so that individuals have specific roles to play in the overall process; (2) the division of time by timetables specifying what people should be doing at any particular time; (3) the use of graduated training programmes in which individuals have to pass through precise stages; and (4) techniques for organizing trained individuals so they operate together like a harmonious machine. The first feature to note here is that disciplinary power does not operate primarily to curb or crush individuals, but rather works to transform them, to train and improve them, making them more capable, productive and efficient than they were before, while simultaneously making possible strict control over these trained, empowered individuals. For example these techniques were implemented in the production process, in order to turn people into trained, useful and reliable workers. Indeed, Foucault argues, they made possible the very capitalist form of ownership and exploitation of labouring activity that Marx focused on. On Foucault's account, they also figured in the reorganization of European armies, schools and hospitals, the state's policing of its population, and its dispensation of justice. In *Discipline and Punish*, Foucault pays particular attention to the implementation of disciplinary techniques in the modern prison.

Crucial to the implementation of these disciplinary techniques is the establishment of a system of surveillance, so that individuals can be continually monitored, trained and maintained in their subjection. Foucault argues that there is a particular architectural figure, the 'panopticon', that embodies many of the techniques of disciplinary control, especially the use of surveillance. It was first envisaged by the utilitarian philosopher Bentham, as a humane way of running prisons, but it is also a highly refined and effective way of doing so. In the proposed arrangement those to be controlled are organized into cells arranged around a central observation tower. They are visible to those in the tower, but they cannot see into the tower. As a result they do not know if they are being observed at any particular time. They have to assume that they are being watched all the time and behave accordingly. They thus become their own jailers, keeping watch over themselves, conspiring in their own subjection. This arrangement is not only a means for controlling a population of prisoners but also lends itself to experimentation on individuals, and the assessment of different forms of training and treatment. Employed not only in prisons but also in workshops, hospitals, schools and so on, it turned these institutions into laboratories for the study of human beings. And the importance of surveillance in maintaining disciplinary control brings us to the second distinctive feature of this kind of power, that it involves not falsification but knowledge. The exercise of this kind of disciplinary control requires that individuals be made visible, so that their behaviour can be known about and regulated; and the ongoing production of knowledge about individuals, which extends to keeping records, files, registers and, more recently, computerized records, allows for ever more sophisticated disciplinary control.

A number of cinematic portrayals of futuristic prisons have shown a keen appreciation of the role of surveillance in social regulation. Here we can also see how new forms of technology might open up new possibilities for surveillance. *Ghosts . . . of the Civil Dead* (John Hillcoat, 1988) portrays a panoptic prison, promoted as the latest in 'humane containment'. As a disciplinary institution, its very architecture is involved in its system of authority. The space within the prison is carefully organized into cells, and the whole prison into three areas, General Population, High Risk Inmates and Solitary Confinement (the last a punishment area within the prison). Time is organized according to an exact schedule, with the activities of the moment announced by a computerized voice. Most importantly, the prison population is subject to continual surveillance. Bentham's central observation tower has been replaced here by hi-tech observation rooms and constant camera surveillance to ensure that inmates observe the prison rules. Hi-tech surveillance is taken to a new level of sophistication in *Face-Off* (John Woo, 1997). Here, Sean Archer/Castor Troy (Nicholas Cage) becomes an inmate in a prison where, in addition to camera surveillance, the prisoners wear electronic shoes that indicate their identity and their position to the authorities at all times. If there is trouble, the shoes can be magnetized and fixed to the floor. In *Fortress* (Stuart Gordon, 1992), the extent of surveillance seems complete. Round-the-clock camera surveillance extends to monitoring the dreams of the prisoners; and for good measure the prisoners have a device implanted within them which causes pain or death for any violation of the prison rules. As the governor informs the hero (Christopher Lambert), in this prison there really is 'nowhere to hide'.

These are dramatic examples of surveillance, relating to highly disciplined penal institutions; and for Foucault, modern prisons are certainly institutions where disciplinary mechanisms have been intensively implemented. But he also argues that disciplinary mechanisms of one sort or another have become a pervasive feature of everyday life. They are exercised in workplaces, schools, hospitals, welfare offices, families and courtrooms. Through them, employers, doctors, social workers, judges, police and administrators are able to monitor and police the behaviour of individuals and groups. These figures are also instrumental in producing and maintaining detailed records, files and statistics concerning individuals and populations, the detailed knowledge of the population that is part and parcel of modern forms of social regulation and planning. It should be stressed however that we are not being confronted here with the kind of situation portrayed in *Nineteen Eighty-Four*, where the population is under constant surveillance by the state through television screens that double as cameras. There, surveillance is portrayed as the most monstrous weapon of totalitarianism, something that is imposed on society by an all-embracing totalitarian state; and this has very much established the tradition of thinking about governmental surveillance. Even the imaginative *Brazil* (Terry Gilliam, 1985), in which citizens are under constant surveillance by the government's Ministry of Information, follows the tradition of portraying surveillance as an instrument of totalitarianism.

Foucault's point is rather that techniques of surveillance and order are practised by the whole of society, from many different points. A film like *M* (Fritz Lang, 1931) better captures this idea of disciplinary mechanisms as thoroughly absorbed into the practices of everyday life. As Peter Lorre's child murderer Hans Beckert stalks the streets of Berlin striking terror into the population, and the police and public search for him, a dense web of surveillance and disciplinary controls that is already in place in society is thrown into relief. We see that, as Anton Kaes puts it

> [c]riminals and vagrants have identity papers (as the film shows, forgeries are easily detected), they are registered and monitored, their fingerprints are recorded and analysed with the latest technology. Asylums and hospitals keep records of their patients and their medical histories. Telephone lines link the population to the authorities and office buildings maintain alarm systems directly connected to police headquarters. Plain-clothes detectives search in ever-widening circles for every possible irregularity; neighbours watch each other; parents train their children to be wary; and every person in the street is seen as a potential suspect.
>
> (Kaes 1999, 46)

And it is not only the police and the general public who are involved in this network of surveillance; the criminal underworld also joins the hunt for the murderer, and we see that they share techniques of surveillance and control with the police and law-abiding citizens. They establish a network of informers, enlisting the city's beggars to watch the streets and report all suspicious behaviour.

On Foucault's account, these widespread forms of surveillance and discipline are entirely compatible with politically liberal states. Indeed, he argues, it was the emergence and spread of these new, discreet, efficient forms of disciplinary control that made possible the overturning of the old, relatively oppressive monarchical order in Europe, and the establishment of modern liberal governments. The modern state can acknowledge and respect individual rights and liberties because it does not need to be overtly oppressive to maintain social order. It can rely on these disciplinary mechanisms to do the job. This is not to deny that modern governments have access to forms of surveillance far more sophisticated and invasive than anything in *Nineteen Eighty-Four*. Some of these are portrayed in *Enemy of the State* (Tony Scott, 1998), in which a lawyer (Will Smith) who accidentally acquires a piece of politically embarrassing evidence becomes the object of total surveillance by a government intelligence agency. It is a process involving not just spying, hidden cameras and phone taps, but also high resolution satellite imaging and computerized monitoring of credit card transactions. But this film continues to portray surveillance as an aberration in the modern liberal state, a matter of out-of-control government agencies using underhand means to violate individual privacy. Foucault's claim is that the modern liberal state is in fact founded on multiple forms of disciplinary surveillance and regulation which permeate everyday life. They are exercised by a wide range of institutions including health, welfare, education and the police, which the state has come to co-ordinate and control. It is primarily through these agencies that the state is able to acquire its detailed knowledge of the population, and to implement its large-scale social policies.

It also needs to be emphasized that for Foucault the role of surveillance and discipline is not simply to control individuals but to transform them, to develop their skills and capacities in specific ways, to produce useful kinds of individuals. To this end, disciplinary regulation involves the formulation of norms of human behaviour, standards that individuals are required to measure up to. Even the prison does not aim simply to confine and control its inmates, but to rehabilitate them, to transform them into law-abiding, upright citizens. This shaping of individuals through the system of penal discipline is evident for example in *Ghosts . . . of the Civil Dead*. Prisoner Henry Wenzil (David Field) becomes, if not a law-abiding citizen, at least an effective enforcer of the prison's own disciplinary order. After killing a prisoner, he reflects that 'they knew what I'd do. I was trained to do what I did. I did the job for them.' This also gives us another way of thinking about the psychological conditioning Alex undergoes in Kubrick's *A Clockwork Orange*, as a final, drastic attempt to achieve what the prison has failed to bring about, the transformation of a vicious young hoodlum into a 'decent' individual. Transformation in another highly disciplined institutional context, the army, features in Kubrick's Vietnam movie, *Full Metal Jacket* (1987). The first half of the film follows the basic training of a group of marines bound for Vietnam. As is made clear from the start, the intensive training, drills and exercises of basic training are designed not simply to make the recruits compliant but to turn them into strong, efficient killers. As the central character Private 'Joker' (Mathew Modine) observes: 'The Marine Corps does not want robots; the Marine Corps wants killers; the Marine Corps wants to build indestructible men, men without fear.'

In the wider social context, different forms of training serve to turn individuals into good students, proficient soldiers or reliable workers; doctors promote healthy bodies and stable minds; social welfare agencies encourage good mothers and proper fathers; and so on. These are presented as 'normal' ways of being. And just as prisoners watched in the panopticon come to watch over themselves, we have come to monitor, judge and modify our own behaviour in terms of these standards of normality. Here we are at the heart of Foucault's account of modern, disciplinary society. Social control is not maintained by an oppressive political regime, but by a 'regime of normality', something far more pervasive and effective. Individuals themselves participate in it, judging themselves and others in terms of standards of normality which are reproduced and policed by teachers, doctors, social workers and other institutional figures. To stray from these standards is to enter the vast area of behaviour defined as abnormal or deviant, behaviour that is in need of disciplinary attention, surveillance, treatment and rehabilitation. Something of the extent of control that can be exercised through this regime comes across in Ladybird, Ladybird (Ken Loach, 1994), in which an impoverished single mother (Crissy Rock) comes to be categorized by the welfare authorities as a problem parent who has difficulty taking care of her children. As a result the children are taken away from her and placed in foster homes. When she has another child, she becomes the object of renewed attention from social workers, who even enlist neighbours to watch and report on her. Amongst other things they insist that she can only keep the child if she attends a centre where she can be trained to 'cope', to be a good mother; and despite her attempts to convince them of her suitability as a parent, there is the constant threat of having another child taken away.

Foucault is not suggesting that we need to reject all forms of social regulation or training. His point is that a crucial part of modern social regulation is that we are only permitted to be certain kinds of individuals; and that to dismiss all alternative forms of behaviour or ways of being, as forms of deviance or abnormality requiring treatment and rehabilitation, is oppressive.

He questions in particular the manner in which standards of normality are often presented to us as being grounded in some timeless, underlying human nature, reflecting 'who we really are'. Like Isaiah Berlin, he sees claims that certain kinds of behaviour are in keeping with our real or essential nature as playing a role in political control. Such claims provide a justification for these standards of normality, and for viewing those who depart from them as deviants, in need of retraining or rehabilitation. For Foucault, talk of a timeless human nature also serves to conceal the extent to which these standards of normal behaviour are in fact socially constructed, formulated as part of the process of disciplinary regulation. And this brings us to the third distinctive feature of Foucault's notion of power. Foucault rejects the idea that there is a determinate human nature which we need to realize, and which social power prevents us from realizing. What disciplinary power does is to transform human beings into certain kinds of individuals, socially useful kinds of individuals; and notions of our true self or real nature, far from being opposed to power, are in fact key elements in its operation.

We are a long way here from the liberal and Marxist pictures. Instead of the individual being the starting point for understanding society, Foucault's position is that it is social processes, forms of disciplinary control and regulation, that turn human beings into certain kinds of individual. And instead of being able to appeal to notions of human nature in order to oppose power, Foucault argues that to claim that certain ways of behaving are natural or normal is to run the risk of playing into the hands of disciplinary forms of power in which conceptions of 'who we really are' play a crucial role. This brings us to some of the possible problems with Foucault's position. First of all, does this mean that there is no escape from social regulation, that there is nothing outside the sway of social power, that society has won an absolute victory over the individual? In fact, this is not what Foucault argues. As Barry Smart (1985, 91) points out, although Foucault thinks we live in a disciplinary society, this is not the same thing as saying that it is a *disciplined* society. For Foucault attempts to impose discipline are always met with resistance: prison revolts against penal discipline, the resistance of workers against workplace discipline through strikes and machine-breaking, and so on. If human beings are essentially anything, they are essentially recalcitrant, stubborn, difficult to control. Foucault's claim that conceptions of normal or natural ways of being or acting can themselves be part of processes of regulation and control means that resistance to forms of social control will include questioning the claim that only certain ways of being and acting are legitimate, and experimenting with different kinds of selfhood, forms of individuality other than those prescribed to us.

It might still of course be argued that this is an inadequate picture. If Foucault refuses to embrace some positive conception of human nature, then there is no ideal of a fully realized humanity, a fully human life, to fight for. And if so, what is the point of resistance? Doesn't Foucault's account simply deprive resistance of any point or justification? In the end, Foucault's answer seems to be that resistance does not need justification; people will always refuse to be content with socially imposed limitations. Whether in the form of the existentialist individual's rebellion, individual self-assertion against the state, the workers' struggle against conditions imposed by capitalist employers or revolts against prison conditions, human beings will always express their impatience with social constraints in one way or another. From this point of view, intellectual justifications for struggle are rationalizations of a fundamental yearning for freedom. We are perhaps left with the view expressed by the director Lindsay Anderson about his film If . . . (1968). Here Mick (Malcolm MacDowell) and his schoolmates revolt against the strict discipline of their boarding school, with a surrealistic finale in which the students open fire on the schoolteachers. For Anderson, the heroes of If . . . are

> not anti-heroes, or drop-outs, or Marxist-Leninists or Maoists or readers of Marcuse. Their revolt is inevitable, not because of what they think but because of what they are. Mick plays a little at being an intellectual ('Violence and revolution are the only pure acts', etc), but when he acts it is instinctively, because of his outraged dignity, his frustrated passion, his vital energy, his sense of fair play if you like. If his story can be said to be 'about' anything, it is about freedom.
>
> (Anderson 1969, 8)

In this chapter we have looked at a number of ways of thinking about our social and political existence. We began with one of the most distinctive features of our modernity, the rise of individualist forms of social and political thinking, the view that individuals are prior to society and provide the basis for legitimate political authority; and we also looked at social and political accounts which questioned this priority given to the individual, and sought to locate the individual in relation to larger social processes; first of all Marxism, and then the more radical account presented by Foucault. In the next chapter we will continue discussing modern social and political thinking. This time our starting point will be another distinctive feature of our modernity: not the rise of the individual, but rather the modern love affair with science and technology.

5

MODERN TIMES – SOCIETY, SCIENCE AND TECHNOLOGY

Charlie Chaplin in *Modern Times*.
Credit: Chaplin/United Artists (Courtesy Kobal)

In Charlie Chaplin's *Modern Times* (1936) there is a well-known sequence in which Chaplin's tramp is working on an assembly line, tightening nuts. All day long the speed of the conveyer belt has been increasing, until finally, unable to keep up, Charlie has a nervous breakdown. He climbs onto the conveyer belt and is carried along with it into the workings of a gigantic machine. Suddenly the screen is full of enormous turning cogs, with the tramp caught up in the midst of them. Move forward sixty years and we have *Alien Resurrection* (Jean-Pierre Jeunet, 1997). Ripley (Sigourney Weaver), cloned back to life after her demise in the previous *Alien* film, comes across a room filled with earlier, failed attempts to clone her. Floating in tanks are deformed, nightmare versions of herself; and strapped on a table, another monstrous Ripley, alive and begging to be killed. Both these films reflect concerns about the scientific and technological advances of the modern period, and the effects that they are capable of having on human beings. From the unprecedented development in the human capacity to control nature, to the current advances in biotechnology and the manipulation of life itself, science and technology have altered our existence in fundamental ways. But they also raise important questions: are all these changes for the better? Are there dangers in these new forms of technological control? If they have costs, do these costs outweigh their benefits? In this chapter we will look at some of the critical perspectives on science and technology that have emerged in recent years. But first of all it needs to be noted that for a long time the dominant attitude towards science and technology has been that they are central to human progress, unambiguous means for the betterment of the human condition. Indeed, along with its individualism, faith in the progressive character of science and technology is another characteristic feature of our modernity. So let us begin by considering this modern faith.

Scientific utopias

The modern Western world's love affair with science and technology, like its liberal individualism, has its origins in the sixteenth and seventeenth centuries. Here we see the rise of an outlook that we can recognize as scientific in the modern sense. It is an outlook that develops through such diverse thinkers as Francis Bacon (1561–1626), René Descartes and John Locke, and which is confirmed through the scientific successes of Galileo Galilei (1564–1642) and Isaac Newton (1642–1727). It involves a rejection of the idea that we can understand the world through appeal to the authority of tradition, biblical or religious authority. Instead, knowledge is to be acquired through experience and observation, the view of knowledge that, as we saw in Chapter 2, was given philosophical formulation in John Locke's empiricism. With the new scientific perspective, the older religious understanding of the world came into question. That involved a view of nature in general as a structured and meaningful cosmos, having been created by God and imbued with God-given order and purpose. In that world, human beings, along with all other creatures, had their proper place and role in God's great scheme. The new scientific perspective is very different. Now, nature is stripped of all supernatural significance. It is to be viewed as an impersonal mechanism, a great machine that operates in a predictable way. Regularities in nature can be observed, measured and formulated in mathematical terms. This new, impersonal, mechanistic way of understanding nature is also bound up with an increasing capacity to manipulate it, to exercise technological control over it. For the traditional world-view, the goal of knowledge of nature was to decipher the meanings, the God-given purposes, woven into the world in order to better understand one's role in God's great design. Now, knowledge of nature is seen primarily as something that makes our lives more comfortable and secure by improving our ability to predict and control nature.

These developments gave impetus in turn to a widespread philosophical and intellectual movement in eighteenth-century Europe known as the Enlightenment, in which many of the key features of the modern outlook were formulated. A number of the thinkers we have looked at, including Hume, Bentham and Kant, are Enlightenment figures. Hobbes can be seen as an important seventeenth-century precursor of the Enlightenment outlook. This outlook is characterized in general by admiration for the methods and achievements of the new natural sciences. Indeed in many ways truth and knowledge came to be seen as epitomized by science, and reasonable beliefs were those that could claim to be scientific in character. This was also a practical, useful knowledge. For the Enlightenment thinkers, science and technology promised to make it possible to force nature to serve human needs, to vanquish disease and human ills, to improve human life and increase happiness. Along with this admiration for science, there was an increasing assault on the religious world-view, which was seen as at best needing to be reformulated so as to be consistent with the new scientific outlook, and at worst, as mere error and superstition, to be dispensed with. This critique also began to have implications for social reform. Scepticism about religious beliefs extended into a wide-ranging criticism of social practices and institutions that drew support from these beliefs. Traditional beliefs and the institutions they helped justify were now to be put to the test in the light of reason and science, and if they failed, were denounced as fraudulent, the result of error and superstition. In the course of the eighteenth century, this rational critique of society was pursued with increasing assurance and fervour.

Above all, the Enlightenment's message was that 'unassisted human reason, not faith or tradition, was the principal guide for human conduct' (Kramnick 1995, xi). For the Enlightenment, a scientific understanding of human nature and needs would provide a rational basis for moral, social and political life. Christian talk of an immaterial soul was to be dismissed as meaningless, unscientific mumbo-jumbo. It is out of this scientific approach to the understanding of human nature that there emerged the down-to-earth, materialistic view of human beings as creatures of desire, creatures driven primarily to seek pleasure and avoid pain. As we have seen, Hume portrays human beings as primarily creatures of desire and feeling; and this creature of desire provides a basis for Bentham's utilitarianism, which seeks to promote moral and social practices that maximize overall human happiness. Other Enlightenment thinkers, including La Mettrie (1709–1751), Helvétius (1715–1771) and the Baron d'Holbach (1723–1789), also argued for this scientific conception of human nature and made it the basis of their visions for moral and political reform. In this way, scientific thinking not only promised to bring about the kinds of technological innovations that would make life easier and more comfortable, but also to provide a more rational, more scientific basis for morality and political organization. The result, it was widely thought, would be improved, more enlightened moral and social practices, a more rational society.

Even those who questioned this scientific understanding of human nature maintained the view that human reason has the power to organize the world for the better. Kant for example questioned the natural-scientific view of human beings as essentially creatures of desire. For Kant, this view of human beings as more or less blindly driven to maximize pleasure and minimize pain conflicted with the Enlightenment's own central belief that human beings could remake their world in accordance with reason. As we have seen, Kant formulates a picture of the human being which stresses that human beings are more than just creatures of desire; they are also rational subjects, and reason here is capable of formulating standards and goals for human conduct. Out of this comes an alternative to Bentham's utilitarianism, the Kantian moral theory that turns on this notion of the human being as a subject that formulates moral rules for itself. Above all, Kant offers a powerful reassertion of the Enlightenment view that reason should be the principal guide for conduct. Hence in his short piece, 'What is Enlightenment?' he sums up the Enlightenment view in a motto: 'Have courage to use your own reason – that is the motto of the Enlightenment' (Kant 1995, 1). As we shall see, the Kantian concern that science alone might not suffice for the realization of Enlightenment ideals will reappear amongst those who built on his conception of human nature, particularly Marx's twentieth-century successors. But the dominant Enlightenment view remained that the application of scientific principles to society would result in improved, more enlightened moral and social practices.

This Enlightenment faith in the power of human reason to organize the world for the better is in turn closely bound up with the eighteenth century's belief in progress. The Enlightenment was confident that the spread of reason and science would ensure progress on all fronts. Scientific knowledge of external nature would lead to technological and material progress, to progress in the control and exploitation of nature and scientific knowledge of human beings and social processes would lead to moral, social and political progress. One of the strongest expressions of this Enlightenment confidence in progress is to be found in the work of the French thinker Condorcet (1743–1794). Writing at the end of the eighteenth century, Condorcet interprets all of human history as an inevitable process of improvement, and his own time as being but a few steps away from the establishment of an earthly paradise. Confident in the march of progress, Condorcet makes grand claims for the future. He envisages, along with technological advances that will increase productivity and make life more and more comfortable, and progress in medicine that will abolish disease and improve health, the abolition of all prejudices and superstition, and the overcoming of social inequality, slavery and barbarism. After science has eradicated all superstitions from the world, after tyrannical monarchies and priestly power have been abolished, democratic rule and respect for equality will take over, and the only kind of social hierarchy will be that required for civilization, education and industry to continue to develop. Human beings will devote themselves only to rational knowledge and science, including knowledge of the laws of human functioning, the better to improve and perfect themselves and the wider society. Through education, existing knowledge will be passed on to new generations who will add to it, contributing in turn to further progress (see Condorcet 1995, 26–38).

These themes, the admiration for science, the critique of religion and the idea that the application of reason and science will lead not only to technological but also moral and social progress, are very much part of the modern outlook, and familiar to us as children of the Enlightenment. The theme of the rational, scientific mind's confrontation with religious dogma and superstition is projected back into the middle ages in *The Name of the Rose* (Jean-Jacques Annaud, 1986). Here, Sean Connery's Sherlock Holmes-like William of Baskerville investigates a series of murders that are going on in a monastery, which the monks and the Inquisitor Bernardo Gui see as the work of the devil. In contrast to the credulous monks, William's approach is methodical, empiricist, scientific, based firmly on observation and experience-based reasoning. He inspects the evidence and formulates a likely explanation to account for the known facts; and he rejects all appeals to supernatural forces to account for what is happening, insisting on purely natural explanations. It is true that Baskerville himself is also a believer, and that in the end his victory is limited, with the Inquisitor still powerful, and the forces of superstition and ignorance still largely holding sway. But he evokes sympathy and recognition in us because he is in many ways ahead of his time, and the time he looks forward to is the sober, modern, scientific outlook that emerged in the seventeenth and eighteenth centuries.

The confrontation between science and religion appears in more contemporary settings in *Inherit the Wind* (Stanley Kramer, 1960) and *Agnes of God* (Norman Jewison, 1985), with science much more clearly in the ascendancy. *Inherit the Wind* dramatizes the famous 'Monkey Trial' of the 1920s in Tennessee, in which a schoolteacher was arrested for teaching Darwin's theory of evolution. Enlightened reason, represented by the teacher's defence lawyer Henry Drummond (Spencer Tracy), confronts blind religious fundamentalism, in the figure of Matthew Harrison Brady (Fredric March). Where

Brady appeals to the authority of the Bible, insisting that everything in the Bible should be accepted 'exactly as it is given there', Drummond points to contradictions within the biblical account, and the difficulties in reconciling many of its claims with what are by now widely acknowledged scientific facts. *Agnes of God* reprises *The Name of the Rose* in a contemporary setting. Jane Fonda plays Dr Martha Livingston, the court psychiatrist sent to a convent to find out whether Agnes (Meg Tilly), a nun accused of killing her newborn child, is fit to stand trial. Agnes remembers nothing of the conception or pregnancy. Livingston takes the rational, scientific view, that nothing mysterious or supernatural has happened here, that what really happened lies buried in the nun's subconscious, in contrast to the Mother Superior (Anne Bancroft) who is willing to think that a miracle might be involved. However we have travelled a long way from *The Name of the Rose*. There, William has to bow down before the Inquisitor. Now, towards the end of the twentieth century, it is religion that must bow down before the inquisition of scientific investigation.

As for the future that technology might make possible, it is common to find cinematic visions of a world transformed by science and technology, a slick, clean and well-ordered world with robots, flying cars, television phones and food in pill form. These visions have become sufficiently clichéd to be parodied in Woody Allen's *Sleeper* (1973), in which a health food store owner (Allen) is frozen after a failed operation and revived two hundred years later. In this future the robots are fussy butlers, the 'instant pudding' expands uncontrollably and household labour-saving devices include the 'orgasmatron'. But the idea that science and technology might be bound up not just with material but also moral progress, with the improvement and perfection of humanity, is most evident in the various *Star Trek* films and television series. The starship *Enterprise* stands almost as a microcosm of Condorcet's ideal society. In this future world, technological developments have made possible unparalleled control over natural processes; and medical advances mean that everyone's physical well-being is fully taken care of. Moreover it is the calm, rational outlook of the scientist that prevails in social existence. Prejudice and superstition no longer exist, except as anomalies. Slavery and other forms of gross social inequality have been consigned to the past. While there is still a social hierarchy, it is simply the order required for the spaceship to function effectively. Much is made of the harmonious coexistence of the different characters, races and even species amongst the crew. Freed by science and technology from most physical and social ills, these people are able to devote themselves entirely to the acquisition of knowledge, to missions of scientific investigation and to their own development and self-improvement. As the *Enterprise* Captain Jean-Luc Picard puts it in *Star Trek: First Contact* (Jonathon Frakes, 1996): 'we work to better ourselves and the rest of humanity'. And in *Star Trek*, it is not merely that technology has freed us for learning and self-improvement; the very machinery, in the form of *Second Generation*'s android Data, also strives to better itself.

Like Condorcet's vision, *Star Trek*'s technological utopia is relatively democratic and individualist in its orientation. It has its own vision of the horrors of totalitarianism, in the form of the Borg, a collective organism that assimilates all life forms it encounters into itself and erases every trace of individuality. As portrayed in *Star Trek: First Contact*, the assimilative Borg is strongly reminiscent of the alien menace taking over the townspeople in *Invasion of the Body Snatchers*. There is however another version of the technological utopia ideal that is closer to Plato's conception of the ideal society in the *Republic*, in which the population is subordinated to rulers who have knowledge of the best social arrangements. In this version, the organization of society is left to an aristocracy of organizers, a ruling, scientifically informed élite. And the justification for obedience to this scientific élite is similar to Plato's, that one should obey those who speak with the authority of knowledge. Interestingly, this was the kind of society that most of the eighteenth-century Enlightenment thinkers envisaged. The democratically inclined Condorcet is an exception. Generally speaking, the Enlightenment thinkers did not advocate democratic reform. Instead, most looked forward to a kind of enlightened, technocratic despotism, a society ruled by a rational, scientifically informed administration, a strong ruler who imposed reforms and progress upon the population. This is a view that reappears in the 1930s in *Things to Come* (William Cameron Menzies, 1936), based on the work of the novelist H.G. Wells. Wells himself was a believer in science and the scientific organization of society. He advocated scrapping democracy in favour of government by an élite scientific group. In *Things to Come*, the earth, which has almost been destroyed by war and disease, is saved by the Air Men, technologists who fly in from the Middle East and impose a government based on scientific principles. In no time, people are living in sumptuous underground cities and launching rockets to the moon.

Whatever form they take, these visions of technological utopia reflect the confidence that human reason and science will bring about progress, a confidence that is very much part of the modern outlook. The enormous transformations brought about by science and technology, including industrialization and the mechanization of factory production, are plain for all to see. However, the view that science and technology are straightforwardly progressive forces is no longer quite so readily accepted. There may indeed have been enormous technological progress, but it is no longer so evident that moral progress inevitably follows from this. The catastrophic events of the twentieth century, including the technologically efficient carnage of two world wars, Nazi atrocities committed in the heart of an 'enlightened' Europe and a nuclear arms race that at one stage threatened the very existence of humanity, have brought this faith in reason and science into question. The impact of technology and industrialization on everyday life has by no means been unequivocally positive; and new technologies such as genetic engineering bring with them new and unknown challenges and risks. Overall, it is no longer so clear that there is a necessary link between science and progress. Instead, a range of concerns and anxieties have emerged about the role and effects of science and technology on human existence, along with more pessimistic, dystopian visions of the future.

Playing God: scientific hubris

In fact, concerns about science and technology go back a long way. Even as the early modern thinkers were optimistically proclaiming the virtues of scientific knowledge, and the prospect of being able to master nature, less optimistic observers were beginning to express fears at the excess of these ambitions. As David West notes, early expressions of this anxiety range from the 'dramatizations of the Faust legend by Marlowe and Goethe to nineteenth century Gothic tales about the potentially monstrous products of scientific hubris' (West 1996, 14). One of the most famous of these early warnings is Mary Shelley's novel *Frankenstein*. Subtitled *The New Prometheus*, an allusion to the mythological Greek figure who defied the Gods by stealing the secret of fire from them and paid dearly for his arrogance, the novel questions the new powers made available to human beings through technology and industrialization. Here, a rather different view of science's confrontation with religion emerges. Science now is not so much the heroic voice of reason, confronting religious superstition and dogma. Rather, science and technology now appear as an arrogant challenge to the deity, an attempt by human beings to take over powers that are the proper preserve of God. And when human beings try to 'play God' and overreach themselves, they run the risk of creating monsters they cannot control.

Anxieties over science and technology continue to appear in more recent cultural products. The idea of science overreaching itself and straying dangerously into realms properly left to God finds expression in the genre of 'mad scientist' films, starting with the classic *Frankenstein* (James Whale, 1931). Based on though not identical with Shelley's novel, the film recasts the tale in its familiar modern form: scientist Dr Frankenstein (Colin Clive) steals the body parts of corpses to assemble a creature (Boris Karloff) that is to be activated by electricity. Because a criminal's brain is accidentally implanted into the skull, the creature becomes a killer. Frankenstein is very much the arrogant scientist, intoxicated by his own brilliance, who as we are informed in the introductory segment 'sought to create a man after his own image without reckoning on God'. His sin is to stray into the realm of the 'two great mysteries of creation – life and death'. Perhaps even more effective is *Island of Lost Souls* (Erle C. Kenton, 1933), based on an H.G. Wells story. Here, the arrogant scientist Dr Moreau ('do you know what it feels like to play God?'), played by Charles Laughton, has produced a whole herd of creatures by surgically transforming animals into semi-humans. Once again, scientific hubris leads to monstrous creations, which in the end turn on their creator. Similar misgivings surface in the *Dr Jekyll and Mr Hyde* films, where the scientist does not merely interfere with life but seeks to meddle with the 'soul' itself. Is it wise to tamper with the problem of good coexisting with evil in the human soul, the bishop asks Dr Jekyll over dinner in the Victor Fleming version, 'until the creator himself has solved it in his own mysterious way?' But Dr Jekyll refuses to heed religious concerns and give up his researches, with the predictably disastrous results.

Concerns about science and technology are not necessarily tied to a religious position however. Even if in the course of the twentieth century religious objections have come to seem increasingly old-fashioned, and the idea of scientists 'playing God' becomes largely metaphorical, there remains a fear that there will be a price to pay for scientific arrogance, that science and technology may get out of control and turn against us. As one commentator puts it, science and technology remain for many 'tainted by promethean hubris . . . which will lead to human disaster' (Charlesworth 1989, 25). One area in particular where such worries have arisen is in relation to the manipulation and transformation of life, as the purely imaginative visions of such transformation in films like *Frankenstein* and *Island of Lost Souls* have come closer to realization. And it is not simply that we might not be able to control our productions; there is also the issue of the welfare of those experimented on. Amongst the horrors of the Nazi period were the terrible medical experiments carried out on concentration camp inmates, and there is a continuing concern that uncontrolled scientific research may lead to the mistreatment and exploitation of research subjects. The dangers of uncontrolled medical experimentation are amongst the many targets of Lindsay Anderson's O Lucky Man! (1973), a satirical tour of seventies British society and more or less a sequel to If . . . . During his travels Mick Travis (Malcolm MacDowell) finds himself at one point in an isolated medical research centre run by the rather alarming Dr Millar (Graham Crowden). Here he discovers that the experiments being conducted include grafting human heads onto animal bodies. There is a shocking moment when Mick pulls back a fellow patient's sheets to reveal a pig's body. The scenario is straight out of Island of Lost Souls, but this modern Dr Moreau is no longer safely tucked away in a remote island; the development of medical technology has made it possible for this figure to come much closer to us.

Moreover, there are recent developments in medical technology, such as genetic engineering and cloning, to consider. They have made it possible for us to manipulate life in a profound way. Manipulation of DNA, the genetic material of cells, makes it possible to create new species and to modify old ones; and cloning, the introduction of a creature's genetic material into a fertilized egg, makes it possible to produce genetically identical copies of that creature. These emerging technologies have provoked new concerns that scientific arrogance will extend to 'human engineering', to visions of re-engineering and 'improving' the human race. This is the rationale for the medical experiments in O Lucky Man!, where Dr Millar enthusiastically informs Mick that a combination of transplantation and genetic engineering will make it possible 'to produce an entirely satisfactory human breed' without having to rely on the hit and miss approach of ordinary reproduction. The worry here is that as human beings become increasingly subject to experimentation and engineering, they will become little more than raw material, to be shaped and manufactured as required. Along with this, new and disturbing possibilities for the misuse and exploitation of human beings suggest themselves. This is part of the background for Alien Resurrection, in which the researchers have cloned Ripley so they can extract and study the alien life form she carries within her. To these scientists, excited by the commercial and military possibilities of the species they have extracted, Ripley is little more than a 'meat by-product'; and the results of their handiwork are evident when Ripley encounters the room filled with the earlier attempts to clone her. Here, the cloning process is presented not only as reducing the human being to a manu-factured product, but as a violation at the most fundamental biological level.

The other kind of concern, that arrogant scientific meddling may set off events we cannot control, reappears in this context in the idea that genetic tampering in natural processes that have taken millions of years to evolve may have incalculable consequences. Human beings may find themselves funda-mentally altered, with unknowable consequences for future generations; or dangerous organisms, plant and animal, may escape into the environment to cause havoc. The latter concern provides the underlying premise for *Jurassic Park* (Steven Spielberg, 1993). Here, scientist John Hammond (Richard Attenborough) clones dinosaurs from fossilized DNA and sets up a dinosaur theme park, but despite the most elaborate safeguards the creatures still manage to get out of control. As the sceptical mathematician Ian Malcolm (Jeff Goldblum) warns, 'if there's one thing the history of evolution has taught us, it's that life will not be contained'. The idea of human beings themselves being irreparably altered by accidents at the genetic level features in another Goldblum vehicle, *The Fly* (David Cronenberg, 1986). This is a remake of the 1958 Kurt Neumann film in which a scientist's matter transportation experiments accidentally turn him into a half-man, half-fly. In Cronenberg's version the tale is retold as a genetic accident, an uncontrollable transforma-tion set in motion at the genetic level. After travelling through the transporter, scientist Seth Brundle (Jeff Goldblum once again) finds that his genes have become spliced together with those of a fly, and he gradually mutates into the hideous 'Brundle-Fly'.

Modern versions of the Frankenstein scenario have not only suggested themselves in connection with the creation and manipulation of life. The possibility that we might come to be threatened by the products of our scientific and technological ingenuity was amply demonstrated for many by the Cold War's nuclear arms race. In Stanley Kubrick's satire *Dr Strangelove* (1963), it is not merely the weapons that science has made available which prove humanity's undoing. After the insane general Jack D. Ripper (Sterling Hayden) sends bombers into Russia, it is the elaborate system of safeguards and deterrents the Americans and Russians have set up to prevent nuclear war that frustrates their efforts to avert disaster. In the end the 'Doomsday Machine', built by the Soviets as a final deterrent, destroys the world. And lurking in the background as the President's scientific advisor is the ultimate mad scientist, the sinister, wheelchair-bound Dr Strangelove himself (Peter Sellers). Such concerns have also appeared in relation to computer technology.

A recurring theme is that the computers we are becoming so dependent on might one day acquire independent intelligence. Once again science and technology make it possible for human beings to create life, in this case artificial life, but here also we may find that we cannot control what we have created. In *Colossus: The Forbin Project* (Joseph Sargent, 1970), the supercomputer designed to control the American missile defence system takes over and starts to develop plans of its own, including linking up with its Russian counterpart to hold the world hostage. In *Terminator* (James Cameron, 1984) and *Terminator 2: Judgement Day* (James Cameron, 1991) the computers of the future, having achieved independence, are waging a brutal war to obliterate the last traces of humanity. And in *The Matrix* (Andy and Larry Wachowski, 1999) the computers, having conquered most of humanity, now grow them as 'crops' in order to use their body heat as a power source.

So how might we respond to the perceived dangers of scientific hubris? As indicated before, it now seems rather old-fashioned to couch our objections in terms of our trespassing on areas properly left to God. David Hume (1986, 21–5) indirectly highlights another problem with religious objections. In his essay 'Of Suicide', Hume criticizes one of the standard Christian arguments against suicide, that human life is a gift from God, that it is in a sense God's property, and so it falls to God rather than to human beings to say when that life should end. Hume's response is to point out that it seems quite permissible for us to interfere in order to try to lengthen our lives, to seek medical attention when we are ill, so why shouldn't it be permissible for us to shorten it? To reject suicide on this basis would seem to require us to reject all medical intervention, and it is not clear that even devout believers would want to go that far. Hume's point can be extended. If we reject certain kinds of scientific investigation and technological interference, such as interference with life at the genetic level, because they are intruding in areas that are properly God's alone to govern, then it would seem that we would have to abandon a whole range of scientific advances that have improved our existence in various ways. Of course we can also couch our objections to these technologies in non-religious terms and simply note that they carry risks and dangers. But the same basic point could still be made, that abandoning these technologies would also mean losing out on the enormous benefits they have the potential to deliver to humanity.

For advocates of these new technologies, being able to control our basic life processes opens up the possibility of freeing ourselves from all manner of biological limitations. We can treat human diseases and defects that have genetic causes, as well as creating useful non-human organisms, such as pest-resistant plants. Here, the Enlightenment confidence in science and technology reasserts itself. On this more optimistic view, we can acknowledge that scientific research and technological interference in these areas have the potential to lead to abuses and carry certain risks and dangers, but also argue that any possible evils will be outweighed by their benefits. It might then seem that what is required is not the abandonment of these activities, but rather the establishment of proper control mechanisms, such as ethical codes and committees, and accountability to the wider community. There already exist numerous ethical codes designed to protect medical and scientific research subjects. Many are modelled on the Nuremberg Code, formulated in response to the excesses of Nazi medical experimentation. These codes usually stipulate, amongst other things, that research subjects be fully informed about the procedures they are to undergo, and that they freely consent to these procedures, in order to avoid the danger of being reduced to mere objects for scientific exploitation. Similarly, it can be acknowledged that new technologies like genetic engineering have certain dangers: accidents might happen and genetically modified organisms might escape into the environment, or results may be intentionally misused, for example in bio-logical weapons. But once again, it might be argued that by imposing proper controls, enforcing ethical guidelines and exercising the appropriate caution in the use of the technologies, it will be possible to avoid these dangers.

So far we have been looking at concerns with science and technology which have to do with the possible excesses of scientists or technologists – with the possibility that arrogant scientific meddling in nature and human nature might have disastrous consequences for humanity. And one response has been that what we need to do to avoid potential dangers and problems is to ensure that the activities of scientists and technologists are properly controlled, subject to proper ethical standards, and accountable to the wider community. As Max Charlesworth puts it in connection with biotechnology in particular, 'we are not powerless before the possibilities opened up before the new biotechnology . . . we can control it and, as best we can, make it serve human purposes' (Charlesworth 1989, 133). In a liberal democratic society, Charlesworth argues, it is ultimately up to the community as a whole, through public scrutiny and debate, to keep watch over science and technology, and to decide what directions they should take. But let us now turn to another kind of concern with scientific thinking and technology, the concern that technology, in the form of industrial technology and mechanization, has already infiltrated human existence in a pervasive way, and that in doing so it has affected our very capacity to exercise control over our existence.

Alienation in a technological society

Driving this second kind of concern is the idea that modern science and technology have, through industrialization and mechanization, created an inhuman social environment, an alien, impersonal world. In this technological society, human beings have lost their humanity. They live a dehumanized, alienated existence, increasingly subject to the requirements of the machine and those who control the machines. This kind of view draws on the Marxist idea of alienation. As we saw in the previous chapter, Marx argues that in capitalist society workers live an alienated, distorted existence, unable to pursue their true interests and denied control over their lives and working conditions. And Marx himself points towards the role of technology in reinforcing alienation, as capitalism comes to harness the new knowledge of science in the nineteenth century. In his analysis of the stages of development of the work process under capitalism, in Chapter 15 of *Capital*, he argues that technology has come to play a larger and larger role in the work process. This serves the capitalist interest in maximizing profits, because the introduction of machines brings about improvements in efficiency and productivity. In the process however, Marx argues, the worker is further degraded, dehumanized and alienated. The skills of the worker are in some cases taken over, embodied in machines that can do the job more efficiently. Where workers are not simply replaced, they now have to conform to the requirements of the machinery. The speed and rhythm of their work is subordinated to that of the machine. Thus, workers have effectively been reduced to an appendage of the machine. There is also an increase in the degree of control of the capitalist over the work process, since the capitalist owns the machinery.

Marx's analysis anticipates the increasing automation of production, and such developments as the introduction of assembly line production (by the Ford motor company) early in the twentieth century. At this time workers themselves became increasingly subject to the forms of 'scientific work management' known as Taylorism. This involved applying techniques of scientific investigation to the work process itself, in order to distinguish the various stages of the process, even the particular movements being made by the workers, and to organize the overall process for maximum efficiency. The worker's movements thus become fully standardized and repetitive and in the end, the worker becomes just another piece of machinery, another cog in the process of mechanized production. It is this dehumanization of the modern industrial worker that is the target of the first part of Modern Times. Here, Chaplin's assembly-line worker has a single, monotonous task to perform in the overall process, tightening nuts. Efficiency is everything, and he not only has to contend with a conveyor belt that is constantly speeding up; he is also subjected to the automatic 'feeding machine' that is supposed to eliminate the need to break for lunch. When Charlie does finally manage to have a break, he is still subject to the rhythms of the machinery. His arms cannot stop making spasmodic nut-tightening movements. Finally, as we have seen, he himself ends up on the conveyer belt and is conveyed into the bowels of the machinery he has been serving. A number of other films of the period take up this theme, notably René Clair's film A Nous la Liberté (1931), in which the repetitive movements of the assembly-line workers are choreographed to music. Anxieties about workplace mechanization and dehumanization are also reflected in the futuristic vision of Fritz Lang's Metropolis (1926), in which the workers of 2026 trudge to underground factories to tend huge machines. In one memorable image, Lang visualizes the machines as modern versions of the Phoenician god Moloch, to which the workers are being sacrificed just as the Phoenicians once sacrificed their children. Metropolis also envisages the eventual replacement of workers altogether with machinery, when the 'wizard inventor' Rotwang (Rudolph Klein-Rogge) is ordered to construct a race of robots who will never tire or make mistakes.

Marx's critique of the dehumanizing effects of technology and mechaniza-tion on workers and the work process has also provided the basis for a wider critique of the effects of technology on modern social life. A number of twentieth-century commentators have argued that alienation and dehuman-ization in the face of technology is taking place on a broader scale, as technology has a greater and greater effect on social existence. This concern with the wider effects of technology arises as technology transforms all facets of social existence including living arrangements, communication and transportation systems, and efficient scientific management and organization become the order of the day in more and more areas of life. As a result, it has been argued, society has become increasingly technologically sophisticated and efficient, but it has also become strangely impersonal, impoverished and inhuman. Thus Jacques Tati takes over from Chaplin as a wry commentator on modern times, when his character Monsieur Hulot confronts modernity, fifties-style, in the form of his sister's soulless, high-tech, gadget-filled house in *Mon Oncle* (1958); and when he finds himself in a coldly modern, glass and steel Paris in *Playtime* (1973), in which the city is beginning to look like every other modern city, with the same skyscrapers, city blocks and hotels, and the old Paris appears only as reflections in the glass doors and windows.

Cinematic visions of the future have also reflected these concerns about the dehumanizing effects of the technologically transformed society. Alongside the scientific utopias of *Star Trek* and *Things to Come* there are a number of films portraying a technological future in which we are presented with far more pessimistic, dystopian visions. In *2001: A Space Odyssey* (1968) Stanley Kubrick, with characteristic irony, sumptuously invokes the technologically trans-formed world of the traditional scientific utopia and at the same time mocks it. On the face of it we have the familiar vision of a scientific utopia of the future, a technologically sophisticated, well-ordered world in which computers and spaceships are at our disposal, and society runs with cool efficiency. But appearances are deceptive here. Kubrick's future world is far from that envisaged in *Star Trek*. In this world, while the technology is magnificent, human beings have become colourless, almost robotic figures, slaves to their machinery. The two astronauts on the mission to Jupiter in the second half of the film are not heroic adventurers but unemotional, unimaginative functionaries, little more than appendages of their own sophisticated technology. Indeed, they are easily upstaged by their increasingly emotional and anxiety-prone computer HAL who, even though he turns against them, remains the most human character on the vessel.

These pessimistic visions of the future have also embodied concerns that the more technologically sophisticated society becomes, the more political rule will take the form of rule by a 'technocracy' of scientists, engineers and technical experts, rather than by elected representatives. Here, the kind of scientific organization of society advocated by people like H.G. Wells is viewed far more critically, as a new, technocratic kind of totalitarianism. This concern was already evident in the twenties in Lang's *Metropolis*, where the world has become one large city in which science is king and the whole of society has been planned along scientific lines. The ruling scientific and managerial élite live in skyscrapers and run the world in which the workers labour deep underground. Jean-Luc Godard gives us another scientifically organized city in *Alphaville* (1965), in which it is a villainous computer, Alpha 60, that runs the society. In the name of 'logic', an authoritarian social order has been established. In Alphaville everyone has their allotted roles, right down to the 'Seductress Grade 3' who greets hotel guests. Here, the dehumanization of individuals, their reduction to unthinking functionaries, is actively encouraged because it serves to support the existing social order. Expressions of emotion are punishable by death, mind-numbing drugs are distributed to the population, and sources of information are limited by removing words from the dictionary. Godard adds a film noir touch with his central character, hard-boiled intergalactic special agent Lemmy Caution (Eddie Constantine), the only person who has a chance of defeating the computer and liberating the population. Similarly, in *Fahrenheit 451* (François Truffaut, 1966) Truffaut portrays a bland totalitarian society in which independent thinking and knowledge are despised, firemen burn books and the populace is kept entertained and stupefied through television.

Many of these concerns about the broader effects of science and technology on social life appear in the work of Marx's twentieth-century successors, in particular the members of the so-called Frankfurt School. This group of German neo-Marxist intellectuals included Max Horkheimer (1895–1973), Theodor Adorno (1903–1969) and Herbert Marcuse (1898–1979). Of these Marcuse is perhaps the best known. Where Marx argues that the mechanization of production has meant the increasing alienation of workers, their subordination to machines and to their capitalist overseers, Marcuse expands this to the larger social canvas. In his book *One-Dimensional Man* he argues that in the twentieth century, in what he calls advanced or late industrial society, technology and mechanization may have increased productivity enormously, but they have also served to increase humanity's subordination to the technological apparatus of production, and to those who control the technology. As productive activity has expanded, more and more areas of social life have become subject to what Marcuse calls 'rationalization', i.e., to reorganization, mechanization and standardization so as to most efficiently contribute to the production process. Individuals have become increasingly subordinated to their role in the system of production; and social power has been increasingly monopolized by professional élites, the technocratic and bureaucratic managers, who provide the administration and organization required for society to function most efficiently and productively. Modern democracy, the idea that the people govern themselves through their freely elected representatives, is a façade. In the end, we are only free to choose between different representatives of the same administrative-bureaucratic apparatus.

Marcuse also argues that our very thinking is becoming increasingly circumscribed to the point where the only significant questions about society seem to be technical ones, the only considerations those of maximizing efficiency. This 'technological rationality' is the kind of thinking required in order to modernize the production process; and as more and more of social life is reorganized to contribute to increased productivity, it also becomes increasingly subject to this kind of thinking. More and more, Marcuse argues, this is becoming the only acceptable way of thinking about our social existence. In other words, his claim is that such thinking now serves as an ideology, a distorted view of the world that brings individuals to accept the existing social order and their place within it. When all non-technical considerations, about whether such a society serves genuine human needs and interests, are excluded, we are left only with thinking that supports the system. The existing social order, with its technocratic and bureaucratic management, appears justified because it is what is required for the growth of productivity and efficiency. This social order is thus, in a technical sense, perfectly rational; and to question this order and one's place in it is to fall into irrationality. So technological rationality is a way of thinking which serves to justify the subordination of individuals, both to their role in the system of production, and to those groups that control society. The society is totalitarian, not in the sense that it is overtly coercive, but insofar as it is impossible to think except in ways that support the system. Overall, for Marcuse, science and technology, far from making it possible for human beings to remake society in accordance with human needs and interests, and to overcome forms of oppression, as Enlightenment figures like Condorcet hoped, have had the opposite effect. They have produced an inhuman society and new forms of social control.

In these Marxist and neo-Marxist criticisms of society, the underlying claim is that human beings live an impoverished, diminished and alienated life in modern technological society. Society and technology are not organized so as to serve genuine human needs and interests. Rather, human beings are made to serve social and technological requirements. So along with these criticisms there is the idea that we need to recover what we have lost. Now, while we can broadly say that what needs to be recovered is our 'humanity', there are different views as to what this involves and how it is to be achieved. It can mean holding on to or reasserting our individuality, and our capacity to feel and respond to the world on our own terms, in the face of the impersonal gadgetry and soulless uniformity of the machine age. This anti-technological individualism is part of the appeal of Chaplin's tramp in *Modern Times*, and Monsieur Hulot in *Mon Oncle*, both of which portray the lone individual holding out against an increasingly mechanical and impersonal world. Marcuse, working in the Marxist tradition, is interested not so much in the reassertion of the lone individual as of humanity in general; and in not simply retreating from society but taking control of our social existence, overcoming forms of power and subordination and reorganizing society in a way that reflects our true needs and interests. So he looks forward to a broad social transformation through which we will create the conditions for full human self-realization.

But is such a social transformation compatible with technology? At times Marcuse shares with the anti-technological individualists a sense that technology is poisoning humanity, and that it needs to be somehow done away with. For Marcuse, increasing technological mastery of nature seems to lead inevitably to our subordination to the inhuman machinery of production and to technocratic rule. We can only escape from this situation if we make a radical break with existing science and technology and develop a new science, involving a more responsive, receptive and nurturing relationship to nature. Marcuse thus verges on a complete rejection of existing science and technology, as being inherently bad and anti-human. We are familiar enough with the argument that certain technologies, such as nuclear power, threaten our survival and would be better abandoned. But the idea of completely transcending technology is more difficult to envisage, and borders on the mystical. 2001: A Space Odyssey imagines human beings finally leaving behind their tools and spaceships, in order to enter into the ultimate, post-technological stage of their evolution. But as the surviving astronaut of the Jupiter mission is reborn as the 'star child', hovering over the earth, the mystical overtones of such a vision are very much in evidence. Closer to earth, Koyaanisqaatsi (Godfrey Reggio, 1983) uses time-lapse photography to portray the frenetic pace and mechanical patterns of modern city life, and by implication to question the technologically-driven modern world, but the film is only able to gesture vaguely towards an alternative, invoking unspoilt, primordial wilderness and Hopi Indian wisdom.

Claims that we need to abandon existing technology also come up against the point that technology, while it may pose certain dangers, has also delivered enormous benefits to humanity. A less radical view is that technology is not bad or anti-human in itself, that it can in principle be used either in the service of human needs and purposes or against them. Problems arise only when technical considerations become all-encompassing, and human needs and purposes cease to figure in our thinking. What is required then is to supplement technology with some framework of thinking that looks beyond merely technical considerations, a moral framework which takes our needs and interests into account. One possibility here could be a revival of the older religious perspective in some form. *Star Wars* (George Lucas, 1977), while it makes much of the marvels of technology, also refers us to a higher religious perspective, the Jedi religion which supports central human values including respect for life, justice and liberty. Technology without a higher religious dimension is represented by the Empire's Death Star, the moon-sized war machine capable of destroying entire planets. Here, the state itself has become an immense machine, manned by the unthinking, faceless storm troopers. In *Star Wars*, technology is not intrinsically bad or anti-human. The rebels also make use of technology to fight against the Death Star. They however are inspired and guided by something beyond technology, the Jedi religion which gives their struggle a moral basis (see Wilkinson 2000, 132–3).

However, such recourse to religion might be thought to represent a step backwards to a pre-modern position. Interestingly, the whole culture which is held up in *Star Wars* as an alternative to the oppressive Empire has a distinctly medieval character, with its monk-like Jedi masters, its princess, warriors and serf-like underclass of servant-robots (see Rubey 1985, 88–92). But religion is not the only candidate here. For others, the framework of thinking called for in order to supplement technology is that embodied in a humanistic, artistic or literary culture, which gives expression to what is most central to our humanity. Thus in *Alphaville*, Lemmy Caution's fellow agent Henri Dickson (Akim Tamiroff) tells him that in Alphaville people have become mere 'ants and termites', functionaries in an 'entirely technical society', and that what is missing are the artists, writers, musicians, painters, the people who make possible a human society. They were, his informant tells him, banished 'about a hundred and fifty light years ago', the film's poetic use of technical terms perhaps a reflection of its own allegiance to something more than technology. Similarly in *Fahrenheit 451*, literature expresses what is most central to the human soul. People resist the oppressive, TV-addicted society and preserve their humanity by secretly reading books and keeping libraries. When Montag the book-burning fireman questions his role and escapes into the country, he finds a whole mini-society of freethinking people, all of whom are maintaining the heritage of literature by committing books to memory and preserving them for future generations.

The main message here is that we do not need to abandon technology, but the pursuit and realization of human needs and interests requires more than technological progress and a technically efficient society. And for many, a humanistic, literature-centred culture is what is needed, a culture in which human needs, interests and purposes will be able to be articulated, and in which technology will become the servant of humanity. A view along these lines has been formulated by Marcuse's successor, Jürgen Habermas (b.1929), the contemporary representative of the Frankfurt School. Habermas agrees with Marcuse that society has become subject to a process of technological rationalization, with human beings increasingly subordinated to the require-ments of technological production, and to the expert administrators who organize society in the interests of maximum efficiency and productivity. But for Habermas, in contrast to Marcuse, there is no question of our transcending or abandoning science and technology. Technological control and manipula-tion are characteristic of the productive dimension of human existence, in which we work on nature, and we have no other way of relating to the natural world. However, Habermas argues, this is only one dimension of our existence. There is another, equally important dimension, that of our relations with one another, the interpersonal or 'intersubjective' dimension. And what is proper to this intersubjective dimension is not technological manipulation but communication, interpersonal discourse. Through language and collective discussion we are able to articulate our needs and interests, and in the light of them, to agree on the proper values and goals we as a society should pursue.

For Habermas, the problem is not science and technology as such, but rather the inappropriate extension of technological practices and forms of thinking, proper to our dealings with nature, to the interpersonal realm of communication and discourse. Then, not only are human beings subjected to continually refined control and administration, but social questions are increasingly viewed solely as technical problems. Technological thinking thus becomes an ideology that blinds us to the very different character of the interpersonal realm, where collective discussion and consensus should rule. By presenting all social questions as technical questions that only expert administrators can solve, it justifies the concentration of social power in the hands of the technocrats and bureaucrats. For Habermas, a society in which a powerful bureaucratic élite administers the social order without consulting the wider population is a denial of the interpersonal dimension of human existence. A fully human form of existence is only possible if we restore the collective, democratic discussion about social values and goals that is proper to the interpersonal realm. In the ideal society, we will determine the standards and goals that society is to pursue through society-wide discussion, and informed by these values and goals, we will be able to make decisions about how to employ and direct our technology (see Habermas 1971, 102–6,

112–13). The Marxist ideal of collective rational self-determination thus becomes Habermas's vision of collective discussion and consensus about the proper values and goals of life.

With this, we arrive at a position that has some similarities with the kind of position presented by Charlesworth at the end of the previous section. Human beings are not powerless before technology; they can control it, and make it serve human purposes. However for Charlesworth this simply requires that science and technology be made subject to ethical standards and ultimately to public discussion and accountability. From Habermas' perspective such a view fails to take into account the possibility that there may be systematic barriers to public discussion and communal control. In particular, he argues that scientific and technological forms of thinking have themselves helped to disempower the community, and to put control of social and technological developments in the hands of technocratic and bureaucratic élites. They have thus affected our very capacity to exercise control over our existence. For Habermas, we need first of all to restore the realm of public discussion and consensus, which will then make it possible for us to formulate ethical standards and goals, and to take collective control of our science and technology. Habermas thus goes beyond Charlesworth's account to offer a more radical critique. Now Habermas' account, as we have seen, is itself part of a long line of critiques of technology, going back via the Frankfurt School to Marx, which point to the alienating and dehumanizing effects of technology on human beings. But these radical critiques make some important assumptions of their own about the nature of human existence and of technology, and these assumptions need in turn to be critically examined. This will be the concern of the final section.

Recent technology, new views

A central assumption made in these radical critiques of technology is that technology has no place within the interpersonal realm, that there is no room, in our relationships with one another, for impersonal technology and the thinking that goes with it. Technological manipulation may be appropriate for our dealings with a non-human nature, but if the technological enters too deeply into the human realm, it serves only to diminish and dehumanize human beings, to reduce them to mere objects, mere cogs in the machinery, and to promote ever more virulent forms of social control and manipulation. From this perspective, recently emergent technologies can only make matters worse, because they seem to have insinuated themselves particularly deeply into the interpersonal realm. For example, there are new communications and computer technologies that, as we saw in the previous chapter, have opened up new possibilities for monitoring and controlling human beings. Technology has also made possible the control and manipulation of fundamental human processes. I have already mentioned genetic engineering and cloning, which have made possible the manipulation of human life at a basic level. To these biotechnologies we can add new reproductive technologies associated with controlling pregnancy and childbirth, from the pill and abortion techniques, to prenatal screening, in vitro fertilization or IVF (the removal of eggs for fertilization and reimplantation in the womb), prenatal screening and caesareans. And there are increasing opportunities for human beings to be literally mechanized, through the mixing of organic and inorganic body parts, such as mechanical organs, electronic ears, prosthetic limbs and cosmetic surgery implants.

These are forms of technological control, then, which operate in a very direct way on people. And a concern they raise is that they represent a new stage in the subjection of human beings. The new technologies seem to make possible new and ever more powerful forms of social control. This is already suggested in the *Enemy of the State* scenario, where modern communications and computer technologies are seen as making possible new and especially invasive forms of state surveillance. The possibility of mixing organic and inorganic parts raises the spectre of human beings coming to be literally manufactured and reconstructed in accordance with social requirements. Such concerns find their way into a number of futuristic visions. In *Robocop* (Paul Verhoeven, 1987), human beings can be reconstructed to serve the state and powerful corporations. In the film, the Omni Consumer Products Corporation transforms a murdered policeman (Peter Weller) into the formidable Robocop, the half-human, half-robotic crime fighter. To the extent that Robocop is dominated by his technology and programming, he is both dehumanized and completely under the control of the Corporation. It is only when he starts to recover the memories of his former self that his human side returns, and he is able to emerge from behind the technological mask to act for himself. *Terminator* goes a step further. Arnold Schwarzenegger is the terminator, a cyborg with a metal skeleton and human flesh coating. The machines running the world in the future have sent him back to kill the woman (Linda Hamilton) who will bear the child destined to become a great freedom fighter. Here, it is the cyborg's flesh and blood appearance that is the mask; he is an emotionless, implacable and merciless machine. The cyborg reflects the concern that, as one commentator puts it, humanity is 'in danger of becoming entirely absorbed in a wholly technological future within which the machine becomes the paradigm by which the organic itself functions' (Sim 1998, 220). In the sequel, *Terminator 2: Judgement Day*, Schwarzenegger returns as a more 'human' cyborg, but he himself has now been superseded by a new line of entirely inorganic and even more ruthless terminators.

Similar concerns have been raised about the new reproductive technologies. For a number of feminist critics, these technologies represent a particularly powerful means of social control and more specifically, of male control over women's reproductive capacities. Gena Corea, in her book *The Mother Machine* (1985), argues that reproductive technologies make it possible for reproduction to be increasingly controlled by male-dominated medical, legal and state agencies. Another feature of the account is the argument that although women might not be overtly coerced into subjecting themselves to reproductive technologies, they are nonetheless being pressured to collaborate in the process because 'pro-natalist' pressures in society make them see their identity as being bound up with reproduction and motherhood. In other words, a quasi-Marxist notion of ideological or false consciousness is introduced to account for women's desire to have children. Out of these concerns Corea constructs a nightmare vision of the future that reproductive technologies are making possible. Women's bodies will be reduced to mere objects of medical manipulation, controlled by medical technologists and experts for the purposes of reproduction. As Jana Sawicki (1991, 72) points out, what Corea envisages is a high-tech version of *The Handmaid's Tale*, the Margaret Atwood novel filmed by Volker Schlondorff (1990). Here, a future United States chooses 'handmaids', surrogate mothers to give birth on behalf of society, and women in general are reduced to childbearers, domestic servants and mistresses. In this case the state has reverted to a religious fundamentalism, with God invoked to prescribe these roles for women, but Corea's suggestion is that the new reproductive technologies may similarly reduce women to a captive class of 'breeders'. Ultimately, Corea argues, biological women might even become superfluous, to be replaced by the 'mother machines', entirely artificial forms of reproduction such as artificial wombs. In this way, men will achieve absolute control over reproduction.

Genetic engineering also has a role to play in these dark visions, raising the prospect that entire populations will become objects of medical and social manipulation. The ability to manipulate genetic material and rid it of flaws may certainly allow us to treat various genetic diseases; but the concern is that it may also lead to the demand for 'perfect' specimens, human beings tailor-made for social requirements, along with various forms of discrimination against those who fall below the standards required. Genetic engineering, in combination with new reproductive technologies, plays a key role in the dystopian vision of *Gattaca* (Andrew Niccol, 1997). The film portrays a possible future society in which one's profession and social status is determined by genetic inheritance, and those with genetic 'defects' are relegated to the worst jobs. In this society it is best to design one's offspring to make them as perfect as possible. The hero Vincent (Ethan Hawke) is a 'god child', whose genetic make-up was left to chance by his parents, while his younger brother was produced with the help of genetic screening and selection, a process that has itself become the norm. In one early scene we see the parents discussing genetic therapy decisions with a genetic engineer. Here, IVF has been used to extract and fertilize the woman's eggs, which have been screened for genetic diseases, as well as for 'potentially prejudicial' conditions such as baldness, short-sightedness and propensity to obesity. Nothing has been left to chance, so that the child will have the best start in life. Vincent, meanwhile, finds that he is part of a new underclass, one of the so-called 'invalids' rejected by insurers and excluded from the better jobs. As he notes sourly, this society has turned discrimination into a science.

In various ways, then, new technologies have been seen as contributing to new forms of social oppression, and opening up new Orwellian scenarios of total political control. This kind of account is very much in line with the analysis of modern technology as a form of social domination first formulated by Marcuse and the Frankfurt School. However, without denying that issues of social control come up in relation to technology, it is possible to raise questions about this kind of account. As already noted, there is a deep-seated assumption here that technology is essentially alien to the human or interpersonal realm. It can only diminish human beings, dehumanize them and reduce them to objects of oppressive manipulation; so it must be excluded from the human realm. But it is not clear that technology necessarily dehumanizes or oppresses individuals. After all, it also enables, enhances human capacities, empowers individuals. To take the example of new reproductive technologies, there are clear cases where technology has been empowering for women, for example the pill; and it can be argued that the call by some feminist critics to simply reject reproductive technologies and return to a pre-technological management of childbirth is a romanticization of the past that forgets the very real risks of natural childbirth. Second, there is a tendency in these accounts to see people as little more than passive victims, unable to resist forms of social regulation. This makes it possible to envisage technocratic and bureaucratic control as all-powerful, able to completely control individuals and populations; and to imagine that once we adopt various technologies there is no turning back, that any oppressive possibilities they may have will inevitably be realized. But more attention needs to be paid to the idea that people are never simply passive, that they actively engage with, criticize and resist social practices.

Here, some of the social and political insights provided by Foucault are useful. Foucault, like Habermas, is concerned with the interpersonal realm, as a realm that cannot simply be explained in terms of productive activity. But he has a very different view of social power, and this makes possible a different view of the place of technology in the interpersonal realm. As we saw in the previous chapter, Foucault questions the view that social power works in a primarily negative way, diminishing human beings, denying their individuality and preventing them from realizing their true needs and real natures. Rather, power works in a positive, productive way, turning human beings into certain kinds of individuals. It works precisely by enforcing the idea that there is some one set of desires or way of being that is 'true', 'real' or 'natural'. In *Discipline and Punish*, as we saw in the previous chapter, he gives an account of the emergence of the specifically modern disciplinary forms of power which aim to manage the behaviour of individuals in a detailed, continuous way. Discipline works on individuals through a range of techniques including monitoring and surveillance, in order to develop their capacities, to make them stronger and more powerful; while simultaneously making them docile and obedient, bringing them to conform in their behaviour to various disciplinary norms and standards. In the process of normalization, discipline produces individuals, in the sense of producing trained, socially useful individuals. So Foucault shares with the Frankfurt School and Habermas the idea that in the modern era society has undergone a process of rationalization; but on Foucault's account in *Discipline and Punish*, this comes about through the spread of multiple forms of disciplinary control throughout society. For Foucault this is the real legacy of the eighteenth-century Enlightenment. In its vision of rationally reorganizing society in accordance with norms based on human nature and needs, it has promoted the spread of these disciplinary techniques which transform human beings into particular kinds of individuals.

How does Foucault's kind of account affect our view of the new technologies? Let us focus on new reproductive technologies and genetic engineering. As Sawicki (1991, 83) points out, new reproductive technologies associated with pregnancy and childbirth provide a good example of these disciplinary technologies of body management. They often involve sophisticated forms of surveillance, such as ultrasound and electronic foetal monitoring. And they aim not to suppress or eliminate women, as Corea suggests, but to enhance their capacities, particularly their reproductive capacities. Indeed, part of the attractiveness of these new technologies to women is precisely that they are enabling in this way. This is not to deny that these reproductive technologies have a controlling role as well. However as Sawicki (1991, 83–4) goes on to argue, this control can arguably be better understood in terms of normalization, the production of specific, socially useful kinds of individual. That is, they involve bringing human processes and capacities into conformity with various medically defined norms of healthy and responsible motherhood. Defining a realm of normality also defines a range of possible deviations from the norm, for example mothers who are infertile, genetically impaired, biologically or socially unfit for pregnancy, or mothers deemed 'negligent' for failing to undergo tests. Such norms figure not only in the medical regulation of women's bodies, providing standards to be policed and defining deficiencies to be corrected, but also in the exclusion of certain groups of women, such as lesbians and single mothers, from access to fertility programmes.

Genetic engineering can also be seen as being linked with processes of normalizing control. Here once again the aim is primarily to improve human functioning, to enhance capacities, to produce socially useful and productive kinds of individual; and this is inseparable from the imposition of various medically defined notions of genetic normality and abnormality. As *Gattaca* suggests, the range of conditions and attributes that can be considered deviant in this way is potentially very wide. Not merely genetic diseases but a whole range of conditions might come to be seen as 'potentially prejudicial', i.e., abnormal or deviant. The film also indicates how such medically defined norms could be taken up and used by other social institutions, particularly in the workplace and by insurance agencies, for the purposes of regulation and exclusion. Moreover, we are shown the widespread forms of surveillance through which norms of genetic correctness could be policed and enforced. Not only one's blood and urine, but also samples from door handles, computer keyboards or handshakes, even the saliva on a stamp, could be tested and monitored. Much of the film is in fact taken up with the central character Vincent's efforts to evade this surveillance, since he has sought to escape from his genetically ordained social position and make his way into the higher echelons of society, by taking on the identity of another, genetically superior individual.

At this point it might seem that these new technologies, even if enabling, also threaten to establish forms of social control more pervasive and total than anything we have seen so far. But a second feature of Foucault's account that needs to be stressed is that individuals are never simply passive and malleable, unable to resist forms of social control. Rather than seeing power as a one-way process in which power is imposed on passive victims, Foucault stresses that power always encounters resistance, that the social realm is one of dynamic power relations, of continuous battles and conflicts. Thus as Sawicki (1991, 80–2) notes, the medical imposition of new reproductive technologies on pregnancy and birth has been contested at every step of the way, and this has led to changes in the way medical practices are conducted and medical technologies employed. For example campaigns have been mounted to make medical experts and technicians who run IVF programmes more accountable; and groups excluded from fertility treatments as 'unfit' have challenged such classifications and demanded access to these services. These struggles have been part of a longer history of struggles over the medical interventions in pregnancy and childbirth since the eighteenth century, when midwives began to be ousted in favour of medical supervision and hospital-ization. From the very beginning modern medical interventions in childbirth have been attacked and contested, by individuals, by organized groups, even by doctors. Especially in the second half of the twentieth century, there have been continual demands for alternative models of childbirth, such as challenges to the ways babies are delivered, from the routine use of drugs for pain and induction of labour to unnecessary caesareans.

The same kind of consideration can be invoked to question the idea that to adopt particular technologies means that there is no turning back, and that any possibilities for oppression or social manipulation inherent in a technology are inevitably going to be realized. Such 'slippery slope' arguments are sometimes invoked against new reproductive technologies, genetic engineering and the like. But these arguments depend heavily on the idea that individuals and populations will passively and uncritically accept what-ever is imposed upon them, no matter how extreme, and this seems highly questionable. One of the unconvincing features of dystopian visions like *Gattaca* is that they are able to accept that a system of control might be completely imposed on a society, and portray most of the population as passively acquiescing to their subordination, while at the same time allowing room for the heroic central character to resist, to try to escape from or find ways around the situation. The position that Foucault argues for is that real populations have more in common with the cinematic hero. People have a dynamic relationship with their social environment; they will always resist, criticize, seek to change or develop alternatives to the way in which social practices are organized and conducted. The current status of genetic engineering bears this out. Like the new reproductive technologies, it has not simply developed unchecked and unquestioned, but has been the subject of considerable scrutiny, critical attention and demands for accountability in recent times.

We thus have a perspective that does not simply reject recent technological developments like the new reproductive technologies and genetic engin-eering, as being inherently dehumanizing, or as necessarily leading to new ways of subjugating human beings. It acknowledges the role of such tech-nologies in empowering people, as well as the role that people can play in determining how the technologies are implemented. Indeed this appears to be Foucault's position on technology more generally, insofar as it impinges on social life. In the modern period technologies have certainly brought with them forms of social control, regulation and normalization, but they have also served to enhance human capabilities. What is required is not the complete rejection of technologies but rather a critical awareness of the role they can play in forms of social power, in order to work towards disconnecting the 'growth of capabilities' from 'the intensification of power relations' (Foucault 1984, 48). Ongoing critical scrutiny and resistance make it possible to modify and transform processes of technological development and implementation, to have a say in how they are administered, to democratize them. In very broad terms then, Foucault is in agreement with Habermas and Charlesworth. Technology is capable of being controlled and used by human beings in positive, beneficial ways.

This is by no means to suggest that we can ever return to the straightforward Enlightenment belief that science and technology, applied to society, will lead inevitably to moral progress and the betterment of the human condition. Too much has happened to allow us to be comfortable with this optimistic view, and the potential risks and dangers of technology are now widely acknowledged. The Western world's outright love affair with science and technology is over. But it can certainly be argued that being critical of technology does not mean that we have to abandon it altogether. The bleak assessments we sometimes find of it can be questioned, and the dystopian futures we have seen are not necessarily on the cards. Given a critical spirit, it is possible to hold on to and make use of the increased possibilities that modern technology provides. It is to the issue of critical thinking in general that I would now like to turn, and this will be the topic of the final chapter.

6

THE HOLY GRAIL – CRITICAL THINKING

Monty Python and the Holy Grail.
Credit: Python Pictures (Courtesy The Ronald Grant Archive)

In *Monty Python and the Holy Grail* (Terry Gilliam, Terry Jones, 1975), the Monty Python comedy about King Arthur and his intrepid knights, there is a scene early on in which a mob of villagers come up to Sir Bedevere (Terry Jones) in a state of high excitement. The villagers insist that they have found a witch and want to know if they may burn her. 'But how do you know she is a witch?' asks Sir Bedevere. It turns out that the villagers have rather limited grounds for their claim. The only justification they can come up with is that 'she looks like one', and even this evaporates when it turns out that they themselves have given her a false nose and dressed her as a witch. All is not lost, however. Sir Bedevere tells them that 'there are ways of telling whether she is a witch' and helps them to formulate an argument (of sorts) to back up their claim.

Amongst the many pleasures of this scene is the absurdity of the idea that a crazed witch-burning mob of villagers would stop in their tracks until they had satisfied themselves that what they were doing was reasonable. But this is what they do; and the activity they are engaging in here is critical thinking, the kind of activity in which one stands back from one's views and beliefs and seeks to evaluate them, to establish whether there are good arguments for them, or to determine whether those arguments that have been put forward for them are adequate. As I indicated in the Introduction, critical reflection is central to philosophy. In this book we have looked at a range of philosophical positions, a series of general accounts regarding what we can know, the nature of our selves, morality and our social and political existence. But philosophy is not just a series of general accounts of the world and ourselves, a set of doctrines to learn and repeat. These accounts emerge when we no longer simply accept our situation, when we stand back from our habitual ways of thinking and acting in order to critically examine and test the basic assumptions about the world and ourselves that we normally take for granted. Philosophy is above all an exercise in thinking, the critical examination and weighing up of beliefs, claims and positions, including its own accounts of the world and ourselves. In this final chapter I want to focus on critical reflection itself, and to look at what in general is involved in critical thinking.

Reasoning and arguing

In its most general sense, thinking critically is a matter of determining whether beliefs, claims or positions are rationally justified, whether they are supported by arguments that conform to the principles of sound reasoning. The notion of reasoning being invoked here is reasoning in its most basic and minimal sense: reasoning as a matter of engaging in clear, connected thinking, of making appropriate connections between ideas. To be able to reason is to be able to see that if we accept certain ideas or claims, other ideas follow. It is to see that certain ideas provide a basis or ground for accepting other ideas. The importance of this ability is evident when we consider cases where the ability is missing or limited. For example, in *Beavis and Butthead Do America* (Mike Judge, 1997) the limited reasoning skills of the 12-year-old protagonists are made entirely evident in the film's opening scene. Here, Butthead wakes to see that the television set is missing. He notices that there is a broken window, footprints on the carpet, and men outside loading a television set onto a truck, but he finds it very difficult to connect all these together and come to the obvious conclusion: that his television set has just been stolen. Similarly, limited reasoning ability is suggested if we are unable to see that certain ideas are inconsistent, that if we hold certain ideas we cannot hold others without falling into contradiction. For example, in *Rain Man* (Barry Levinson, 1988) the mental competence of the autistic Raymond (Dustin Hoffman) is called into question by a psychiatrist because he affirms two conflicting claims: both that he wants to stay with his brother, and that he wants to go back with the doctor to the home for the mentally disabled.

To be able to reason in this minimal sense of being able to see that if we accept some ideas, others follow, means that we can use certain ideas or claims to support others. That is, we can provide arguments for those claims, in the philosophical sense of the term. This is not argument in the sense of a heated discussion or a quarrel. We may be trying to change the beliefs of others, but we are trying to convince them that a certain conclusion ought to be believed because there are good reasons for it. An argument, as philosophers understand the term, is a chain of reasoning in which reasons are put forward to justify claims. So another way of characterizing reasoning is as the activity of developing good arguments, in which initial claims, or 'premises', provide good reasons for the conclusion we seek to establish. Being able to reason in this way also means that we are in a position to think critically about claims or positions that are put forward. Critical thinking asks whether there are good reasons for holding a belief or a position, as well as whether reasons that are put forward in support of them are adequate or relevant, whether there are other considerations that might call these beliefs or positions into question, and whether they are compatible or consistent with other positions held. Through such critical reflection we can not only evaluate the beliefs and arguments of others, but also assess our own views to see if they are worth holding.

In critical thinking, then, we are assessing arguments, various chains of reasoning that are put forward to support a conclusion, in accordance with standards of sound reasoning. These standards are themselves articulated in the area of philosophy known as logic, which seeks to provide an account of when, in general, ideas follow from other ideas, and thus when arguments work properly. This is not to say that when you are actually involved in arguing, you are explicitly referring to these standards or rules, having them in mind and then applying them to particular cases – any more than when you speak, you start with rules of grammar, and then apply them in order to construct sentences. Rather, logical principles, like grammatical rules, are usually followed implicitly and unreflectively in our language and thought. Logic seeks to make these rules explicit, in the same way that linguistics makes explicit the grammar of a language. Moreover, it is not to say that these rules can always be used to describe arguments as they unfold in practice. Although logical rules may be made explicit and set out, it is not always clear how they apply to actual arguments. Real arguments are not usually formulated with absolute clarity. However by setting out some of these ground rules, it is possible to say in general terms what kinds of arguments there are, and what counts as a good argument.

To begin with, there are clear cases where what is going on fails to amount to an argument at all. Arguments are more than mere assertions, and also more than straightforward disagreements. Assertions are bald claims, without any kind of justification or grounds, whereas an argument builds up a case for the claim being made. To return to the witch scene in Monty Python and the Holy Grail, the initial claim of the villagers, that they have found a witch, is little more than an assertion. As we saw earlier, what evidence they do put forward initially to back up their claim quickly evaporates. Sir Bedevere helps them to construct an argument in support of their claim, which we will have a closer look at in a moment. Arguments should also be distinguished from mere disagreements, in which one party asserts an opinion, and the other either denies it or asserts an opposing opinion. This distinction comes out in the *Monty Python* television show's 'Argument Clinic Sketch' (episode 29). Michael Palin pays for a five-minute argument with John Cleese and finds that Cleese's response to everything he says is: 'no it isn't'. Eventually Palin quite rightly makes the point that Cleese is not arguing, because argument is more than simply 'the automatic gainsaying of anything the other person says'. An argument, Palin insists, is a 'connected series of propositions designed to establish a conclusion' (to which Cleese replies 'No it isn't!') (see Chapman *et al.* 1989, 86–9).

Now if arguments are indeed a connected series of propositions designed to establish a conclusion, there are some arguments where, given the supporting reasons or premises, the conclusion is guaranteed as a matter of logic. In these cases, if we accept the initial premises, the conclusion simply must follow. It can be relied upon as being absolutely certain. There is an example of this in the argument clinic sketch, where Palin is trying to argue that Cleese is not arguing with him. We can formulate the argument that Palin is running against Cleese in the following way: to simply deny whatever I say is not to argue with me; Cleese is simply denying whatever I say; therefore, Cleese is not having an argument with me. Here, once we accept the two premises, that Cleese is simply denying whatever I say, and that to deny whatever I say is not the same as having an argument with me, the conclusion follows inescapably that Cleese is not arguing with me. It is not just very likely or highly probable that this is the case, but necessarily so. If these premises are true, the conclusion simply must be true. To put this another way, given these premises, it cannot possibly be false. To accept the premises and deny the conclusion would be to fall into complete inconsistency.

Now this might seem to suggest that if we employ these sorts of arguments, where the conclusion follows with logical necessity from the premises, we will always reach absolutely reliable conclusions. However this is not quite true. To explore this further we can go back to Sir Bedevere's lesson on argument in the *Holy Grail*. After pointing out that there are ways of telling if someone is a witch, he asks the crowd: 'what do you do with witches?' Their reply: 'burn them!' What else, he asks, do you burn apart from witches? Along with cries of 'more witches', someone suggests: 'wood'. So why, asks Sir Bedevere, do witches burn? The crowd: 'because . . . they're made of wood?' Sir Bedevere: 'good!' But despite Sir Bedevere's confidence, this is an absurd conclusion. Let us look more closely at what is going on here. What is the underlying argument in this case? Presumably the following: there is a claim that if something burns, then it is made out of wood; a further claim that witches burn; and the conclusion that witches, in order to burn, must be made out of wood. And this is one of those arguments in which the conclusion follows from the premises as a matter of logic. In that respect it is like Michael Palin's argument. In this case, once I accept the claim that if something burns, then it is made of wood, and the claim that witches burn, then I am committed to the conclusion that witches are made out of wood. In these circumstances, I cannot deny that witches are made of wood without falling into inconsistency.

So if the witch argument is one of these absolutely reliable kinds of arguments, why have we ended up with an unacceptable conclusion? What is the difference between this and Palin's argument? Well, it is true that in both cases the conclusion follows necessarily given the premises, but there is one key difference: in Palin's argument, the premises are true. It is true that an argument is more than just denying whatever Palin says, and it is true that Cleese is simply denying whatever Palin says. In the witch argument however, one of the premises is false. It might be true that witches burn, but it is not true that if something burns, it is made of wood. There are many things not made of wood that also burn. So this is where the witch argument goes wrong, why its conclusion is unacceptable. One of its premises is false. This means that we can only completely rely on such arguments to the extent that their premises are true. Good reasoning requires true premises. At the same time however, we can still say that to question the premises of the argument is not an objection to its logic, which has to do only with the form of the argument. As far as the form of the witch argument goes, how the premises relate to the conclusion, it is perfectly okay. Indeed, the witch argument and the Palin argument are identical in form, a form that can be expressed in the following schematic way:

> if p then q
> p
> therefore q

Any argument that has this form is said to be logically valid, and what this means is precisely that if the premises of the argument are true, the conclusion must be true. If an argument has a valid form and its premises also happen to be true, the argument is said to be sound. So whereas the witch argument is valid, Palin's argument is not only valid but sound.

The argument form we have just been looking at is known as *Modus Ponens* (Latin for 'affirmative mood'). There are a number of other logically valid forms of argument, arguments where the conclusion is guaranteed to be true if the premises are true, a few of which can be noted here. A second logically valid kind of argument, known as *Modus Tollens* ('denying mood'), has the following schematic structure:

> if p then q
> not-q
> therefore not-p

In *Dr Strangelove* (Stanley Kubrick, 1964), group captain Lionel Mandrake (Peter Sellers) uses a *Modus Tollens* argument to try to convince General Jack D. Ripper (Sterling Hayden) that there is no Russian attack and the planes that have been sent in to bomb Russia can be recalled. If a Russian attack were in progress, Mandrake points out, we would not be hearing a civilian radio broadcast; but since the radio he is holding is indeed playing ordinary music, there cannot be any Russian attack in progress. (Unfortunately Ripper is unimpressed by Mandrake's impeccable logic, since he has become completely insane.) One further logically valid form of argument is the hypothetical syllogism, an argument that takes the following form:

> if p then q
> if q then r
> therefore, if p then r

We can extract an argument along these lines from the *Holy Grail* witch scene. As the discussion continues, Bedevere gets the crowd to accept a number of premises: if something weighs the same as a duck, then it is made of wood; and if something is made of wood, then it is a witch. From this it follows that if the accused weighs the same as a duck, then she is a witch. As before, the content of Bedevere's argument is questionable, but this is not an objection to its form, which is perfectly valid. In the end, however, it remains the case that good reasoning requires both acceptable premises and valid logical form.

In general, arguments of this sort, in which the conclusion follows with absolute certainty given the premises, are known as deductive arguments. If the truth of the premises of a deductive argument can be established, that leaves no room for doubt about the argument's conclusion. The conclusion can be said to have been proved. However many of the arguments we employ in ordinary life are not of this sort. We are more likely to encounter another kind, in which the premises provide evidence for the conclusion, but do not guarantee it. This is the kind of reasoning often employed by movie detectives. *Sherlock Holmes in Washington* (Roy Neill, 1943) opens with the famous detective (played by Basil Rathbone) in good form. He expresses surprise that Watson (Nigel Bruce) has decided not to go to the cricket that afternoon, even though Watson has said nothing about his intentions. When Watson, amazed, asks how he knew this, Holmes replies

> Elementary, my dear Watson; invariably when you go to a cricket match you fill your flask with my best whisky. Just now I noted in passing that the flask was empty. A single whiff informed me that it had recently been filled. Obviously after filling it you had poured the contents back into the bottle. Therefore, you had changed your mind about the cricket match.
>
> (see Davies 1978, 73)

Here, Holmes is working on the basis of what he has observed of Watson's behaviour, and also of the behaviour of whisky and flasks. He has seen that Watson regularly fills his whisky flask before going to a cricket match. Had he simply seen that the flask was filled, he would have surmised that Watson intended to go to the cricket. But now he notes that the flask is empty, though it smells of whisky, which allows him to infer that it was filled and then the whisky returned to the bottle. And this allows him to further surmise that Watson, having filled the flask, was intending to go to the cricket, but having emptied it, has changed his mind.

Clearly there is a process of reasoning going on here, but despite Holmes referring to what he does as 'deduction' (the film itself announces him at the beginning as the 'supreme master of deductive reasoning') it is not that sort of reasoning. Unlike deductive reasoning, the conclusion here is not guaranteed given the premises. There is no necessary link between Watson filling his whisky flask, and his going to the cricket. We can perfectly well imagine that Watson might fill his whisky flask and not go to the cricket, without falling into inconsistency. This is simply a regular sequence of events that Holmes has observed. On the basis of this experience, Holmes has made a generalization, that whenever Watson fills his whisky flask, he is going to go to the cricket. Given this, he is able to argue that if Watson now fills his whisky flask, this provides evidence that he will be going to the cricket. Similarly, there is no necessary relation between smelling whisky on the flask, and its having been filled earlier with whisky. Holmes has observed that whenever whisky flasks are emptied, the smell of whisky tends to linger for a little while. And he makes a generalization on this basis, that whenever he smells whisky on an empty whisky flask, that flask has not long since been emptied. So smelling the whisky on Watson's empty flask now provides evidence that he has recently emptied his flask. It is these two lines of reasoning, together, that lead Holmes to his conclusion that Watson was going to the cricket, but has changed his mind.

This kind of reasoning, in which we take a number of specific cases and generalize from them, is known as inductive reasoning. Our most basic expectations about the world arise from it. We reason in this way when we conclude that the sun will rise tomorrow, that bread will nourish us, that objects will fall when dropped, because they have done so in the past. But it is important to remember that this kind of reasoning is never foolproof. Various things can go wrong. The examples I am basing my generalization on may be in some way unrepresentative. For example, Watson may come to think that all detectives are musically-inclined eccentrics, but this might be because he has not had the opportunity to meet other detectives like *The Name of the Rose*'s William of Baskerville, or *Chinatown*'s J.J. Gittes. He has generalized about all detectives on the basis of an unrepresentative sample. A further problem, discussed by David Hume in Section 4 of his *Enquiry Concerning Human Understanding*, arises with this kind of reasoning when we consider whether the future will always be like the past. Inductive arguments tend to rely on what has happened in the past to predict what will happen in the future, and there is an underlying assumption here, that the future will, at least in all relevant aspects, always be like the past. But there is nothing to guarantee that this will be so. We cannot argue, for example, that because the future has always been like the past in the past, it will continue to be so. To think that, we would have to assume precisely what we are trying to establish, namely that the future will always be like the past. We can only be sure that the future has, so far, turned out to be like the past; we cannot be sure that it will continue to be so (see Hume 1975, 32–9).

190

Yet even if these inductive arguments are never foolproof, even if they do not establish their conclusions with absolute, deductive certainty, they none-theless provide evidence for their conclusions. They make the conclusion more probable or likely. We can speak of degrees of likelihood that the conclusion is correct, given the evidence; and we can say that some inductive arguments are stronger than others. The basic rule here would be to generalize as little as possible. An inductive argument is stronger, the less one generalizes from experience. For example, having observed Watson's behaviour with the whisky flask, Holmes would have strong grounds for saying that whenever Watson fills his whisky flask he is heading out to the cricket, but less strong grounds for the more audacious generalization, that whenever anyone fills their whisky flask they are heading for the cricket. Equally, inductive argu-ments can be strengthened by increasing the number of cases from which we generalize. So to improve his argument, Holmes could look at the behaviour of a large number of people. If he studied the bulk of the population and found that whenever they filled their whisky flasks they headed out shortly after for the cricket, he would have a stronger basis for the generalization that whenever anyone fills their whisky flask, they are heading for the cricket. Still, it remains the case that no matter how strong the evidence, we can never have complete certainty in inductive reasoning. The Princess (Robin Wright) in Rob Reiner's *The Princess Bride* (1987) is sure that she and her dashing rescuer Westley (Cary Elwes), on the run from the unpleasant Prince, will never survive the dreaded Fire Swamp. But Westley's response shows the right degree of caution about inductive inferences, no matter how strongly based: 'Nonsense, you're only saying that because no one ever has.'

When arguments go wrong

It is possible, then, to discern two basic types of argument, deduction and induction. We have also seen some of the possible problems that can arise with inductive arguments. Let us now look at some of the other ways arguments can fall short of being good arguments; and in particular, at various fallacies that can afflict reasoning. A fallacy is an argument that appears to be reasonable and which thus tends to persuade us, even though it is in fact a bad argument. For example, an argument can appear to be deductively valid, to have the form of a valid argument, but in fact be deductively invalid. Where the problem is in the form of the argument, we speak of formal fallacies. Informal fallacies involve no violation of logical form, but suffer from some other kind of problem. We will shortly look at three kinds of informal fallacies: to do with language and linguistic confusion, to do with using premises in your argument that are irrelevant to what is at issue, and to do with inadequacies in the evidence being put forward for the conclusion we are trying to establish. But first, let's look at some formal fallacies.

Formal fallacies

Amongst the fallacies resulting from the form of the argument, the formal fallacies, are the two known as 'affirming the consequent' and 'denying the antecedent'. In the fallacy of affirming the consequent, we present an argument which looks like the valid *Modus Ponens* form 'if p then q; p; therefore q'. However in affirming the consequent we put things backwards and argue:

> if p then q
> q
> therefore p

An example of this appears in *Rear Window* (Alfred Hitchcock, 1954). L.B. Jefferies (James Stewart) has been watching his neighbour, whom he suspects of murder, wrapping a butcher knife and a small saw in newspaper. He tells his girlfriend Lisa (Grace Kelly) about it, adding that there's 'something terribly wrong'. He fancies indeed that this proves his suspicions about his neighbour. However to think this way is to fall into the fallacy of affirming the consequent. It is to argue along the following lines: if his neighbour was a murderer, he would have a knife and saw; he has a knife and saw; therefore he is a murderer. But as Lisa points out, this establishes nothing. Many people have knives and saws around their houses, but it does not follow that they intend to commit murder. After all, knives and saws can be used for quite innocent purposes. Later on his sceptical detective friend Doyle (Wendell Corey) joins in, reminding him of the hundreds of knives Jefferies himself has owned in his lifetime, and telling him quite rightly that 'Your logic is backward' (see Sharff 1997, 129–30, 149).

In the fallacy of denying the antecedent, we have an argument that looks like the valid *Modus Tollens* form 'if p then q; not q; therefore not p', but instead we are arguing:

> if p then q
> not p
> therefore not q

The fallacy of denying the antecedent appears in *Interiors* (Woody Allen, 1978), when Pearl (Maureen Stapleton) says at one point: 'You'll live to be a hundred if you give up all the things that make you want to.' This is a nice, humorous line but at the risk of ruining it let us take it completely seriously and look at the reasoning behind such a statement. The reasoning here is presumably as follows: if you do enjoyable things like smoking, drinking and having sex, this will shorten your life span; therefore, if you give up these pleasures, you will live a long life (but also a thoroughly boring one). However this is fallacious reasoning. To give up these things only means that you will not die from them, but there are plenty of other causes of premature death, such as being hit by a bus. All that can validly be said here is that if doing enjoyable things like smoking, drinking and having sex shortens your life, then if you do happen to end up living a long life, we can be sure that you didn't do these enjoyable things.

Informal fallacies of language

Turning now to informal fallacies, which involve a problem other than violation of logical form, let us begin with informal fallacies of language. These can arise from unclarity in the way things are expressed or formulated. One kind of unclarity is vagueness. A vague term or claim is one whose meaning is not precisely determined. For example, we speak of people as being bald, but there are degrees of baldness, and it is not always clear at what point one can be said to be bald. Vagueness becomes a problem for argument when vague terms or expressions are used to try to persuade people, in place of argument. In *The Next Best Thing* (John Schlesinger, 2000), Madonna's boyfriend Ben (Benjamin Bratt) exploits vagueness to get a table in a restaurant by saying 'would it make a difference if I said that Harrison Ford was in our party?' Later, when the maître d' complains that a trick has been played on the restaurant, Ben can rightly point out that strictly speaking he never said that Harrison Ford *was* in their party. But although vagueness can mislead, it is not easy to remove it completely from language, as Dudley Moore discovers in *Bedazzled* (Stanley Donen, 1967). Here, chronically shy Stanley Moon (Moore), infatuated with a waitress (Eleanor Bron), sells his soul to the Devil (Peter Cook) in return for seven wishes. It seems that Stanley is now in a position to realize his desires; but each time he describes a situation he wants realized, the Devil exploits vagueness and other shortcomings in his description to frustrate him. Thus for example when Stanley specifies that he wants himself and his waitress to be living in the country, each in love with the other, he finds that she is married to a saintly husband (played by the Devil) and that neither she nor Stanley can engage in adultery because they both admire her husband too much (see Wilmut 1980, 111–14).

Another form of unclarity is ambiguity, which refers to words (as well as phrases and sentences) that have more than one meaning. For example, 'bank' can mean a river bank or a financial institution. *Being There* (Hal Ashby, 1979) is based largely on ambiguity and the resultant misunderstanding. Here, the child-like gardener Chauncey (Peter Sellers), having lived all his life in his employer's house, finds himself on the street after his employer dies and the house is sold. After being hit by a limousine carrying Mrs Rand (Shirley Maclaine), he recuperates at the house of her powerful businessman husband (Melvyn Douglas); and here he rises to political influence because his naive pronouncements about life and gardening are ambiguous enough to be interpreted as examples of great profundity. Thus when he says 'my house was shut down', Mr Rand takes him to mean that his business house was closed down; when he says 'I'm a good gardener', Rand replies that that's what a businessman is, a good gardener; when he tells Mrs Rand that he 'likes to watch', meaning watch television, she takes this to mean that his sexual tastes run to voyeurism; and so on. When a word is used ambiguously in an argument, and the argument depends on that ambiguity, we have the informal fallacy of equivocation. In the trial over the teaching of evolution portrayed in Stanley Kramer's *Inherit the Wind* (1960), fundamentalist Matthew Brady responds to Henry Drummond's (Spencer Tracy's) cross-examination with equivocation. Drummond points out that according to physical laws, if the earth had stopped spinning as the Bible reports at one point, it would have had catastrophic consequences. Brady's response is that since these laws were made by God they can be changed, cancelled or used as God pleases. But this response relies on an ambiguity in the term 'laws'. Laws in the sense of physical laws are descriptions of natural regularities and are discovered, not made; Brady treats them as laws in the sense of enacted rules, which have to be made and which can be changed or altered by their makers. The same ambiguity is exploited in the fallacious argument sometimes used for God's existence, that natural laws must have a law-maker because they are laws and all laws must have a law-maker.

Along with the failure to recognize ambiguity, unclarity arises from the failure to observe the so-called use/mention distinction. Most of the time we simply use words, but sometimes we want to mention them, to talk about the words themselves. If we are not careful about distinguishing between use and mention, misunderstandings can arise. In *Monty Python's Life of Brian* (Terry Jones, 1979), Brian (Graham Chapman), born in a manger just down the road from Jesus, becomes a reluctant messiah. The stoning scene early on in the film indicates the importance of observing the use/mention distinction. Official (John Cleese): 'You have been found guilty by the elders of the town of uttering the name of our lord and so as a blasphemer you are to be stoned to death.' Man: 'Look, I'd had a lovely supper and all I said to my wife was, "That piece of halibut was good enough for Jehovah".' Cleese: 'Blasphemy!' As neither Cleese nor the crowd make any distinction between merely mentioning as opposed to actually using the offending word, it is impossible even to discuss the issue. Eventually Cleese himself becomes the victim of this confusion. Cleese (to Man): 'I'm warning you, if you say "Jehovah" once more. . . .' Someone throws a stone at him. 'Right. Who threw that? . . . Stop it, will you. Now look, no one is to stone anyone until I blow this whistle. *Even* . . . and I want to make this absolutely clear . . . *even* if they do say "Jehovah".' At this point the crowd rain stones on him and crush him with a huge rock (see Chapman *et al.* 1979, 11–12).

Language can also be involved in fallacious thinking when things are labelled in such a way that the conclusions we want the audience to draw about them are suggested by the labels, rather than being supported by reasons. For example, to speak of an individual in non-personal or inhuman terms, as an 'it', or an 'animal', is already to load any debate concerning that individual in a certain way. Something of this goes on in the *Star Trek* 'Measure of a Man' episode where the issue is whether the android Data is property, able to be dismantled, studied and replicated, or a person, with the right to refuse such treatment. The very way the defendant is referred to becomes significant. The scientist who wants to dismantle Data repeatedly refers to the android as 'it', which loads things in favour of the android being considered property, a mere thing. For his part, Captain Picard (Patrick Stewart) who is defending Data continually uses 'he', pushing the idea that Data is a person. The ensuing discussion also points to another way in which labelling can be used to sway an audience. This is through the use of euphemistic labels to replace words that might come across as too harsh, painful or offensive, and thus to sanitize what we want to talk about and promote. Picard's arguments on Data's behalf include the claim that to talk as the scientist does of creating and using a whole generation of Datas, and of treating them as disposable property, is to employ a comfortable euphemism, 'property', to obscure what would really be going on, namely slavery.

Euphemism can thus play a pernicious role in shielding things from critical examination or evaluation. Government agencies and the military seem particularly adept at this sort of whitewashing, a fact highlighted in a number of films. In Francis Ford Coppola's hallucinatory Vietnam movie *Apocalypse Now* (1979), Martin Sheen is told that his mission is to go into the jungle, not to kill the mad Colonel Kurtz, but to 'terminate' him 'with extreme prejudice'. In *Dr Strangelove*, General Buck Turgidson (George C. Scott) turns military euphemism into an art form. Discussing the options for the United States now that the insane General Ripper has sent nuclear bombers into the Soviet Union, he urges President Muffley (Peter Sellers, again) to 'back them up with everything we've got' before the Soviets have a chance to retaliate. To support his claim, he argues:

> We have to choose between two admittedly regrettable but distinguishable post-war environments, one where you have a hundred and fifty million dead and one where you have twenty million killed . . . I'm not saying we wouldn't get our hair mussed. But I do say no more than ten to twenty million people killed, tops, depending on the breaks.

Here the military language is euphemistic in the extreme. There are 'post-war environments'; we may 'get our hair mussed'. As the President points out, what the general is actually talking about is mass murder, death on a colossal scale. Even 'war' here has become a sanitizing euphemism.

Informal fallacies of relevance

A number of informal fallacies, then, involve confusion in language. Another general kind of informal fallacy has to do with using premises in your argument that are irrelevant to what is at issue. One such fallacy of relevance is the *ad hominem* argument. Here, instead of trying to disprove the truth of what has been claimed, one attacks the person making the claim, or the group to which they belong. A number of such *ad hominem* arguments can be found in *Twelve Angry Men* (Sidney Lumet, 1957). In this Hollywood classic, Henry Fonda plays juror #8, the architect, the only person on a jury holding out for a not guilty verdict for a boy accused of killing his father, and who uses argument to gradually turn the case around for the defendant. As the discussion unfolds, various forms of fallacious reasoning are exposed in the other jurors, including examples of the *ad hominem* fallacy. These come from juror #10 (Ed Begley), the bigoted juror. At one point #10 says:

> Now you're not going to tell us that we're supposed to believe that kid, knowing what he is. Listen, I've lived among 'em all my life. You can't believe a word they say. You know that. I mean, they're born liars.
>
> (Garrett et al. 1989, 180)

So his argument is that the testimony of the defendant, a slum kid from an unidentified minority, that he is innocent, should not be believed, because he is one of 'them'. Later, he adds: 'Look, you know how these people lie! It's born in them! . . . That's how they are! By nature! You know what I mean?' (312–15). But as the old man, juror #9 (Joseph Sweeney), rightly points out: 'I don't think the kind of boy he is has anything to do with it. The facts are supposed to determine the case' (281).

Another fallacy of relevance is the appeal to authority. We often need to rely on experts, but it is possible to rely too heavily on authority and to fail to take other considerations into account, or to appeal to an expert who is not an expert in the relevant field or otherwise untrustworthy. To use improper appeals to authority to support our conclusion is to commit the fallacy of appeal to authority. For example, in *Inherit the Wind* the fundamentalist Matthew Brady underpins his opposition to evolution by appealing to the invincible authority of the Bible. His view is that everything in the Bible should be accepted exactly as it is given there. Here we have an instance of excessive reliance on authority, a reliance that excludes all other considerations. In *Twelve Angry Men*, a fertile source of informal fallacies of all kinds, juror #1 (Martin Balsam), the foreman, appeals to the testimony of the court psychiatrist to the effect that the defendant has 'strong homicidal tendencies', as evidence for the boy's guilt. In this case however the expert evidence is considered more critically. Juror #11 (George Voskovec), the immigrant, points out that other considerations need to be taken into account, in particular that psychiatric tests can only indicate a potentiality to kill, which proves nothing; many of us may be capable of murdering, but few of us go ahead and do it (see Garrett *et al.* 1989, 296–9).

A further fallacy of relevance is the appeal to anger or pity. Here we attempt to persuade people not through reason but by arousing their anger in support of a position, or by making them feel sorrow, sympathy or anguish, where such feelings are simply not relevant to the issue at stake. In *Twelve Angry Men*, when Henry Fonda begins to win people over to his side, juror #3 (Lee J. Cobb), the angry juror, tries to discredit him by accusing him of committing this kind of fallacy, of swaying the other jurors through an appeal to pity. Hence when juror #5 (Jack Klugman), the slum-dweller, changes his view from guilty to not guilty, #3's response is:

> Brother, you're really something! You come in here and vote guilty like everyone else, and then this golden-voiced preacher here starts to tear your heart out with stories about a poor little kid who just couldn't help becoming a murderer.
>
> (216)

Later, as others start to vote not guilty, juror #3 accuses them of giving into pity: 'This is getting to be a joke . . . I mean everybody's heart is starting to bleed for this punk little kid . . .' (258). Eventually, he accuses Fonda directly:

> You come in here with your heart bleeding all over the floor about slum kids and injustice, and all of a sudden you start getting through to some of these old ladies in here! Well you're not getting through to me! I've had enough!
>
> (272)

Finally, the fallacy of irrelevant conclusion (also known as *non sequitur*) arises when an argument purporting to establish a certain conclusion in fact proves something different. The premises of the argument and the supposed conclusion are then essentially unrelated, and the whole argument becomes logically irrelevant. In *Star Trek: The Next Generation*'s trial of Data, Picard argues that the prosecution has not established its case for this very reason. The point at issue is whether Data is a person, which the prosecution seeks to show is not the case by arguing that the android is a machine, and was created by a human. Picard, for the defence, argues that these arguments do not do what they purport to do because they are entirely irrelevant to the question of Data's personhood. They may establish that Data is a machine, but then human beings are also machines of a certain type; and they may also establish that Data was created by a human being, but human children are also created by human beings, out of the building blocks of their parents' DNA. Whether Data is a person or not can only be established using quite different considerations, by determining whether the android satisfies the conditions of personhood, which Picard then goes on to argue for.

Informal fallacies of evidence

The third general kind of informal fallacy to be considered here is the fallacy of evidence, which involves inadequacies in the evidence being put forward for the conclusion we are trying to establish. A common fallacy of evidence is simply jumping to conclusions, accepting a conclusion as settled before all the relevant evidence is in. There are a number of instances of this in *Twelve Angry Men*. When the jurors are first asked why they think the accused is guilty, juror #6 (Edward Binno), the working man, supports his view as follows:

> I was looking for a motive . . . that testimony from those people across the hall from the kid's apartment, that was very powerful. Didn't they say something about an argument between the father and the boy around 7 o'clock that night?

In response Fonda points out that this is an overhasty conclusion:

> I don't think that's a very strong motive. This boy has been hit so many times in his life that violence is practically a normal state of affairs for him. I can't see two slaps in the face provoking him into committing murder.
>
> (Garrett *et al.* 1989, 189–90)

Soon after, juror #4 (E.G. Marshall), the stockbroker, offers another overhasty argument for the boy's guilt: 'He was born in a slum. Slums are breeding grounds for criminals . . . Children from slum backgrounds are potential menaces to society.' Juror #5 rightly points to the reckless generalization this involves: 'I've lived in a slum all my life . . .' (192–3). In other words, he points out that living in a slum does not automatically turn you into a criminal, or even a potential criminal.

There are a number of other fallacies of evidence. Begging the question is the fallacy of assuming as a premise the very conclusion that the premise is supposed to prove. In effect, one is arguing in a circle, arguing that something is true because it is true. In *Twelve Angry Men*, juror #3, the angry man, comes up with the following argument: 'D'you feel like seeing a proven murderer walking the streets?' (217). This is entirely circular because his argument for the boy's being a murderer is that to acquit him would be to set free a proven murderer. Another fallacy of evidence is the appeal to ignorance, the fallacy of supposing that if there is no evidence against a certain claim, then this is a reason for believing that the claim is true. In *Twelve Angry Men*, juror #2 (John Fiedler), the bank-teller, falls into this fallacy: 'I thought it was obvious [that the boy was guilty] from the word go. I mean nobody proved otherwise' (183). In other words, the failure to prove the boy not guilty is wrongly put forward here as evidence for the view that the boy is guilty. The fallacy of false dichotomy operates by presenting a range of alternatives on an issue that are merely assumed or are misleadingly represented as exhaustive. As a result, the number of possible alternative positions there might be on the issue is unjustifiably restricted. An example comes from *The Crucible* (Nicholas Hytner, 1996), an adaptation of Arthur Miller's play about the 1692 Salem witch trials. When John Proctor (Daniel Day-Lewis) tells the trial judge Danforth (Paul Scofield) that the girls making the accusations of witchcraft are frauds, and that he has proof, the judge's response is that 'a person is either with this court or against it. There be no road in between. Only good and evil' (Miller 1996, 67). The fallacy here is to hold that the only alternatives are to support the court's hunt for witches, or to stand opposed to it and thus show oneself to be in league with the witches, if not a witch oneself. There is a third option being excluded here, which Proctor is trying to present, namely that the witch hunt is itself misconceived and without foundation.

Another fallacy of evidence is that of false analogy. We often argue by analogy, to the effect that if two things are similar in some respects, they will be similar in other respects as well. This is a form of inductive inference, and so it is not a foolproof, deductively valid approach, but properly used it provides evidence for a claim. In *Twelve Angry Men*, Fonda uses an argument by analogy to question one of the most important pieces of evidence against the boy: that his alibi did not seem to hold up. Though he claimed to be at the movies at the time of the killing, he could not remember the name of the film or who starred in it when questioned by the police. Fonda asks juror #4, the stockbroker, whether he can remember the movie he has seen a few days before, or who was in it. The stockbroker has some difficulty doing so, and Fonda points out that if it's possible for this gentleman to have difficulties remembering details of films he has just seen, then it is also perfectly possible for this boy to have done so (Garrett *et al.* 1989, 295). The fallacy of false analogy would arise if there were significant differences between the two cases. Fonda is careful to stress the similarities between the stockbroker and the boy, that both have difficulties remembering the same kind of event after a similar period of time. But if he had tried to argue, for example, that it is possible to be unable to remember vitally important details soon after an event because most people cannot remember trivial details many years later, the two cases are now too dissimilar for the analogy to reasonably hold, and he would have fallen into the fallacy of false analogy.

A final fallacy of evidence is the so-called *post hoc* fallacy (from the Latin 'post hoc, ergo propter hoc', i.e., 'after this, because of this'). This is the fallacy of presuming that something that precedes an event is the cause of that event, or that something which comes after an event is caused by that event. The two events may regularly occur one after the other, but this is not the same thing as one event causing the other. The most flagrant examples of such thinking occur when there is not even a regular correlation to speak of, where one event has simply occurred after the other, and we imagine that one has brought about the other. We may pray for the traffic lights to change, and they do change, but this does not mean that our prayers brought about the change. An example of such thinking appears in *Dr Strangelove*. General Ripper, having sent the bombers into Russia, explains his views on the evils of fluoridation to Captain Mandrake: 'Do you realize that fluoridation is the most monstrously conceived and dangerous communist plot we've ever had to face . . . Do you know when fluoridation first began? 1946. How does that coincide with your post-war commie conspiracy?' Here, Ripper commits the *post hoc* fallacy by arguing that because fluoridation was introduced after World War Two around the time of the emergence of the Soviet state as a world power, it must be part of a communist plot.

Closed thinking

In a number of ways, then, bad arguments can have the appearance of good ones, and can thereby have persuasive power. The use of these deceptive arguments can be unintentional, the result of lack of understanding or carelessness, or it can be part of a deliberate attempt to mislead or manipulate. Whatever the reason, fallacious reasoning can give unjustifiable positions the appearance of being justified, or persuade us of positions that are not in fact defensible. One of the important tasks of critical reflection is to evaluate the arguments being used to justify or promote various positions in order to determine whether dubious forms of reasoning are involved. We come now to another general kind of problem that can arise in our thinking, which has to do with the grip that positions, once they have been acquired, can have on our arguments and reasoning.

It might seem that a view of the world that is confirmed by everything we encounter, and which can explain away any inconsistencies we come across, would be a desirable thing. This however is the error that conspiracy theorists typically fall into. For them, everything is part of the great conspiracy. If there is no evidence to support the conspiracy, or important evidence is lacking, it has obviously been removed to hide what is going on. If anyone criticizes the conspiracy theorist, they show themselves to be part of the conspiracy. Every objection can be dealt with. But this unshakeability is not so much a sign of the superiority of the conspiracy theorist's views, as of the difficulty of putting these views to any kind of test since there is no way in which they can possibly fail. The problem here is sometimes referred to as the fallacy of the irrefutable hypothesis, or the fallacy of invincible ignorance. It can involve a straightforward refusal to consider evidence that is contrary to some cherished belief; or we might interpret whatever evidence, even the most hypothetical, that might be put forward to falsify a claim, in a way that twists it into evidence for the claim. Either way, we end up with a closed, dogmatic, irrefutable system of thinking in which everything that we encounter seems to confirm our beliefs, and nothing can be put forward to call them into question.

Such closed thinking is not confined to conspiracy theorists. It appears whenever a viewpoint or a belief system becomes all-consuming and unquestionable, as for example in religious fundamentalism and political fanaticism. Such thinking becomes an object of parody in *The Life of Brian*. On the religious side, Brian (Graham Chapman), forced to pose as a prophet to escape from pursuing Roman soldiers, finds himself being hailed by the crowd as the Messiah. There is nothing he can say or do to dissuade his new admirers. The more he protests, the more this is taken as proof of his divinity. When Brian tells the crowd to go away, this is taken as a blessing; they tell Brian he has given them a sign of his divinity because he has 'brought them to this place', even though they have simply followed him; finally, when he says, point blank, 'I am not the Messiah, will you please listen!', the response is: 'Only the true Messiah denies his divinity' (see Chapman *et al.* 1979, 41–3). Even outright denial is thus interpreted in a way consistent with the original belief. Political fanaticism also comes in for attention in the film, in the form of the Judean People's Front, an anti-Roman guerrilla organization. Convinced of the rightness of their cause, the Front is not interested in anything that might bring their struggle into question. When their leader Reg (John Cleese) asks rhetorically 'what have the Romans ever done for us?', and his followers come up with a long list, he remains unmoved: 'Alright, but *apart* from better sanitation and medicine and irrigation and public health and roads and a freshwater system and baths and public order . . . what have the Romans done for us?' (20).

Cleese himself has stated that *The Life of Brian* 'is about closed systems of thought . . . systems by which whatever evidence is given to a person, he simply adapts it, fits it into his ideology' (Cleese quoted in Wilmut 1980, 250). And once established, such thinking is clearly hard to shake. If all opposing considerations and arguments are either ignored or interpreted so as to confirm or reinforce one's position, criticism becomes enormously difficult. In *The Name of the Rose*, once the Inquisitor has accused someone of devil-worship and heresy, no counter-argument is possible. It is impossible to dispute the claim and defend those accused without oneself being suspected of complicity in the crime. Thus, when William of Baskerville tries to defend those accused of the murders taking place in the monastery, Inquisitor Bernard Gui accuses him of heresy, of 'having sought to shield a heretic from just punishment by the Inquisition'. Similarly in *The Crucible*, once someone is accused of witchcraft, it is impossible to dispute this. If the accused protests their innocence, this is only to be expected, for a witch will of course deny the crime; and anyone who questions the veracity of those doing the accusing, or who speaks up for those accused, runs the risk of themselves being accused of witchcraft. Even the trial judge, when he questions the girls who have been accusing people of witchcraft to test their honesty, finds himself threatened with complicity by their leader Abigail Williams (Winona Ryder): 'do you think you are so mighty that the devil cannot turn your wits?' (Miller 1996, 74).

In the end, such closed thinking cannot tolerate any contrary evidence or argument, any consideration or viewpoint that differs from it. In *The Crucible*, as we saw earlier on, if one is not for the court one is against it, and hence likely to be in league with evil. No further alternatives are possible. But this intolerance of alternatives also comes at a cost. Such thinking is also closed to any new or different thinking, to any ideas that go beyond the limits of the existing system of beliefs. It is thus unable to develop or expand. This immobility is evident for example in *Inherit the Wind* during Henry Drummond's cross-examination of the fundamentalist Matthew Brady. Here, Brady makes heroic efforts to maintain the literal truth of biblical claims, however outlandish they might seem. When questioned about unlikely events reported in the Bible such as a man being swallowed by a whale, or the sun standing still in the sky, Brady remains unfazed. 'The Bible satisfies me', he proclaims, to which Drummond replies sarcastically: 'It frightens me to think of the state of learning in the world if everyone had your driving curiosity.' Drummond's point is that thinking of the fundamentalist sort is closed to new ideas and new forms of understanding which do not fit into the preferred view of the world; and that as a result, this is a form of understanding that cannot develop or grow. It is condemned instead to stand still, to repeat itself, and the closed system of beliefs becomes a prison.

We might perhaps want to dismiss closed thinking as the province of conspiracy theorists, blind fanatics, dogmatic fundamentalists and the like. But as the twentieth-century thinker Karl Popper (1902–1994) has pointed out, such thinking can also afflict perspectives that claim to be scientific (see Popper 1972, 34–5). He cites amongst his examples certain psychoanalytic theories which can provide a story to account for any human behaviour, and which no conceivable human behaviour is thus able to contradict; and those Marxists who endlessly reformulate their theory to keep any threatened falsification by historical events at bay. In both cases, the theories have the unfalsifiable certainty of religious faith. Their ability to explain everything they encounter, Popper argues, is precisely what is wrong with these theories. It means that they can never really be put to the test. Popper also points to the psychological appeal of these unfalsifiable theories. Their ability to explain everything means that their holders know in advance that everything that happens to them will be understandable. This provides not only a sense of intellectual mastery but also, the emotional sense of secure orientation in the world (see Magee 1973, 45). Here perhaps is the great attraction of closed thinking in general. An unquestionable system of beliefs keeps all uncertainty and risk at bay. It allows us to enjoy complete security and certainty, and provides a firm standpoint from which to understand and to proceed in the world.

It might even be argued that we have a general tendency towards closed thinking, or at least a degree of resistance to critical questioning of our beliefs, because of our need for some standpoint from which to proceed. We need some framework of beliefs in order to make sense of the world and to function within it. Otherwise, we would be confronted with a meaningless, unintel-ligible confusion of experiences and events. Our belief structures provide a frame of reference in terms of which to interpret our experiences, to pick out what is important to us and ignore what is not. But what this also means, as Joel Rudinow and Vincent Barry point out, is that '[t]he way we deal with incoming information is determined in large part by what we already believe' (Rudinow and Barry 1994, 12). As a result it is not easy to question these beliefs in the light of new experiences, since they provide the frame of reference in terms of which we evaluate these experiences. We are more likely to view the world, and ourselves, in a way that confirms our existing outlook. For the same reason, we are more likely to steer clear of or dismiss beliefs, values and attitudes that are widely contrary to the ones we hold, than to consider that our views might be limited or questionable. And the emotional benefits of this cannot be discounted. For all of us, having a framework in terms of which things make sense gives us emotional security. To have one's world-view called into question is often acutely painful, unsettling and threatening.

So, far from being confined to fanatics and fundamentalists, a tendency towards closed thinking, a resistance to anything that might unsettle and change our existing beliefs, is arguably a widespread tendency in our thinking. The stubborn jurors in *Twelve Angry Men* are, at least initially anyway, resistant to considerations that might challenge their positions, but they are not fanatics. Far from it. They are recognizably ordinary individuals. They each bring a certain perspective to the proceedings, a way of thinking about the world which colours how they view the accused and the evidence presented in the trial, and which their various arguments and justifications are designed to preserve. This is a very understandable way of proceeding. However, to point to a widespread tendency is not to say that it is impossible for us to critically scrutinize and question our beliefs, simply that it requires effort. And it remains important that we make this effort, to the extent that fixed perspectives and closed forms of thinking imprison our understanding and make us intolerant of alternative ways of thinking. Critical scrutiny which shows up the limits of an existing way of thinking, its inability to deal with certain facts or arguments, opens up the possibility of escaping from its confines, recognizing that there might be different ways of seeing things, and coming to think in new and different ways.

This critical scrutiny of closed forms of thought can even be applied to critical thinking itself, understood as a matter of weighing up our beliefs and positions to determine whether they are rationally justified. It is possible to become closed and dogmatic in the very demand for rational accountability, to insist that positions are only ever acceptable if they can be rationally grounded or justified. Arguably there are always limits to what we can rationally justify and make over in our views and beliefs. While we may provide reasons or arguments for particular beliefs, any argument must itself proceed on the basis of premises that are not themselves argued for, and which cannot be justified within the argument without falling into circularity. And while these premises may themselves be argued for elsewhere, it does not seem possible for us to rationally justify every single aspect of our thinking. On what basis could we do so? That would seem to require that we be able to stand outside all our beliefs and principles; but if we were somehow able to do that, we would have no beliefs or principles in terms of which to proceed. In other words, we would no longer have a place to stand. What this suggests is that in our thinking there will always be certain background beliefs and principles that remain outside the scope of rational justification at any particular time, beliefs and principles that we have to rely on in order to reason and argue.

Nonetheless, philosophers have sometimes argued that reason itself can provide the first principles from which to proceed, the ultimate standpoint in terms of which to organize our thinking. We then have a position from which to critically evaluate all our beliefs and principles, to rationally ground and justify them, and to exclude those that cannot be rationally grounded. Such thinking is characteristic of 'rationalist' philosophies of various sorts. Thus a rationalist philosopher like Plato insists that reason alone provides a reliable basis for knowledge, and criticizes all beliefs about the world based on the senses; in a similar spirit, Kant argues that only reason can provide an adequate basis for morality, and excludes desire and emotion from the scene. But it is important to note that the rationality being invoked to provide this ultimate standpoint is rather more complex than the basic notion of reason as connected thinking in accordance with principles of sound reasoning. And since the reason being called for here amounts to an absolute principle that everything else has to conform to, and which is itself supposedly beyond question, the problem of closed, dogmatic thinking reappears, along with the need for the kind of critical scrutiny that challenges dogmatic thinking. As we have seen in earlier chapters, the rationalist emphasis on reason as the only legitimate basis for knowledge or morality has in fact been a recurring object of criticism in philosophical thinking, insofar as the dogmatic insistence on the primacy of reason ignores or devalues other factors, such as the role of the senses in relation to knowledge, and of feeling and emotion in connection with morality.

The importance of being critical

At the beginning of the chapter I suggested that critical reflection is at the very heart of philosophy. To do philosophy is above all to philosophize, to stand back from and think critically about things rather than simply accepting them. In the ensuing discussion, at least two roles have emerged for critical thinking. The first is to weigh up positions, beliefs and arguments, to ask whether there are good reasons for holding a belief or position, whether reasons that are put forward in support of them are adequate or relevant, and whether the arguments being presented conform to principles of sound reasoning. The second role is to question beliefs or positions that have become closed and dogmatic, to show up the limits of such thinking, its failure or inability to deal with certain facts, considerations or arguments, and to open the way to thinking differently. In the Introduction I suggested that philosophy, understood as critical thinking, is linked in an important way with our freedom, and it is how these forms of critical reflection contribute to our freedom that I want to focus on in this final section.

Critical reflection in the first sense, as a matter of rationally assessing beliefs and positions to determine whether there are good reasons or arguments for holding them, allows us not only to evaluate the beliefs and arguments of others, but also to think about what positions we ourselves should accept and make our own. And one of the reasons it is important to undertake this kind of critical activity is that it provides us with a way of defending ourselves against manipulation and control by others. That is, when we become self-critical in this way, we are no longer simply at the mercy of whatever others tell us to believe. We no longer take things at face value. We can critically weigh up the positions being presented to us, to see if there are in fact good reasons for believing them. We can also weigh up arguments that might be presented to us in support of these positions, in order to ensure that we are not being taken in by spurious argument. Whether through carelessness or as part of a deliberate attempt to manipulate, fallacious reasoning can make unjustifiable positions appear justified. Critical reflection allows us to see through this deceptive semblance of justifiability.

As we saw in Chapter 1, Plato's image of the cave, right at the beginning of philosophy, invites us to do precisely this, to critically reflect on what is presented to us, rather than simply accept the way things appear. For Plato, this is the beginning of the road out of imprisonment, imprisonment within the cave of received ideas. We also saw how Plato's story of escape from imprisonment through critical reflection has implications for a number of areas of our existence. Critical reflection plays an important part in our growing up, insofar as we come to think about ideas, beliefs and attitudes that we have picked up along the way from parents, teachers and friends. When we are young we tend to absorb beliefs and attitudes unthinkingly, and to that extent we are little more than passive products of our environment. But it is also possible for us to think critically about them. We may end up accepting or rejecting them, but whatever position we end up with, it will be one that we have decided for ourselves, for our own reasons. Critical reflection thus contributes to the development of our intellectual independence. And given that we continue to be subject to various social and cultural influences, critical reflection continues to have a role to play. In the face of influences from advertising, the mass media, cultural pressures and political propaganda, along with the seductive messages coming from all manner of experts, gurus and demagogues, a capacity to be critical, to critically weigh up the claims and arguments we are presented with, remains vital if we are to maintain a degree of independence.

Here, critical reflection helps us escape from the imprisonment that comes from being under the sway of the ideas, attitudes and views of others. In so doing, it contributes to our freedom, not merely in the sense of independence from the sway of external forces, but in the more positive sense of being able to determine ourselves, to rationally decide things for ourselves. Isaiah Berlin has given an eloquent formulation of the ideal of freedom as self-determination:

> I wish my life and decisions to depend on myself, not on external forces of whatever kind. I wish to be the instrument of my own, not of other men's, acts of will. I wish to be a subject, not an object; to be moved by reasons, by conscious purposes, which are my own, not by causes which affect me, as it were, from outside. . . .
>
> (Berlin 1969, 131)

As we saw in Chapter 3, the eighteenth-century philosopher Kant is one of the great advocates of this 'positive' notion of freedom, freedom as rational self-determination. Perhaps we can never completely dictate the terms of our existence, a feat that would be like trying to pull ourselves up by our own bootstraps; but critical reflection on our beliefs and attitudes means that we can go a long way towards taking an active part in determining who we are and what we stand for, as opposed to being the mere product of external forces.

The second role for critical reflection is to confront closed, dogmatic forms of thinking. If we can be imprisoned by uncritically accepting the views of others, we can also be imprisoned by our own views, to the extent that we interpret whatever we encounter in terms of them and refuse to consider any evidence that is inconsistent with them. Such thinking is to be found in various kinds of fanaticism and fundamentalism, but it is arguably also a more widespread tendency, given that we view the world in terms of some frame of reference which we rely on to make sense of things and to interpret new experiences. The cost of such closed thinking, however, is imprisonment within its confines. Unable to pass beyond it, we are doomed to repeat ourselves; and we are closed and intolerant towards alternatives, towards that which does not fit into our way of thinking. The role of critical thinking here is to point up the limits of closed thinking, and to encourage an open-mindedness towards that which is outside of or inconsistent with it. We will then be open to the possibility of thinking differently, of appreciating different ways of looking at the world. This kind of critical thinking is also linked to freedom, not now the freedom from the undue influence of others, the freedom of self-determination, but rather freedom from the undue influence of our own views, freedom from the grip of closed, dogmatic thinking, and the freedom to explore other, alternative forms of thinking.

As we have seen, this form of critical reflection can also be applied to critical thinking itself, to the extent that the demand for rational accountability itself becomes closed and dogmatic. I have argued that we cannot stand wholly apart from and rationally dictate the terms of our existence. There are always background beliefs and principles we have to rely on in order to reason and argue, and which thus remain outside the scope of rational justification. But if we invoke a more complex notion of reason capable of providing the ultimate principles for our thinking and action, we run the risk of succumbing to a dogmatic rationalism, of becoming intolerant of whatever does not conform to standards of rational accountability, and of becoming prisoners of a rationality that has become tyrannical. Indeed this is one of the potential dangers that Berlin sees in the positive notion of freedom, freedom as living in accordance with the dictates of our reason. The more we turn reason into the central principle of our being, the more we see it as entitled to devalue, discipline and repress the 'lower' aspects of ourselves, our desires and emotions. This is the rationalist view of the self which, as we saw in the second chapter, is present in Kant and goes right back to Plato. But as we also saw, thinkers like Hume and Freud are on hand to criticize such dogmatic rationalism, to help free us from a rationality that has become tyrannical, and to open our eyes to the profound role that desire and emotion play in our individual existence.

The importance of criticizing dogmatic rationalism is also evident in relation to our social and political existence. In Chapter 5 we saw how modern thinking, from the Enlightenment onwards, sought to provide a rational critique of traditional beliefs and institutions, and to remake the individual and social world in rational terms. For the Enlightenment, reason, rather than faith or tradition, was to be the proper guide to human conduct. Once again, the notion of reason being invoked is more than just the minimal idea of connected thinking. Reason here is either identified with science and technology, or it is understood in Kantian terms, bound up with some notion of our 'real' or 'essential' nature. Recent critiques of Enlightenment visions of a rational society are not directed at rationality in the minimal sense. They are not calling into question logical principles, but the more complex Enlightenment notions of rationality. And here also, the concern is essentially to criticize a dogmatic conception of rationality, which only accepts that which conforms to its standards, and is intolerant of anything that falls outside them. Critical reflection once again seeks to challenge a way of thinking that is imprisoning, and intolerant of alternatives. For the Frankfurt School the target is the technological rationality for which efficiency is the only criterion for organizing social practices; for Foucault it is the vision of rational social organization that imposes notions of normal behaviour and simultaneously defines a vast range of behaviour as deviant or abnormal. In both cases the aim of the critique is to help free us from an imprisoning form of thinking and to open up a space for something else, either for principles of social organization other than those dictated by technical efficiency, or for forms of life that go beyond the possibilities dictated by a regime of normality.

Philosophical thinking, as critical reflection, can thus be seen as contributing in various ways to our freedom. This is the freedom that comes from not simply accepting our situation, from standing back from received views, assumptions and forms of thinking, and thinking things through for ourselves; and also the freedom that comes from refusing to turn any position we might hold into fixed, unquestionable dogma, closed to the possibility of other ways of thinking. In the end this liberating aspect of philosophy gives us another way of thinking about what philosophy itself is, another way of answering the question posed in the Introduction: what is philosophy? Philosophy is the kind of thinking that helps set one's thinking free. This is why viewing philosophy as no more than doctrines to be learnt or repeated misses what is most important about it. It is to turn its own pronouncements into views to be taken for granted and assumed without question, to imprison the mind in a new set of dogmas. The best way of understanding what philosophy is, is by engaging critically with the views it presents, thinking things through for yourself, coming to your own views about the matters it deals with; and also, never imagining that you have found the final, definitive answer, but always remaining open to the possibility of thinking differently. To understand philosophy in this way is to experience the limitless freedom of thought.

GLOSSARY

This glossary contains key terms that have been used in the book. It also lists the main thinkers discussed, along with the particular texts referred to and their original dates of publication. In the book I have cited recent editions of these texts, so the dates there are not always the original ones.

absurd   Without point or justification. For existentialism, the world is absurd. There is no reason for the way the world is or what happens in it, and human beings in particular have no reason or justification for existing.

alienation   A term employed by Marx to describe the state of people under capitalism, separated from a properly human existence, unable to pursue their true interests and denied control over their lives and working conditions.

argument   A chain of reasoning in which reasons are put forward to justify claims. See also deductive argument and inductive argument.

autonomy   Self-rule or self-determination. For Kant, the ability of the person to rationally determine their existence rather than being determined by external forces. Kant contrasts it with heteronomy, where we are determined in what we do by non-rational factors.

Bentham, Jeremy (1748–1832)   English philosopher. Founder of utilitarianism. Author of *An Introduction to the Principles of Morals and Legislation* (first published 1789).

Camus, Albert (1913–1960)   French novelist and philosopher. An important figure in the development of existentialism. Author of *The Myth of Sisyphus* (first published 1942).

cognitive relativism   The view that knowledge, what can be said to be true, varies relative to individual, social or cultural conditions.

Condorcet, Marquis de (1743–1794)   French mathematician and social theorist, who embodied the Enlightenment confidence in human progress through reason and science. Author of *Sketch for a Historical Picture of the Progress of the Human Mind* (first published 1795).

deductive argument   A deductive argument is one in which the conclusion follows necessarily given the premises. A deductive argument is *valid* if it follows an approved logical form, but it is only *sound* if, in addition, it has true premises.

Descartes, René (1596–1650)   French philosopher and the 'father of modern philosophy'. A central figure in the theory of knowledge, and the best-known modern proponent of a dualist view of the human being. Author of the *Meditations on First Philosophy* (first published 1641).

discipline   The name given by Foucault to techniques of social regulation he sees as characteristic of the modern period, techniques for controlling individuals and populations including the detailed division and organization of space and time, and the use of surveillance.

divine command theory   An account of morality that sees moral rules as God's laws or commandments. The morally right action is that which is commanded by God; the morally wrong action is that which God forbids.

dualism   The view that the human being is composed of two very different sorts of things, an immaterial mind (or soul) and a material body. Both Plato and Descartes are dualists.

empiricism   The account of knowledge which holds that all knowledge of the world is derived from sense experience and observation. Empiricists typically hold that reason by itself, independently of experience, cannot establish truths about the world. Locke and Hume are two classic empiricists.

Enlightenment   A philosophical and intellectual movement in eighteenth-century Europe which formulated key features of the modern outlook, including faith in reason, belief in the progressive character of science and technology and a critical attitude towards religion.

epistemology   The area of philosophy concerned with giving an account of knowledge, of the nature, scope and limits of what we can know.

ethics   Moral philosophy, the area of philosophy concerned with how we ought to conduct ourselves and deal with one another, and why we should be moral at all.

existentialism   The philosophy of human existence which holds that there is nothing outside of or within ourselves that we can appeal to in order to justify our values and moral rules. If there are moral rules and values it is because we have freely chosen them, and nothing can guide us in these choices. Prominent figures include Jean-Paul Sartre, Simone de Beauvoir and Albert Camus.

fallacy   An argument that appears to be reasonable and which thus tends to persuade us, but which is in fact a bad argument. A formal fallacy appears to be a valid deductive argument but is in fact invalid. An informal fallacy involves no violation of logical form, but has some other kind of problem.

feminism   The area of social and political thinking that criticizes the subordination and oppression of women.

Foucault, Michel (1926–1984)   French philosopher, responsible for an influential reformulation of the notion of power. Author of *Discipline and Punish* (first published 1975).

Frankfurt School   The name given to a group of twentieth-century German neo-Marxists, who were particularly concerned with analysing the effects of science and technology on social life. Prominent members include Max Horkheimer, Theodor Adorno, Herbert Marcuse and, more recently, Jürgen Habermas.

freedom   According to the distinction formulated by Isaiah Berlin, negative freedom is 'freedom from', freedom from external interference by other individuals, governments and so on; positive freedom is 'freedom to', freedom to live in accordance with rules we define for ourselves. Hobbes is the classic advocate of the former, and Kant of the latter.

Freud, Sigmund (1856–1939)   Viennese thinker and founder of psychoanalysis. Author of *The Ego and the Id* (first published 1923).

Habermas, Jürgen (1929–)   German philosopher and leading contemporary representative of the Frankfurt School. Author of *Toward a Rational Society* (first published 1969).

Hobbes, Thomas (1588–1679)   English philosopher, advocate of reductive materialism, and an early proponent of liberal thinking. Author of *Leviathan* (first published 1651).

Hume, David (1711–1776)   Scottish philosopher, one of the first modern empiricists and an advocate of a view of human beings as primarily creatures of desire. Author of the *Treatise of Human Nature* (first published 1739) and *An Enquiry Concerning Human Understanding* (first published 1748).

ideology   The Marxist term for false consciousness, a false or limited understanding of one's social situation, needs and interests which serves to maintain the existing social order.

inductive argument   An inductive argument is one in which we take a number of specific cases and generalize from them. Inductive arguments do not establish their conclusions with absolute certainty, but they can be said to provide evidence for their conclusions.

Kant, Immanuel (1724–1804)   German philosopher, a key figure in modern theory of knowledge, and an influential moral theorist. Author of the *Critique of Pure Reason* (first published 1781) and *Groundwork of the Metaphysics of Morals* (first published 1785).

liberalism   The tradition in social and political philosophy which holds that individuals should be as free as possible to pursue their interests. Some political and legal constraints are necessary to maintain social order, but the liberal view is typically that these should be as minimal as possible. The main architect of modern liberal thinking is Locke.

Locke, John (1632–1704)   English philosopher, founder of modern empiricism and a central figure in the development of modern liberal thinking. Author of the *Essay Concerning Human Understanding* (first published 1689) and *The Second Treatise of Government* (first published 1689).

logic   The area of philosophy which seeks to provide an account of when, in general, ideas follow from other ideas, and thus when arguments work properly.

Marcuse, Herbert (1898–1979)   German philosopher and member of the Frankfurt School. Author of *One-dimensional Man* (first published 1964).

Marx, Karl (1818–1883)   German philosopher and founder of Marxist social and political thinking. Author of *Capital* (first volume published 1867).

Marxism   The social and political account formulated by Karl Marx which sees the individual as existing necessarily in a community, and emphasizes the role of the economic in accounting for our social existence. His twentieth-century successors include the Frankfurt School thinkers and Jürgen Habermas.

Mill, John Stuart (1806–1873)   English philosopher. A key figure in the development of utilitarianism, and of liberal thinking. Author of *On Liberty* (first published 1859) and *Utilitarianism* (first published 1863).

Nietzsche, Friedrich (1844–1900)   German philosopher. Along with Søren Kierkegaard, an important precursor of twentieth-century existentialism. Author of *The Gay Science* (first published 1882).

normalization   For Foucault, the process of bringing individuals to conform in their behaviour to various norms and standards, through disciplinary techniques.

person On Locke's account, a thinking, intelligent being; for Kant, a rational agent. In both cases a person is to be distinguished from a biological human being. It is widely held that persons have a special value and that they deserve particular moral respect.

personal identity The problem of what makes a human being the same person over time.

philosophy of mind The area of philosophy that considers questions such as: what is the nature of the mind? Is the mind distinguishable from the body? Are reason and the passions in conflict within us?

Plato (c.429–327 BC) Greek philosopher, a central figure in the emergence and development of the theory of knowledge, moral thinking, and social and political thought. Author of the *Republic*.

Popper, Karl (1902–1994) Viennese philosopher of science. Author of *Conjectures and Refutations* (first published 1963).

psychoanalysis An account of the self developed by Sigmund Freud which divides the self into the ego or rational 'I', the superego or moral conscience, and the id, consisting of instinctual drives.

rationalism The account of knowledge which downplays the role of sense experience and holds that by employing certain procedures of reason alone, we can attain at least some important truths about the world. Plato and Descartes are examples of rationalists. Kant offers a rationalistic account of morality, one that holds that reason alone can provide the basis for moral rules and principles.

reasoning In its most basic sense, a matter of engaging in clear, connected thinking, making appropriate connections between ideas. To be able to reason is to be able to see that if we accept certain ideas or claims, other ideas follow.

reductive materialism The view that all mental phenomena can be reduced to and identified with material processes.

Sartre, Jean-Paul (1905–1980) French philosopher and central figure in the development of twentieth-century existentialism. Author of *Being and Nothingness* (first published 1943).

scepticism The view that calls into question the possibility of knowledge.

social and political philosophy The area of philosophy that looks at the individual's relationship to society, the nature and justification of political authority and notions of political power, amongst other topics.

state of nature The state that human beings would find themselves in if all social authority were absent, envisaged by Hobbes and Locke to provide a justification for organized society. Society is justified as a remedy for the problems and shortcomings experienced in the state of nature.

technological rationality   A form of thinking oriented purely towards maximizing efficiency. For the Frankfurt School, this has become the dominant form of rationality in the modern period.

theodicy   The part of theology that seeks to reconcile a good and all-powerful god with the existence of suffering and evil in the world.

theory-dependence   The view that experience varies with the expectations and knowledge of the observer.

universalizability   A central principle of Kant's moral theory. In order to act morally we need to determine that the principle we are thinking of acting on is universalizable, that it could consistently be followed by all individuals in relevantly similar situations.

utilitarianism   The moral theory which holds that the moral character of an act depends on its consequences, on how much pleasure or happiness it produces. For utilitarianism, an action is right insofar as it tends to create the greatest happiness for the greatest number of people. Key figures in the development of utilitarianism are Bentham and Mill.

FURTHER READING

Introduction

Useful introductions to philosophy include Emmet, *Learning to Philosophize* (1968), Hollis, *Invitation to Philosophy* (1985), Pojman, *Philosophy: The Pursuit of Wisdom* (1998), Popkin and Stroll, *Philosophy* (1986) and Rosenberg, *The Practice of Philosophy* (1996).

1 Plato's picture show – the theory of knowledge

A good introduction to Plato is Annas, *An Introduction to Plato's* Republic (1981). For more on *Descartes*, his method and motivations, see Cottingham, *Descartes* (1986) and Williams, *Descartes: The Project of Pure Enquiry* (1978). Woolhouse's *The Empiricists* (1988) provides a clear introduction to the empiricists Locke and Hume. Kant's theory of knowledge is discussed in Körner, *Kant* (1955). A general introduction to theories of knowledge is provided by Trusted, *An Introduction to the Philosophy of Knowledge* (1997).

2 *All of Me* – the self and personal identity

A good general introduction to theories of human nature, including chapters on Plato and Freud, is Stevenson, *Seven Theories of Human Nature* (1974). For a clear discussion of Hobbes' account of human nature, see Peters, *Hobbes* (1956). Descartes' dualism and some possible alternatives are discussed in Churchland, *Matter and Consciousness* (1988) and Dennett, *Consciousness Explained* (1991). There are interesting discussions of personal identity in Glover, *I* (1988) and Noonan, *Personal Identity* (1989), and of personhood in Goodman (ed.), *What is a Person?* (1988) and Midgley, 'Persons and Non-persons' (1985).

3 *Crimes and Misdemeanors* – moral philosophy

There are many good general guides to moral philosophy including Frankena, *Ethics* (1973), MacIntyre, *A Short History of Ethics* (1966), Norman, *The Moral Philosophers*

218

(1983), Rachels, *The Elements of Moral Philosophy* (1993) and Raphael, *Moral Philosophy* (1981). Useful guides to Kant's ethics are Acton, *Kant's Moral Philosophy* (1970) and Sullivan, *An Introduction to Kant's Ethics* (1994). Dinwiddy's *Jeremy Bentham* (1989) provides an accessible introduction to Bentham's thinking. A clear introduction to the work of J.S. Mill is Ryan, *J.S. Mill* (1974). Good general introductions to Sartre and existentialism include Barrett, *Irrational Man* (1958), Charlesworth, *The Existentialists and Jean-Paul Sartre* (1974) and Molina, *Existentialism as Philosophy* (1982).

4 *Antz* – social and political philosophy

A good general introduction to political philosophy is Plamenatz, *Man and Society* (1992). Hobbes' political philosophy is discussed in Peters, *Hobbes* (1956) and Watkins, *Hobbes's System of Ideas* (1989). Social contract views of society are discussed in Raphael, *Problems of Political Philosophy* (1976). McLellan, *The Thought of Karl Marx* (1980) provides a useful guide to the main elements of Marx's thought. Berlin, in 'Two Concepts of Liberty' (1969) offers a famous defence of negative freedom. A feminist perspective on political philosophy is presented in Jagger, *Feminist Politics and Human Nature* (1983). Smart's *Michel Foucault* (1985) provides a good general introduction to Foucault.

5 *Modern Times* – society, science and technology

For a general introduction to the thought of the eighteenth-century Enlightenment, see Hampson, *The Enlightenment* (1968) and Cassirer, *The Philosophy of the Enlightenment* (1951). Kramnick (ed.), *The Portable Enlightenment Reader* (1995) is a useful collection of readings, including excerpts from Condorcet. Modern biotechnology is discussed from a liberal perspective in Charlesworth, *Life, Death, Genes and Ethics* (1989). A clear introduction to Marxism, the Frankfurt School and Habermas is West, *An Introduction to Continental Philosophy* (1996). For discussion of Foucault, feminism and new reproductive technologies, see Sawicki, *Disciplining Foucault* (1991).

6 *The Holy Grail* – critical thinking

A good general introduction to critical thinking is Rudinow and Barry, *Invitation to Critical Thinking* (1994). A clear introduction to logic is Copi, *Introduction to Logic* (1982). Pirie, *The Book of the Fallacy* (1985) and Thouless, *Straight and Crooked Thinking* (1959) concentrate on how arguments can go wrong. For discussions of Popper and falsifiability, see Magee, *Popper* (1973) and Chalmers, *What is this Thing called Science?* (1986).

BIBLIOGRAPHY

Acton, H.B. (1970) *Kant's Moral Philosophy*, London: Macmillan.

Anderson, Lindsay (1969) 'Notes for a Preface', in Lindsay Anderson and David Sherwin, *If . . .*, Melbourne: L & S Publishing.

Annas, Julia (1981) *An Introduction to Plato's* Republic, Clarendon Press: Oxford.

Barrett, William (1958) *Irrational Man*, New York: Doubleday.

Bentham, Jeremy (1987) *An Introduction to the Principles of Morals and Legislation*, in John Stuart Mill and Jeremy Bentham, *Utilitarianism and Other Essays*, ed. Alan Ryan, Harmondsworth: Penguin.

Berlin, Isaiah (1969) 'Two Concepts of Liberty', in Isaiah Berlin, *Four Essays on Liberty*, Oxford: Oxford University Press.

Biskind, Peter (1983) *Seeing is Believing: How Hollywood Taught us to Stop Worrying and Love the Fifties*, New York: Pantheon.

Blackburn, Simon (1994) *Oxford Dictionary of Philosophy*, Oxford; New York: Oxford University Press.

Camus, Albert (1975) *The Myth of Sisyphus*, Harmondsworth: Penguin.

Cassirer, Ernst (1951) *The Philosophy of the Enlightenment*, Princeton, N.J.: Princeton University Press.

Chalmers, Alan (1986) *What is this Thing called Science?* St Lucia, Queensland: Queensland University Press.

Chapman, Graham, Terry Jones, Terry Gilliam, Michael Palin, Eric Idle and John Cleese (1977) *Monty Python and the Holy Grail (Book)*, London: Eyre Methuen.

—— (1979) *The Life of Brian*, London: Eyre Methuen.

—— (1989) *Monty Python's Flying Circus: Just the Words*, vol. 2, London: Methuen.

Charlesworth, Max (1974) *The Existentialists and Jean-Paul Sartre*, St Lucia, Queensland: Queensland University Press.

—— (1989) *Life, Death, Genes and Ethics*, Maryborough, Victoria: ABC Enterprises.

Christensen, Terry (1987) *Reel Politics: American Political Movies from Birth of a Nation to Platoon*, Oxford; New York: Basil Blackwell.

Churchland, Paul (1988) *Matter and Consciousness: A Contemporary Introduction to the Philosophy of Mind*, revised edition, Cambridge, Massachusetts: MIT Press.

Condorcet, Marquis de (1955) *Sketch for a Historical Picture of the Progress of the Human Mind*, trans. J. Barraclough, London: Weidenfeld & Nicolson.

—— (1995) 'The Future Progress of the Human Mind', in Isaac Kramnick (ed.), *The Portable Enlightenment Reader*, New York: Penguin.

Copi, Irving (1982) *Introduction to Logic*, 6th edition, New York: Macmillan.

Corea, Gera (1985) *The Mother Machine: Reproductive Technologies from Artificial Insemination to Artificial Wombs*, London: The Women's Press.

Cottingham, John (1986) *Descartes*, Oxford: Basil Blackwell.

Cowie, Peter (1982) *Ingmar Bergman*, London: Secker & Warburg.

Davies, David (1978) *Holmes of the Movies: The Screen Career of Sherlock Holmes*, New York: Bramhall House.

Dennett, Daniel (1991) *Consciousness Explained*, Boston: Little, Brown & Co.

Descartes, René (1986) *Meditations on First Philosophy*, trans. John Cottingham, Cambridge; New York: Cambridge University Press.

Dewey, Robert E. and James A. Gould (eds) (1970) *Freedom: Its History, Nature and Varieties*, New York: Macmillan.

Dinwiddy, John (1989) *Bentham*, Oxford; New York: Oxford University Press.

Durgnat, Raymond (1968) *Luis Buñuel*, Berkeley: University of California Press.

Emmet, E.R. (1968) *Learning to Philosophize*, Harmondsworth: Penguin.

Foucault, Michel (1977) *Discipline and Punish*, trans. Alan Sheridan, Harmondsworth: Allen Lane.

—— (1984) 'What is Enlightenment?' in Paul Rabinow (ed.), *The Foucault Reader*, New York: Pantheon.

Frankena, William (1973) *Ethics*, 2nd edition, Englewood Cliffs, N.J.: Prentice Hall.

Freiberger, Eric (1996) 'Projecting the Real: Tornatore's *Cinema Paradiso*', in *Film and Philosophy* 3: 107–22.

Freud, Sigmund (1986) *The Ego and the Id*, in Anna Freud (ed.), *The Essentials of Psychoanalysis*, trans. James Strachey, Harmondsworth: Penguin.

Garrett, George P., O.B. Hardison Jr and Jane R. Gelfman (eds) (1989) *Film Scripts Two: High Noon, Twelve Angry Men, The Defiant Ones*, New York: Irvington Publishers.

Giannetti, Louis (1996) *Understanding Movies*, 7th edition, Englewood Cliffs, N.J.: Prentice Hall.

Glover, Jonathon (1988) *I: The Philosophy and Psychology of Personal Identity*, Harmondsworth: Penguin.

Goodman, Michael (ed.) (1988) *What is a Person?*, Clifton, N.J.: Humana Press.

Gunning, Tom (2000) *The Films of Fritz Lang: Allegories of Vision and Modernity*, London: British Film Institute.

Habermas, Jürgen (1971) 'Technology and Science as "Ideology"', in Jürgen Habermas, *Toward a Rational Society*, London: Heinemann Educational Books.

Hampson, Norman (1968) *The Enlightenment*, Harmondsworth: Penguin.

Hanley, Richard (1997) *The Metaphysics of Star Trek*, New York: HarperCollins.

Hobbes, Thomas (1968) *Leviathan*, ed. C.B. Macpherson, Harmondsworth: Penguin.

Hollis, Martin (1985) *Invitation to Philosophy*, Oxford: Blackwell.

Hume, David (1969) *A Treatise of Human Nature*, ed. Eric C. Mossner, Harmondsworth: Penguin.

—— (1975) *Enquiries Concerning Human Understanding and Concerning the Principles of Morals*, ed. L.A. Selby-Bigge, revised by P.H. Nidditch, Oxford: Clarendon Press.

—— (1986) 'Of Suicide', in Peter Singer (ed.), *Applied Ethics*, New York: Oxford University Press.

Irwin, Terence (1989) *Classical Thought*, Oxford: Oxford University Press.

Jagger, Alison (1983) *Feminist Politics and Human Nature*, Totowa, N.J.: Rowman & Allanheld.

Jarvie, Ian (1987) *Philosophy of the Film: Epistemology, Ontology, Aesthetics*, New York: Routledge & Kegan Paul.

Kaes, Anton (1999) *M*, London: British Film Institute.

Kant, Immanuel (1929) *The Critique of Pure Reason*, trans. Norman Kemp Smith, London: Macmillan.

—— (1964) *Groundwork of the Metaphysic of Morals*, trans. H.J. Paton, New York: Harper Torchbooks.

—— (1995) 'What is Enlightenment?', in Isaac Kramnick (ed.), *The Portable Enlightenment Reader*, New York: Penguin.

Körner, S. (1955) *Kant*, Harmondsworth: Penguin.

Kramnick, Isaac (1995) 'Introduction', in Isaac Kramnick (ed.), *The Portable Enlightenment Reader*, New York: Penguin.

Le Doeuff, Michèle (1989) *The Philosophical Imaginary*, trans. Colin Gordon, London: Athlone.

Locke, John (1993) *The Second Treatise of Government*, in John Locke, *Political Writings*, ed. David Wootton, Harmondsworth: Penguin.

—— (1997) *An Essay Concerning Human Understanding*, ed. Roger Woolhouse, Harmondsworth: Penguin.

MacIntyre, Alasdair (1966) *A Short History of Ethics*, London: Routledge & Kegan Paul.

McLellan, David (1980) *The Thought of Karl Marx*, 2nd edition, London: Macmillan.

Magee, Bryan (1973) *Popper*, London: Fontana.

Marcuse, Herbert (1964) *One-Dimensional Man*, London: Routledge.

Marx, Karl (1967) *Economic and Philosophical Manuscripts*, in Karl Marx, *The Writings of the Young Marx on Philosophy and Society*, trans. and ed. Loyd D. Easton and Kurt H. Guddat, New York: Anchor.

—— (1976) *Capital*, vol. 1, trans. Ben Fowkes, Harmondsworth: Penguin.

Midgley, Mary (1985) 'Persons and Non-persons', in P. Singer (ed.), *In Defence of Animals*, New York: Blackwell.

Mill, John Stuart (1975) *Three Essays: On Liberty, Representative Government, The Subjection of Women*, Oxford; New York: Oxford University Press.

—— (1987) *Utilitarianism*, in John Stuart Mill and Jeremy Bentham, *Utilitarianism and Other Essays*, ed. Alan Ryan, Harmondsworth: Penguin.

Miller, Arthur (1996) *The Crucible: A Screenplay*, London: Methuen.

Molina, Fernando (1982) *Existentialism as Philosophy*, Englewood Cliffs, N.J.: Prentice Hall.

Nietzsche, Friedrich (1974) *The Gay Science*, trans. Walter Kaufmann, New York: Vintage.

Noonan, Harold (1989) *Personal Identity*, London; New York: Routledge.

Norman, R. (1983) *The Moral Philosophers: An Introduction to Ethics*, Oxford: Clarendon Press.

Perkins, V.F. (1972) *Film as Film: Understanding and Judging Movies*, Harmondsworth: Penguin.

Peters, Richard (1956) *Hobbes*, Harmondsworth: Penguin.

Pirie, Madsen (1985) *The Book of the Fallacy*, London: Routledge & Kegan Paul.

Plamanatz, John (1992) *Man and Society: Political and Social Theories from Machiavelli to Marx*, revised by M.E. Plamenatz and R. Wokler, London; New York: Longman.

Plato (1961) *Phaedrus*, trans. R. Hackforth, in Edith Hamilton and Huntingdon Cairns (eds), *The Collected Dialogues of Plato*, Princeton, N.J.: Princeton University Press.

—— (1974) *Republic*, 2nd revised edition, trans. Desmond Lee, Harmondsworth: Penguin.

Pojman, Louis (1998) *Philosophy: The Pursuit of Wisdom*, 2nd edition, Belmont, CA: Wadsworth.

Popkin, Richard and Avrum Stroll (1986) *Philosophy*, 2nd revised edition, Oxford: William Heinemann.

Popper, Karl (1972) *Conjectures and Refutations*, 4th edition, London: Routledge & Kegan Paul.

Rachels, James (1993) *The Elements of Moral Philosophy*, 2nd edition, New York: McGraw-Hill.

Raphael, D.D. (1976) *Problems of Political Philosophy*, revised edition, London: Macmillan.

—— (1981) *Moral Philosophy*, Oxford: Oxford University Press.

Rosenberg, Jay (1996) *The Practice of Philosophy: A Handbook for Beginners*, 3rd edition, Upper Saddle River, N.J.: Prentice Hall.

Rubey, Dan (1985) 'Star Wars: Not So Long Ago, Not So Far Away', in Peter Steven (ed.), *Jump Cut: Hollywood, Politics and Counter-Cinema*, Toronto: Between the Lines.

Rudinow, Joel and Vincent Barry (1994) *Invitation to Critical Thinking*, 3rd edition, Fort Worth, Texas: Harcourt Brace College Publishers.

Ryan, Alan (1974) *J.S. Mill*, London: Routledge & Kegan Paul.

Sartre, Jean-Paul (1958) *Being and Nothingness*, trans. Hazel E. Barnes, London: Methuen.

Sawicki, Jana (1991) *Disciplining Foucault: Feminism, Power and the Body*, New York; London: Routledge.

Schirato, Tony and Susan Yell (1996) *Communication and Cultural Literacy: An Introduction*, St Leonards, N.S.W.: Allen & Unwin.

Schrader, Paul (1985) 'Blue Collar', in Dan Georgakas and Lenny Rubenstein (eds), *Art, Politics, Cinema: The Cineaste Interviews*, London: Pluto Press.

Sharff, Stefan (1997) *The Art of Looking in Hitchcock's Rear* Window, New York: Limelight Editions.

Sim, Stuart (ed.) (1998) *The Icon Critical Dictionary of Postmodern Thought*, Cambridge: Icon Books.

Smart, Barry (1985) *Michel Foucault*, Chichester: Ellis Horwood.

Stam, Robert, Robert Burgoyne and Sandy Flitterman-Lewis (1992) *New Vocabularies in Film Semiotics: Structuralism, Post-structuralism and Beyond*, New York: Routledge.

Sterrit, David (1999) *The Films of Jean-Luc Godard: Seeing the Invisible*, New York: Cambridge University Press.

Stevenson, Leslie (1974) *Seven Theories of Human Nature*, New York; Oxford: Oxford University Press.

Sullivan, Roger (1994) *An Introduction to Kant's Ethics*, Cambridge: Cambridge University Press.

Taylor, Charles (1985) *Philosophy and the Human Sciences: Philosophical Papers 2*, Cambridge; New York: Cambridge University Press.

Thouless, R.H. (1959) *Straight and Crooked Thinking*, London: English Universities Press.

Trusted, Jennifer (1997) *An Introduction to the Philosophy of Knowledge*, 2nd edition, London: Macmillan.

Warnock, Mary (1970) *Existentialism*, London: Oxford University Press.

Watkins, John (1989) *Hobbes's System of Ideas*, Aldershot, Hants: Gower Publishing Company.

West, David (1996) *An Introduction to Continental Philosophy*, Cambridge: Polity Press.

Wilkinson, David (2000) *The Power of the Force*, Oxford: Lion.

Williams, Bernard (1978) *Descartes: The Project of Pure Enquiry*, Harmondsworth: Penguin.

Wilmut, Roger (1980) *From Fringe to Flying Circus: Celebrating a Unique Generation of Comedy 1960–1980*, London: Eyre Methuen.

Wilson, George (1986) *Narration in Light: Studies in Cinematic Point of View*, Baltimore: Johns Hopkins University Press.

Woolhouse, R.S. (1988) *The Empiricists*, Oxford: Oxford University Press.

INDEX